HIKE LIST

MENASHA RIDGE PRESS
Birmingham, Alabama

60 HIKES
WITHIN 60 MILES

PORTLAND

INCLUDES
THE COAST, MOUNTS HOOD
AND ST. HELENS, AND
THE COLUMBIA RIVER GORGE

THIRD EDITION

PAUL GERALD

DISCLAIMER

This book is meant only as a guide to select trails in the Portland area and does not guarantee hiker safety in any way—you hike at your own risk. Neither Menasha Ridge Press nor Paul Gerald is liable for property loss or damage, personal injury, or death that result in any way from accessing or hiking the trails described in the following pages. Please be aware that hikers have been injured in the Portland area. Be especially cautious when walking on or near boulders, steep inclines, and drop-offs, and do not attempt to explore terrain that may be beyond your abilities. To help ensure an uneventful hike, please read carefully the introduction to this book, and perhaps get further safety information and guidance from other sources. Familiarize yourself thoroughly with the area you intend to visit before venturing out. Ask questions, and prepare for the unforeseen. Familiarize yourself with current weather reports, maps of the area you plan to visit, and any relevant park regulations.

 Printed on recycled paper

Library of Congress Cataloging-in-Publication Data

Gerald, Paul, 1966–
   60 hikes within 60 miles, Portland: including the Coast, Mounts Hood and
   St. Helens, and the Columbia River Gorge/Paul Gerald. —3rd ed.
      p. cm.
   Includes bibliographical references and index.
   ISBN 13: 978-0-89732-975-0 (alk. paper)
   ISBN 10: 0-89732-975-9 (alk. paper)
   1. Hiking—Oregon—Portland Region—Guidebooks. 2. Portland Region (Or.)—
   Guidebooks. I. Title. II. Title: Sixty hikes within sixty miles, Portland.

   GV199.42.O72P6738 2007
   796.5109795—dc22
      2007005337

Cover and text design by Steveco International
Cover photo by Paul Gerald
Author photo by Cheryl Juetten
All other photos by Paul Gerald
Maps by Steve Jones, Scott McGrew, and Paul Gerald

Menasha Ridge Press
P.O. Box 43673
Birmingham, AL 35243
www.menasharidge.com

WITH IMMENSE GRATITUDE AND RESPECT, I DEDICATE THIS BOOK TO THE PEOPLE WHO BUILD AND MAINTAIN TRAILS. —PAUL GERALD

TABLE OF CONTENTS

ACKNOWLEDGMENTS

Whenever people ask me what it's like to write a book, I tell them it's such a pain that by the time the thing arrives, you feel nothing but relief. There's a *lot* of work in this thing, and I am far from the only person who contributed.

I processed a lot of information for this book, much of which came from the United States Forest Service, Oregon State Parks, PortlandHikers.org, the Columbia Gorge Visitors Center, the Mount Hood Visitors Center, the Mazamas, and the amazing book *Oregon Geographical Names* from the Oregon Historical Society Press. I own the sixth edition, revised and updated by Lewis L. McArthur, and I recommend it highly. Other helpful tidbits and charm came, along the way, from Laurie MacArthur at Opal Creek, Walt Dunn and Carole Wendler at Mount St. Helens National Volcanic Monument, Howard Harrison at Cascade Head, and all the nice people at Nature of the Northwest.

The book includes words I wrote and photographs I took, but many others have put it all together: Susan Cullen Anderson, Travis Bryant, Ritchey Halphen, Russell Helms, Steve Jones, Annie Long, Molly Merkle, Myra Merkle, and Galen Schroeder. Without these folks, the book is just a set of files on my Macintosh.

Of course, a hike is a lonely experience without good friends to share it with. Here— listed alphabetically to avoid controversy—is a list of the folks who made "researching" this third edition such an enjoyable experience: Keanu Allridge, Corky Corcoran, Christie Dewey, Mike Fesenmeyer, Craig Frerichs, Jane Garbisch, Stefan Henry-Biskup, Beth McNeil, Eric Miller, Steve Moellering, Jean Nelson, Diana Robinson, Brandon Rydell, Craig Schuhmann, Rick Schmitt, Rick Vazquez, and Chela Zini-Caban. (I have done a horrendous job of keeping notes on this, so I apologize to anybody I left out.) I do need to give major thanks to everybody with the Mazamas, especially Tom Eggers and Leslie Wood, and even greater thanks to all the cool people with the Adventurous Young Mazamas.

Special thanks, and Sunday brunch, to Cheryl Juetten for taking my author photo. And to Jenny Boyce, who made life pleasant as the book was wrapped up.

A lifetime of love and thanks to my family back east: Marjorie and Barry Gerald; Lee, Lela, and Jack Gerald and Max Simpson; Lucy, Becky, David, Jeff, and Charlie Cook. And, finally, thanks to my Oregon family, the Thursday Night Boys, for keeping me (reasonably) sane.

—*Paul Gerald*

FOREWORD

Welcome to Menasha Ridge Press's *60 Hikes within 60 Miles*. Our strategy was simple: First, find a hiker who knows the area and loves to hike. Second, ask that person to spend a year researching the most popular and very best trails around. And third, have that person describe each trail in terms of difficulty, scenery, condition, elevation change, and all other categories of information that are important to hikers. "Pretend you've just completed a hike and met up with other hikers at the trailhead," we told each author. "Imagine their questions, and be clear in your answers."

An experienced hiker and writer, author Paul Gerald has selected 60 of the best hikes in and around his adopted hometown of Portland. From the civilized hikes of downtown Portland to the rugged trails of volatile Mount St. Helens, Gerald provides hikers (and walkers) with a great variety of trails—and all within 60 miles of the city.

You'll get more out of this book if you take a moment to read the Introduction explaining how to read the trail listings. The "Topographic Maps" section will help you understand how useful topos will be on a hike, and will also tell you where to get them. And though this is a "where-to" rather than a "how-to" guide, those of you who have hiked extensively will find the Introduction of particular value.

As much for the opportunity to free the spirit as well as to free the body, let Paul Gerald's hikes elevate you above the urban hurry.

All the best,
The Editors at Menasha Ridge Press

ABOUT THE AUTHOR

PAUL GERALD's writing career began in the sports department of the much-missed *Dallas Times Herald.* He later worked for the *Memphis Commercial Appeal* and the *Memphis Flyer* before setting out as a freelancer. Since then, he has written some 300 travel articles for the *Flyer,* and along the way his work has also appeared in Northwest Airlines' *WorldTraveler,* Portland's *Willamette Week, Dish Magazine,* Nike.com, Weissmann Travel Reports, and numerous newspapers around the country.

He's also worked in and around landscaping, restaurants, public relations, social work, an amusement park, Alaskan fishing boats, the YMCA, corporate marketing, and most recently as a package handler for FedEx. Such is the life of a writer who really, really wants to avoid having a regular job.

Paul's hiking life started at age 12, when he went to a summer camp in the Absoraka Mountains of Wyoming. He became a trail and road hound at that point, and his hometown of Memphis never looked the same. He's hiked in the Rocky Mountains from New Mexico to Montana, as well as in Appalachia, Alaska, Nepal, and Argentina. In 1996 he moved to Portland to be close to the ocean, the mountains, and the big trees.

This is his first book; his second is *Day and Overnight Hikes: Oregon's Pacific Crest Trail,* also published by Menasha Ridge Press in 2007. He has greatly enjoyed meeting people using his books out on the trails; he's also grateful that none of them appeared to be lost or angry. He does hope, however, that any feedback will be directed to him, care of the publisher, or at **www.paulgerald.com.** And he hopes people will continue to enjoy and benefit from the fruits of his labor.

PREFACE

IT'S EARLY MARCH in Portland, and the rising sun glows directly behind Mount Hood. Aside from being an inspiring sight—the rays of sun spreading out from behind the mountain, the red glow on the underside of the clouds, the shadow stretching across the city—it's also an inspiring sign. It's confirmation that the sun is moving northward through the sky; warm and dry days are coming, and another hiking season is dawning.

I usually see this wonderful sight from a StairMaster at the YMCA on Barbur Boulevard, where I try to keep my legs and lungs strong over the winter so I can walk up and down hills for the next eight months or so. Sure, you can hike in the winter around here, but who needs it? Short days, muddy trails, rainy skies, few views—I get out there occasionally, because I'm addicted to trails. But the true hiking season starts when that March morning sun rises behind the mountain. That's when I know that very little snow will fall below 3,000 feet, the wildflower show will start in the eastern end of the Columbia River Gorge, the waterfalls will start to go nuclear, and somewhere, up on a hill or out on a trail, a trillium soon will bloom. And once the trillium blooms, I know it's time to get out and hike.

The book you're holding is intended to accompany you into the wonderful world that is day hiking in and around the Portland area. Within these pages are 60 trails that you can hike between breakfast and dinner in the City of Roses. Sixty hikes: at one per week, you've got more than a year of hiking here.

Compared with the pantheon of trails in the area, 60 doesn't seem like many. This corner of America is a hiker's dream, with a wide variety of accessible, well-maintained trails and no shortage of places to find maps, gear, and walking companions. But here are 60 select trails that give you a little of everything there is to enjoy around Portland: mountain

The morning sun rises over Portland, as seen from Washington Park.

views, forest solitude, picturesque streams, strenuous workouts, casual strolls, fascinating history, fields of flowers, awesome waterfalls, and ocean beaches.

This book makes it a point to tell you much more than just which direction to go. Think of it as a pack-sized hiking partner, something you can learn from and enjoy as you go. It points out not just which turns to take, but also what to look for along the way. And it strives to educate: Why is Dog Mountain called Dog Mountain? Why are there cables attached to trees along the Clackamas River? Where do all these trails on Lookout Mountain go? What's with that trail above McNeil Point, the one that's not on the official map? Where is the tallest tree in Portland? How do I find the hidden waterfall near the "Throne of the Forest King?" And for this third edition, I've included driving times to the trailhead and elevations for each trail.

Even if you've hiked some of these trails, hiking them with this book will be a new experience for you. And if you've never laced on a pair of hiking boots, or if you've just arrived in Portland, here are 60 great places to start. Whether you want a convenient city bus ride to the flat and fascinating Washington Park, a bumpy drive to Lookout Mountain, or the thigh-burning experiences that are Kings and Elk mountains, this book will tell you what to bring, how to get to the trailhead, where to go on the trail, and what to look for while you're hiking.

In fact, here's one of my favorite hints—just to get you going—that isn't found elsewhere in this book (or any other): when driving to Mount Hood, don't

Suspension bridge over Drift Creek Falls

follow the signs that say "Mount Hood." I know that sounds odd, but if you are traveling east on Interstate 84, Exit 16/Mount Hood leads you through the heart of Gresham, a tangle of strip malls, fast-food joints, and traffic lights that only slow you down. Forget that. Instead, take Exit 17/ Troutdale, make a right at the second light onto 257th Avenue, and after 4 miles turn left onto Southeast Orient Road. It will drop you back onto US 26 just 1 mile before Sandy, after taking you through the kind of country that Gresham replaced: farms, nurseries, country stores, creeks, and a plain two-lane country road.

Every time I take people this way, they usually say two things: First, "Where are we?" and, later, "Man, this is much nicer than the way I usually go."

I suppose that if I am to be your guide, you may want to know some things about me. While hiking has long been one of my favorite activities, I find that when inviting people to come along, I must often assure them that I am not embarking on a major expedition or a speed event. I am, to put it simply, not fast. The hiking times listed in this book are the times I would spend on a trail if I weren't stopping to make notes for a book. But even when I'm not "working," and that's a real stretch of the word, I also stop to eat, drink, look around, relax, take pictures, and eat some more. In other words, I hike to enjoy myself; I go elsewhere for my workouts. Out on the trail, I average about 2 miles an hour with stops included, but the times in the book take into account factors beyond my natural pace: hills, trail condition, altitude, and the number of times needed to stop and say, "Man, look at that (view, waterfall, creek, meadow, etc.)!"

I had hiked more than these 60 trails before I wrote this book, and the toughest decisions I had to make were which hikes to leave out. The range of the book—a rough circle of 60 miles as the crow flies from the edge of the Portland metro area—is bordered on the north by the south side of Mount St. Helens, on the south by Detroit Lake, on the east by OR 35, and on the west by the Pacific Ocean. Hiking these trails, you'll glimpse everything from desert to coastal rain forest, from volcanic aftermath to 1,000-year-old trees.

These things are on my mind when I'm indoors exercising; all the beauty is out there, just waiting. Maybe, during the winter, we hikers slip out a few times, like when we get a "sunbreak," a word surely made up by weather forecasters in the Pacific Northwest—the same people who distinguish between rain and show-ers. These sunbreaks call us out to the city trails like Forest Park, Washington Park, or the Marquam Trail to Council Crest. Or, we just put on our raincoats to see wild birds in Oaks Bottom or if the steelhead run has made it to Tryon Creek. Sometimes we get tantalizingly clear days, when our eyes glaze over and we say foolish things like, "Is it spring?" Then, we insist on going out to the coast to look for whales from Cape Lookout, into the Gorge to see what Angels Rest is like without 57 other people up there, or down to Silver Falls State Park to see the waterfalls at full blast.

But for the most part, winter is a time to stay in shape at the gym or go play in the snow. March is when the snow starts to melt in lower elevations, especially on south-facing slopes like the Washington side of the gorge. March is when you go to Beacon Rock State Park to warm up for Table or Dog mountains. It's when you get the payoff for your winter workout. Or you wallow in the moisture and go see the great waterfalls of the gorge or hike the Multnomah/Wahkeena loop, Triple Falls, or Eagle Creek before the summer crowds inundate them. Or you drive east of the Rain Shroud, out where it really is spring, to see the wildflowers at McCall Preserve or Catherine Creek.

As the snow line rises, so do the hikers. April means you can drive to the Lewis River Trail, or to Siouxon Creek, or to many of the great hikes in the Clackamas and Santiam watersheds—whether it's the old-growth majesty of Opal Creek or the rolling splendor of the Clackamas River itself. April also means there will be spring chinook spawning in the Salmon River, and you might even glimpse some in the underwater viewing structure at Wildwood. And when your legs get those early-season blues, there are always the hot springs at Breitenbush and Bagby.

May means the meadows on top of places like Saddle Mountain, Kings Mountain, and Dog Mountain are exploding with flowers—as well as weekend crowds, so steal away on a weekday. It also means those trails just a little farther up are about to be snow-free, and that the roads to places like Lava Canyon, Ape Cave, Ramona Falls, and Larch Mountain will be open.

By June the hiking panorama is practically wide open, and the problem becomes where to go. The coast is nice for the duration, so the views are clear from Tillamook Head and Cape Lookout. But back to the east the rhododen-drons are blooming on the trails to Salmon Butte and Mirror Lake. You can prob-ably tackle south-facing Ape Canyon on the flanks of Mount St. Helens by now, too. And if you really want to see how well you're conditioned, take a shot at some of the Mazama trails at Trapper Creek—and remember, when you're done, there are more hot springs just across the river in Carson.

On July 16, a red-letter date on the hiker's calendar, the road opens to the mind-boggling bluffs of Cascade Head out on the coast. And not long after that the rising temperatures make taking a dip in Trillium Lake or Serene Lake seem like a good idea.

And then there's August, which to me means one simple thing: wildflowers up high. Every time I arrive in Wy'east Basin, Paradise Park, Elk Meadows, or the ponds below McNeil Point on an August morning, I say to myself, "This is why I live here!" When people in other places say to me, "How can you handle all that rain?" I answer with one word: "August."

In August, it's sunny and around 85 degrees. You're in shape; the meadows on Hood are snow-free and flower-filled; the butterflies are flitting among the blooms; and all is right with the world. And as August yields to September, the sadness is more than made up for by the ripening huckleberries. Anybody who goes for a late-August walk around 5,000 feet elevation in the Pacific Northwest and doesn't want to move here is either stubborn or insane.

The nice thing about fall is that most people think hiking season is over, so the trails—compared to summer weekends, at least—are practically empty. And September is, in some ways, a sad month, because you know the clear skies are about to end. It feels that way, at least; the truth is that you've still got at least two months before the snows come again, and in the meantime there are the fall colors—the big-leaf maples in Forest Park, the vine maples at Opal Creek, and the mountain ash on the ridge above the Toutle River. The blackberries on the way to Warrior Rock are so numerous you'll think it's an industrial crop, and it's always nice to go back to Silver Falls for a look at the trees and the falls without the throngs of people.

What starts with the sun glowing behind Mount Hood ends with me high up on it. I love the energy of a mountain under threat of winter, and my favorite way to say thanks to the trail gods at the end of the hiking season is to make the long drive to Cloud Cap Saddle, then the long hike to Cooper Spur. I like to sit there with most of the state below me, the October wind blowing a cloud off the summit above me, the Eliot Glacier calving next to me, and about ten of the hikes I've done in my field of vision. I sit and remember the morning I was on the StairMaster, looking up at this mountain and saying, "I can't wait to get up there."

Now, I'm there, and it's time to go back down. By early November, the little rock-walled sitting area at the top of Cooper Spur will be under a foot of snow, and I'll pant once more at the gym, or maybe I'll stroll along the Clackamas or in the Gorge, stealing a few more miles of hiking before the first showers turn to rain. Then I'm living for sunbreaks once again, dreaming of flowers and butterflies and meadows and waterfalls, watching the rising sun retreat back to the south through the windows of the YMCA.

HIKING RECOMMENDATIONS

HIKES GOOD FOR CHILDREN

FLAT HIKES

STEEP HIKES

STEEP HIKES *(continued)*

URBAN HIKES

RURAL HIKES

SECLUDED HIKES

HIKES GOOD FOR WATCHING WILDLIFE

HISTORIC TRAILS *(continued)*

TRAILS FEATURING WATERFALLS

In the following categories, parentheses indicate a shorter option within a longer hike.

HIKES LESS THAN 1 MILE

HIKES 1 TO 3 MILES

HIKES 3 TO 6 MILES

HIKES MORE THAN 6 MILES

60 HIKES
WITHIN 60 MILES

PORTLAND
INCLUDING

THE COAST, MOUNTS HOOD
AND ST. HELENS, AND
THE COLUMBIA RIVER GORGE

INTRODUCTION

Welcome to *60 Hikes within 60 Miles: Portland!* If you're new to hiking or even if you're a seasoned trailsmith, take a few minutes to read the following introduction. We'll explain how this book is organized and how to use it.

HIKE DESCRIPTIONS

Each hike contains seven key items: an In Brief description of the trail, an At-a-Glance Information box, directions to the trail, a locator map, a trail map, and a hike description. Combined, the maps and information provide a clear method to assess each trail from the comfort of your favorite chair.

IN BRIEF

Here you'll get a "taste of the trail." Think of this section as a snapshot focused on the historical landmarks, beautiful vistas, and other interesting sights you may encounter on the trail.

KEY AT-A-GLANCE INFORMATION

The At-a-Glance information boxes give you a quick idea of the specifics of each hike. There are 13 basic elements covered.

LENGTH The length of the trail from start to finish. There may be options to shorten or extend the hikes, but the mileage corresponds to the described hike. Consult the hike description to help decide how to customize the hike for your ability or time constraints.

CONFIGURATION A description of what the trail might look like from overhead. Trails can be loops, out-and-backs (that is, along the same route), figure eights, or balloons. Sometimes the descriptions might surprise you.

DIFFICULTY The degree of effort an "average" hiker should expect on a given hike. For simplicity, difficulty is described as "easy," "moderate," or "strenuous."

1

SCENERY Rates the overall environs of the hike and what to expect in terms of plant life, wildlife, streams, and historic buildings.

EXPOSURE A quick check of how much sun you can expect on your shoulders during the hike. Descriptors used are self-explanatory and include terms such as shady, exposed, and sunny.

TRAFFIC Indicates how busy the trail might be on an average day, and if you might be able to find solitude out there. Trail traffic, of course, varies from day to day and season to season.

TRAIL SURFACE Indicates whether the trail is paved, rocky, smooth dirt, or a mixture of elements.

HIKING TIME How long it took the author to hike the trail. Paul Gerald is a self-described dawdler who often easily fritters away time eating or admiring wildflowers. On average, he covers 2 miles an hour (more mileage hiking downhill, less on steady ascents, particularly during hot weather). If you're an experienced hiker in great shape, you'll finish the hikes with time to spare, but if you're a beginner or like to stop and take in the views, allow a little extra time.

SEASON Time of year when a particular hike is accessible. In most cases, the issue is snow.

ACCESS Notes fees or permits needed to access the hike.

MAPS Which map is the best, or easiest (in the author's opinion) for this hike.

FACILITIES What to expect in terms of restrooms, phones, water, and other niceties available at the trailhead or nearby.

SPECIAL COMMENTS Provides you with those little extra details that don't fit into any of the above categories. Here you'll find assorted nuggets of information, including whether or not your dog is allowed on the trails.

DIRECTIONS

The directions will help you locate each trailhead. When pertinent, numbered exits are included in the driving directions for each hike.

DESCRIPTIONS

The trail description is the heart of each hike. Here, the author provides a summary of the trail's essence and also highlights any special traits the hike offers. Ultimately, the hike description will help you choose which hikes are best for you.

NEARBY ACTIVITIES

Not every hike will have this listing. For those that do, look here for information on nearby sights of interest.

WEATHER

For most folks, hiking season around Portland starts in March or April, when flowers and temperatures start to rise. Unfortunately, that's the least stable of seasons where the weather is concerned. Weather forecasts are notoriously off the mark during spring, so if they aren't absolutely, positively sure it will be clear, plan for 50-something degrees and drizzling into June.

Snow is a different matter; the higher hikes in this book won't be completely clear most years until July. Also beware that in the Columbia River Gorge, wind is a constant reality, so even on a sunny June day a hike like Dog Mountain can have you reaching for hat and gloves. By mid- to late June, and all the way into October, you'll see mostly sunny skies, mild temperatures, and happy hikers. Then winter comes and, for all intents and purposes, it rains until spring. We try to think of it as "waterfall loading."

Average Daily (High) Temperature by Month: PORTLAND

	Jan	Feb	Mar	Apr	May	Jun
High	46	51	56	61	68	74
	Jul	Aug	Sep	Oct	Nov	Dec
High	80	81	75	64	53	46

MAPS

The maps in this book have been produced with great care and, used with the hiking directions, will help you stay on course. But as any experienced hiker knows, things can get tricky off the beaten path.

The maps in this book, when used with the route directions present in each hike profile, are sufficient to direct you to the trail and guide you on it. However, you will find superior detail and valuable information in the United States Geological Survey's 7.5-minute series topographic maps. Topo maps are available online in many locations. The easiest single Web resource is located at **terraserver.microsoft .com**. You can view and print topos of the entire United States there, and view aerial photographs of the entire United States, as well. The downside to topos is that most of them are outdated, having been created 20 to 30 years ago. But they still provide excellent topographic detail.

If you're new to hiking you might be wondering, "What's a topographic map?" In short, a topo indicates not only distance but elevation as well, using contour lines. Contour lines spread across the map like dozens of intricate spiderwebs. Each line represents a particular elevation, and at the base of each topo a contour's interval designation is given. If the contour interval is 200 feet, then the distance between each contour line is 200 feet. Follow five contour lines up on a map and the elevation has increased by 1,000 feet.

In addition to outdoors shops and bike shops, you'll find topos at major universities and some public libraries, where you might try photocopying the ones you need to avoid the cost of buying them. But if you want your own and can't find them locally, contact map retailers (see Appendix C).

TRAIL ETIQUETTE

Whether you're on a city, county, state or national park trail, always remember that great care and resources (from nature as well as from your tax dollars) have gone into creating these trails. Treat the trail, wildlife, and fellow hikers with respect.

Here are a few general ideas to keep in mind while on the trail.

- **Hike on open trails only. Respect trail and road closures (ask if you're not sure), avoid possible trespass on private land, and obtain all permits and authorization as required. Also, leave gates as you found them or as marked.**

- **Leave no trace of your visit other than footprints. Be sensitive to the ground beneath you. This also means staying on the trail and not creating any new ones. Be sure to pack out what you pack in. No one likes to see the trash someone else has left behind.**

- **Never spook animals. An unannounced approach, a sudden movement, or a loud noise startles most animals. A surprised snake or skunk can be dangerous to you, to others, and to themselves. Give animals extra room and time to adjust to your presence.**

- **Plan ahead. Know your equipment, your ability, and the area in which you are hiking—and prepare accordingly. Be self-sufficient at all times; carry necessary supplies for changes in weather or other conditions. A well-executed trip is a satisfaction to you and to others.**

- **Be courteous to other hikers, or bikers, you meet on the trails.**

WATER

"How much is enough? One bottle? Two? Three? But think of all that extra weight!" Well, one simple physiological fact should convince you to err on the side of excess when it comes to deciding how much water to pack—a hiker working hard in 90-degree heat needs approximately ten quarts of fluid every day. That's two and a half gallons—12 large water bottles or 16 small ones. In other words, pack along one or two bottles even for short hikes.

Serious backpackers hit the trail prepared to purify water found along the route. This method, while less dangerous than drinking it untreated, comes with risks. Purifiers with ceramic filters are the safest, but also are the most expensive. Many hikers pack along the slightly distasteful tetraglycine hydroperiodide tablets (sold under the names Potable Aqua, Coughlan's, and others).

Probably the most common waterborne "bug" that hikers face is giardia, which may not hit until one to four weeks after ingestion. It will have you passing noxious rotten-egg gas, vomiting, shivering with chills, and living in the bathroom. But there are other parasites to worry about, including E. coli and cryptosporidium (both of which are harder to kill than giardia).

For most people, the pleasures of hiking make carrying water a relatively small price to pay to remain healthy. If you're tempted to drink "found" water, do so only if you understand the risks involved. Better yet, hydrate prior to your hike, carry (and drink) six ounces of water for every mile you plan to hike, and hydrate after the hike.

FIRST-AID KIT

A typical kit may contain more items than you might think necessary. But these are just the basics:

- **Ace bandages or Spenco joint wraps**
- **Antibiotic ointment (Neosporin or the generic equivalent)**
- **Aspirin or acetaminophen**
- **Band-Aids**
- **Benadryl or the generic equivalent, diphenhydramine (an antihistamine, in case of allergic reactions)**
- **Butterfly-closure bandages**
- **Gauze (one roll)**
- **Gauze compress pads (a half-dozen 4- by 4-inch pads)**
- **Hydrogen peroxide or iodine**
- **Matches or pocket lighter**
- **Moleskin/Spenco "Second Skin"**
- **A prefilled syringe of epinephrine (for those known to have severe allergic reactions to such things as bee stings)**
- **Snakebite kit**
- **Sunscreen**
- **Water purification tablets or water filter (see note above)**
- **Whistle (more effective in signaling rescuers than your voice)**

Pack the items in a self-sealing waterproof bag. You will also want to include a snack for hikes longer than a couple of miles. A bag full of GORP ("good ol' raisins and peanuts") will kick up your energy level fast.

HIKING WITH CHILDREN

No one is too young for a hike in the woods or through a city park. Be careful, though. Flat, short trails are probably best with an infant. Toddlers who have not quite mastered walking can still tag along, riding on an adult's back in a child carrier. Use common sense to judge a child's capacity to hike a particular trail, and be prepared for the possibility that the child will tire quickly and need to be carried.

When packing for the hike, remember the needs of the child as well as your own. Make sure children are adequately clothed for the weather, have proper shoes, and are protected from the sun with sunscreen. Kids dehydrate quickly, so make sure you have plenty of fluid for everyone.

To assist an adult with determining which trails are suitable for children, a list of hike recommendations for children is provided on page xv.

Finally, when hiking with children, remember the trip will be a compromise. A child's energy and enthusiasm alternate between bursts of speed and long stops to examine snails, sticks, dirt, and other attractions.

THE BUSINESS HIKER

Whether you're visiting or a resident in the Portland area, these hikes are the ideal opportunity for a quick getaway from your everyday demands. Many of the hikes are classified as urban and are easily accessible from downtown areas.

Instead of grabbing a burger down the street, pack a lunch and head out to one of the area's many urban trails for a relaxing break from the office or that tiresome convention. Or plan ahead and take a small group of your business comrades on a nearby hike in one of the area forests. A well-planned half-day getaway is the perfect complement to a business stay in Portland.

SNAKES

The most common snakes you'll encounter in and west of the Cascades are non-poisonous garter snakes. The only venomous snakes in Oregon are rattlesnakes, but sightings of these pit vipers are generally infrequent, occurring most commonly in dry, rocky, or exposed zones east of the mountains. The standard rules for hiking in rattlesnake territory are:

- **Do not put your hands (or feet) where you can't see them—for example, on top of a rock outcrop or in a log pile.**
- **Be extra-cautious in hot weather, as snakes are more active.**
- **Scan the trail continuously as you hike.**
- **Keep children from running ahead on trails. Bites to children are more severe than to adults.**
- **Avoid tall grass where you can't see your feet (or a potential snake).**

Should you encounter a rattler, its body language will reveal its mood. A coiled rattler is primed for a strike, while a stretched rattler is more sanguine (although snakes have been reported to "lunge"). If the snake is within striking distance, stand motionless and wait for the snake to calm down and move. Taking small, slow steps backward is also an option. If you're out of immediate range, you can either skirt the snake or wait for it to move. Some people believe tapping the ground with a stick (from a safe distance, rather than in the snake's face) will encourage the snake to move on.

RATTLESNAKE

TICKS

Ticks like to hang out in the brush that grows along trails. I've noticed ticks mostly in the eastern Gorge, but you should be tick-aware during all months of the spring, summer, and fall. Ticks, actually arthropods and not insects, are ectoparasites, which need a host for the majority of their life cycle in order to reproduce. The ticks that light onto you while hiking will be very small, sometimes so tiny that you won't be able to spot them. Primarily of two varieties, deer ticks and dog ticks, both need a few hours of actual attachment before they can transmit any disease they may harbor. I've found ticks in my socks and on my legs several hours after a hike that have not yet anchored. The best strategy is to visually check every half hour or so while hiking, do a thorough check before you get in the car, and then, when you take a posthike shower, do an even more thorough check of your entire body. Ticks that haven't latched on are easily removed, though not easily killed. If I pick off a tick in the woods, I just toss it aside. If I find one on my person at home, I make sure to dispatch it down the toilet. For ticks that have embedded, removal with tweezers is best.

POISON OAK

Poison oak is a deciduous plant that grows as sparse groundcover, vine, or shrub; regardless of its form, poison oak always has three leaflets. It is easiest to spot in summer and early autumn, when the leaves flush bright red. Beware of unknown bare-branched shrubs and vines in winter—the entire plant can cause a rash no matter what the season.

The rashes are caused by urushiol, the oil in the sap of poison oak. Reactions may start almost immediately, or may not appear until a week after exposure. Raised lines and/or blisters appear, accompanied by a terrible itch. Refrain from scratching because bacteria under fingernails may cause infection. Wash and dry the rash thoroughly, and apply a calamine lotion to help dry out the rash. If itching or blistering is severe, seek medical attention.

Recognizing and avoiding poison oak is the most effective way to prevent painful, itchy rashes. Most people come into contact with the plant while they're bushwhacking or traveling off-trail, so you can minimize your encounters with poison oak by staying on established trails. If you do knowingly contact poison oak, you must remove the oil within 15 to 20 minutes to avoid a reaction. Showering on the trail with cool water (hot water spreads the oil) is impractical, but some commercial products such as Tecnu clean the oil off skin.

If you come into contact with poison oak, remember that oil-contaminated clothes, pets, or hiking gear can easily inflict an irritating rash on you or someone else, so wash not only any exposed parts of your body but also clothes, gear, and pets if applicable.

POISON OAK

IN THE COLUMBIA RIVER GORGE

01 ANGELS REST-DEVILS REST

KEY AT-A-GLANCE INFORMATION

LENGTH: 4.6 miles

CONFIGURATION: Out-and-back

DIFFICULTY: Moderate, due to altitude gain and a little rock scrambling at the top

SCENERY: Forest most of the way, waterfall, creek crossing, panorama at the top

EXPOSURE: Shady except for one section

TRAFFIC: Heavy; on a nice weekend day this trail will have more dogs on it than many trails have hikers.

TRAIL SURFACE: Packed dirt with some roots, rocks

HIKING TIME: 2.5 hours

DRIVING DISTANCE: 28 miles (30 minutes) from Pioneer Square

SEASON: Year-round

ACCESS: No fees or permits needed

WHEELCHAIR ACCESS: None, but nearby Bridal Veil State Park has some accessible trails

MAPS: Trails of the Columbia Gorge; Green Trails #428 (Bridal Veil); USGS Bridal Veil

FACILITIES: Restrooms and water 0.5 miles west at Bridal Veil State Park

SPECIAL COMMENTS: If you're going on a weekend, consider starting out early to avoid traffic.

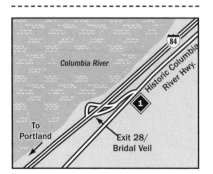

IN BRIEF

There's a reason for all the parking at this trailhead: it's one of the finer hikes around, with a gentle grade to a spectacular lookout point above the Columbia River. It also connects with the Wahkeena Trail, making longer loops or one-way hikes with shuttles possible.

DESCRIPTION

As you drive out Interstate 84, you can actually see Angels Rest, a flat-topped rock outcropping sticking out over the road at the end of a ridge. What looks like a building on top is in fact a clump of trees. And if it looks like it's way up there, just remember that if you take your time on the way up you'll have plenty of breath left to be taken away by the view up top.

The trail starts with a climb that is only steep for a moment and leads through the woods to an early reward: a rare view down at a waterfall, in this case 100-foot Coopey Falls. Soon thereafter, the trail crosses a wooden bridge over Coopey Creek and then starts climbing just a little more steeply.

After about a mile, you'll start switching back through an area that burned in 1991; note the blackened trunks of some of the bigger trees. It was mostly just the underbrush and smaller trees that burned, opening up the forest floor to the sun and letting wildflowers

Directions ───────────────►

From Portland on I-84, drive 21 miles east of I-205 to Exit 28/Bridal Veil. After less than a mile, park in the parking area at the intersection with the Historic Columbia River Highway; there's a second parking lot down the road to the right. The signed trailhead is on the old highway between the two parking lots.

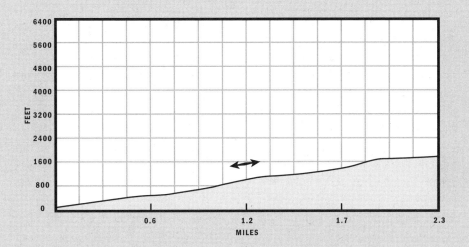

Columbia River just east of Mosier Tunnel from Historic Columbia River Highway

come in to take your mind off the climb. Follow a series of small switchbacks into more open country, getting a view of the rocky face of Angels Rest as you go, and when the trail traverses a rockslide for 100 yards, you're almost done.

Just past the slide, the trail goes back into the woods briefly, and you turn left out onto the final ridge. This last stretch of the trail is why you might think twice about bringing small children: It gets a little narrow, with cliffs to the east falling away a few hundred feet, and in one spot you'll have to scramble up about ten feet of rocks. When a trail goes back and to the right on the ridgetop, stay straight.

The reward for this small effort is a view to rival any other in the Gorge. To the east, you can see Beacon Rock and the high walls on either side of the river. To the west you can see Vista House (built in 1916 as a pioneer memorial and rest stop for travelers, now an interpretive center, museum, and gift shop) and the hills falling away toward Portland and the Willamette Valley. The Columbia River, right below you, seems so close that you could get a running start and jump into it. You might see some windsurfers out there; on one trip, I watched a floatplane practicing touch-and-go landings on this stretch of the river. If it's really clear, you'll have a view of Silver Star Mountain right across the river. You can also see two other hikes from this book: Right next to Beacon Rock is the step-shaped Hamilton Mountain, and the big flat-topped mountain looming behind that is Table Mountain. There's even a nice bench to sit on out there. All in all, it's hard to imagine a better place to have lunch.

If you're up for more hiking, you can turn this into a longer out-and-back or do a one-way hike with another car parked farther east. To do this, as you walk back down the ridge, veer left (east) instead of keeping straight, which is where you came from. After a few minutes you'll come to a junction; go left to head for the Wahkeena Trail or straight 1 mile up the Foxglove Trail to Devils Rest.

If you turn left, you'll come to Wahkeena Spring in 2.6 miles, and 0.1 mile later you'll intersect the Wahkeena Trail (#420). Here, you can turn left (down-hill) and follow Wahkeena Creek 1.6 miles down to the picnic area at Wahkeena Falls, or you can go straight and, in 1.2 miles, intersect the Larch Mountain Trail. Go down that one for 1.8 miles, and you'll be at Multnomah Falls. There's a more detailed description of this trail section in the Wahkeena Falls to Mult-nomah Falls profile (page 57).

NEARBY ACTIVITIES

Vista House, and the road that leads to it, are both worth a visit. To get there, simply drive back toward Portland on the Historic Highway, rather than on I-84. Follow the 90-year-old road and its moss-covered stone guardrails past a few other waterfalls and then up the hill to Crown Point, where you can step into Vista House and take in a postcard view and historic displays about the building of the road. Keep going west on that road past Vista House, and in a couple of miles you'll see a sign leading you down a steep hill back to I-84.

02 BEACON ROCK-HAMILTON MOUNTAIN

KEY AT-A-GLANCE INFORMATION

LENGTH: 1.6 miles to top of Beacon Rock; 7 miles to Hamilton Mountain

CONFIGURATION: Out-and-back, loop

DIFFICULTY: Moderate (Hamilton Mountain is strenuous).

SCENERY: Overlooks of the Columbia River, close-up view of a waterfall, spring wildflowers, amazing trail construction

EXPOSURE: Fairly open

TRAFFIC: Heavy on weekends

TRAIL SURFACE: Packed dirt with rocks, pavement

HIKING TIME: 1 hour for Beacon Rock, 3.5 hours for Hamilton Mountain

DRIVING DISTANCE: 51 miles (1 hour and 10 minutes) from Pioneer Square

SEASON: Year-round; call for trail conditions in winter.

ACCESS: No fees or permits needed.

WHEELCHAIR ACCESS: None

MAPS: Green Trails #428 (Bridal Veil)

FACILITIES: Water and restrooms

SPECIAL COMMENTS: For more information, phone Washington State Parks at (360) 902-8844.

IN BRIEF

One of the most recognized symbols of the Columbia River Gorge, Beacon Rock is also an amazing, if short, hiking experience—and it's not even all this state park has to offer. There's also a rigorous climb to scenic Hamilton Mountain and an amazing waterfall on the way.

DESCRIPTION

Beacon Rock got its name—well, its white man's name—on Halloween 1805, when William Clark described it in his journal. For the Corps of Discovery as well as the people who then lived along the Columbia River, Beacon Rock meant two important things: the last of the rapids on the Columbia and the beginning of tidal influence on the river. Today, it means a unique hiking experience to its summit, and the state park around it means a chance to take in more nice views of the Columbia River.

To go up Beacon Rock, which is a climb of nearly 600 feet in less than a mile, start walking at a sign on the south side of WA 14

Directions

From Portland on I-84, drive 37 miles east of I-205 and take Exit 44/Cascade Locks. As soon as you enter the town, take your first right to get on the Bridge of the Gods, following a sign for Stevenson, Washington. Pay a $1 toll on the bridge, and at the far end turn left (west) on WA 14. Proceed 6.6 miles to Beacon Rock State Park. To climb Beacon Rock, park on the left; to go toward Hamilton Mountain, turn right on the access road to the campground and drive 0.25 miles to the trailhead. The gate to the upper trailhead is closed in winter and spring, but the trail is open; you'll just have to park on WA 14 and walk up the access road.

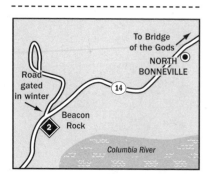

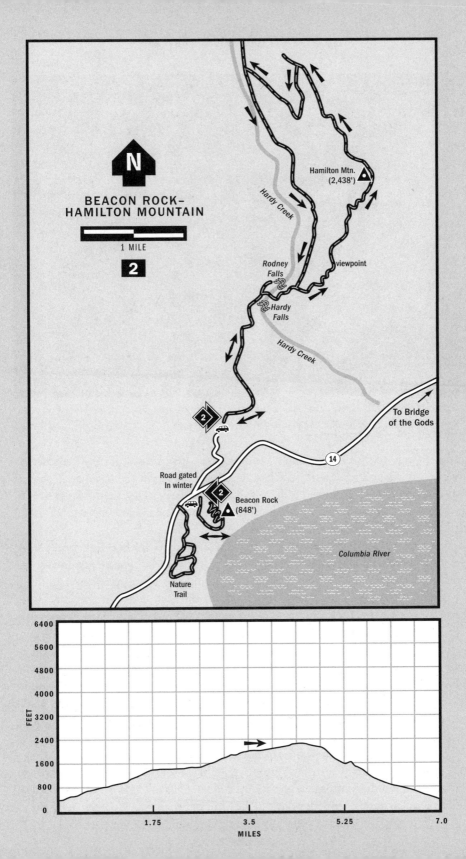

N

BEACON ROCK–
HAMILTON MOUNTAIN

1 MILE

2

Hamilton Mtn.
(2,438')

Hardy Creek

Rodney
Falls

viewpoint

Hardy
Falls

Hardy Creek

2

To Bridge
of the Gods

14

Road gated
In winter

2

Beacon Rock
(848')

Columbia River

Nature
Trail

FEET

6400
5600
4800
4000
3200
2400
1600
800
0

1.75   3.5   5.25   7.0

MILES

Hardy Falls, on the way to Hamilton Mountain

and get ready to give thanks and admiration to a man named Henry J. Biddle. It was he who bought the rock (which is what's left of the inside of an ancient volcano) specifically to build the trail you're about to hike. That he did so is simply amazing; that he did it with the help of just one other person from October 1915 to April 1918 is almost beyond comprehension.

To get to the top, just keep it up and, if heights bother you, don't look down. It's virtually all rails and bridges and platforms until you're just below the summit, where you'll have a view east to Bonneville Dam, north to Hamilton Mountain, and straight down the other side to the boat docks of the state park. Keep an eye out for rock climbers, and don't throw anything from the top.

For a more challenging and more rewarding hike, drive (or walk, if the gate is closed) up the road across WA 14 to the campground and the Hamilton Mountain trailhead. You'll climb gently through forest until you reach a bench to take a break, although the power lines you're under aren't all that scenic. At 0.5 miles, stay straight at a trail leading left to the campground, and 0.9 miles later you'll come to a trail leading down and to the right for 100 yards to two viewpoints of Hardy Falls. A minute past that on the main trail, you'll see a sign that says "Hamilton Mountain"—and, oddly enough, points downhill.

For a sight to remember, and also if you'd like a soaking to cool you down, go left a couple hundred yards and check out Rodney Falls (also known as the Pool of Winds), which almost explodes out of a bowl in the rock face. You can get right in its spray, if you don't mind essentially wading throughout the last part of the trail.

If you don't feel like climbing anymore, turn back here, as it gets tougher quickly. For Hamilton Mountain, follow the signed trail as it drops down to, then crosses, Hardy Creek and then heads up the hill. After 0.2 miles of climbing, you'll come to a trail junction with two wonderful options: difficult and more difficult. To the left is the return portion of a possible loop hike, but keep to the right (the more difficult way), and after some sturdy climbing you'll reach a spectacular rock lookout. There's nothing wrong with turning around here, but be careful as you walk around on these rocks—in some spots it's more than 200 feet straight down.

But if you want the real view, keep going up, and in the first few minutes watch for side trails leading to the top of the ridge. After gaining 700 feet in just over a mile, reach a junction on top of the mountain. The view south is somewhat blocked by brush, but you can see up to Table Mountain (see page 49) to the northeast, Mount Adams just east of that, and Mount St. Helens to the northwest. The scenery is better on the route you just came up, but if you want to complete the loop, continue back along the ridge for 0.9 miles, turn left onto an old road, pick up the Hardy Creek Trail less than a mile later, and follow that trail through the woods for another mile. That puts you back at the junction mentioned above, just east of Rodney Falls. Turn right and you'll be back at the trailhead in 1.6 miles.

NEARBY ACTIVITIES

The Columbia Gorge Interpretive Center, a few miles east on WA 14 in Stevenson, features historical displays ranging from the geological (formation of the gorge) to the steam engines used on railroads a bit more recently.

03 CATHERINE CREEK

KEY AT-A-GLANCE INFORMATION

LENGTH: Up to 4.1 miles

CONFIGURATION: Loop

DIFFICULTY: Easy–moderate

SCENERY: Wide-open vistas, a geological curiosity, and (in spring) flowers, flowers everywhere!

EXPOSURE: Out in the open most of the way, optional trip to a clifftop

TRAFFIC: Heavy on weekends in late spring and early summer; light otherwise

TRAIL SURFACE: Dirt and some rock, also a small paved section

HIKING TIME: 30 minutes–4 hours

DRIVING DISTANCE: 72 miles (1 hour and 30 minutes) from Pioneer Square

SEASON: Year-round, but late March to early June is the time to go

ACCESS: No fees or permits required.

WHEELCHAIR ACCESS: A series of loops below the parking area offers access to flowers, birds, views of the Columbia River, and a waterfall on Catherine Creek.

FACILITIES: Portable restroom at the trailhead, but no drinkable water around

IN BRIEF

For ten months of the year, there's really no reason to go to Catherine Creek, but in April and May, there's no better place to be, for Catherine Creek at that time is wildflower heaven.

DESCRIPTION

In a typical hiking year, there are usually some hikes that I do before Catherine Creek, but my personal hiking season really starts when the grass widows bloom at Catherine Creek in late March. It gets serious when the camas blooms in early April. And my personal Easter Sunday tradition is to pack a lunch, hike up the hill to a certain spot, spread out my food, take in the view, and listen to the meadowlarks. Then I go back to rainy old Portland.

There's really not much to this hike, physically speaking. In fact, there's a paved and wheelchair-accessible section below the road that you could knock out in about 15 minutes. It's really all about the flowers. From the road, walk through a gate and choose a path that tends to the right toward a small canyon just up the hill. If you're like me, you'll stop within a few feet and start admiring flowers. One enthusiast has counted as many as 82 different species in bloom here on an April day, with

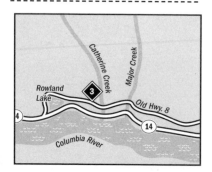

Directions

From Portland on I-84, drive 57 miles east of I-205 and take Exit 64, the third exit for Hood River, Oregon. Turn left at the end of the ramp, following signs for White Salmon, Washington. Pay a 75¢ toll to cross the Columbia River, then turn right onto WA 14. Travel 5.7 miles and turn left onto Old Highway 8. The parking area is 1.4 miles ahead, on the left.

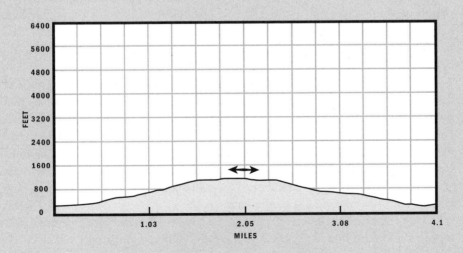

such fantastic names as chocolate lily, common bastard toad flax, rough wallflower, Columbia Gorge lupine, least hop clover, poet's shooting star, rigid fiddleneck, great hound's tongue, slender popcorn flower, small-flowered blue-eyed Mary, and chickweed monkey flower. (I didn't make up any of those names!) I can only identify about five kinds of flowers, but I love them all, and it seems like they're all at Catherine Creek.

Drop into the canyon, then follow the path as it starts up the creek. Watch out for poison oak; it's everywhere, including a stand of it on the right just as you near the creek. After a quarter mile, you'll cross the creek (either by fording it or on a cool, bouncy plank bridge) and 100 yards later arrive at an old homestead. The little white flowers that fill the corral here are called miner's lettuce, and you can eat them. Above you now is the geological curiosity, a natural arch that we'll visit later.

Past the homestead, you'll go up a slight rise and into a meadow. In May, under some of the bushes, you'll find dense thickets of irises—technically not wildflowers, but lovely nonetheless. When you reach the power lines, a total of 0.8 miles since the car, you'll have your first decision to make. There are basically three options: a lower loop, an upper loop, and an exploration. For the lower loop, follow the road to the right here, and your hike will be less than a mile. I'll describe that section later, because you really should at least do the upper loop.

For the upper loop, follow a trail that continues up the ravine to your right (as you came up through the meadow). It will climb gradually for a half mile, through oak trees and past big, yellow balsamroot flowers (among many others), until it eventually pops out into the upper meadows. You might call this the Catherine Creek high country, but it's hardly 500 feet above the trailhead. Just go east into the meadows, and within 100 feet you'll encounter a trail heading up the hill. If you turn right and go downhill, this is the upper loop.

But now that you're up here, you really should do the exploration. For one option, you can strike out to the east and join the flower lovers, photographers, kids, dogs, and couples. I have fond memories of a guy I encountered out here who had a butterfly net and a big, boyish grin, practically skipping along. My favorite option here is to follow the trail up the hill (that's north) to the treeline, where another trail runs east and west. Turn left on that one, and it crosses another line of trees and enters yet another huge meadow. The trail sort of peters out in that meadow, but if you look up and to the right, you'll see a clump of trees that shelters a tiny spring. Just below that is a berm, created to capture the spring water. And on that berm a guy could have himself quite a fine Easter picnic, with the Columbia River laid out at his feet, flowers all around, and Mount Hood right across the way.

For the sake of being complete, I have included this longest option on my elevation profile, making a 4.1-mile loop.

Now, for heading home. From the trail we first encountered in the upper meadow, just head downhill, and if all the trails confuse you (people tend to wander here) just aim between the island in the Columbia and the orchards on the far side. You'll cross back under the power lines and come into a few more trees, then

April-blooming camas in the high country above Catherine Creek

pick up a clearer trail, tending right, that hugs the top of the ridge above Catherine Creek. Following this, you'll get a view down into the canyon where the homestead is, and then you'll be at the top of the arch. You can get out on top of it (it's wider than it looks, but be careful), and you can also walk down through it to get back to the homestead. But why should you? There's more to see up here.

Keep going down the hill, and when in doubt stay close to the cliff edge. You'll enter a little draw filled with purple camas, with creek access on your right, and a few minutes later you'll be at the road—and probably as close to power lines as you'll ever be in your life. Turn right here, and a little rock scramble will put you on the shoulder of the road, on which you'll cross the creek again and see the parking lot, just up the hill.

You could go up there and call it quits, but Catherine Creek has one more surprise for you. On the other side of the road, at the far end of the guardrail, take a little trail that goes back down toward the creek. You'll get to visit a lovely little waterfall down there, then you can climb a hill to a bench. That bench is on the paved section of the trail that's below the road where you parked, and if you keep turning right you'll be back at the car in no time. Be sure to stop and read some of the interpretive signs, especially the one that explains a little of the history of the area you've just wandered through.

Catherine Creek has a neighbor hike to the west called Coyote Wall (see next section), and the two hikes share a pair of secret doors to one another.

I shall now give the secret away. The upper one is described in reverse on the following pages; for the lower one, start at the Catherine Creek trailhead and go left on another old road, which climbs gently through marshy areas and over small hills. After a quarter mile, it arrives at an uphill turn back to the right, at the top of a cliff. For many years, a big dead tree has been lying here, and if you go behind that tree, you'll see a small trail heading down to the west, along the face of the cliff. Didn't see *that,* did you?

This little trail hugs a steep, rocky hillside for a short time, then drops down into a grassy bowl, where it intersects yet another old road heading steeply uphill. Follow this road as it climbs, then swings to the left and becomes a trail. You'll pass a series of rock pits that Native Americans used as vision quest sites—don't disturb them!—and the trail keeps winding west, up through the oaks. I call it a "faith trail," because it seems to be going nowhere. Trust me, it does.

Where it goes is through several meadows some 700 feet above Rowland Lake, then past a freaky tree known as the Coyote Tree (complete with bones hanging in it) and finally down into a mess of trails, all of which lead into an area called the Labyrinth. For a description of that area, see the Coyote Wall–Labyrinth profile that follows. Combining these two hikes into about a 10-mile round-trip (I usually start at Coyote Wall) is one of my absolute favorites and an annual tradition each April.

For more information, contact the Columbia River Gorge National Scenic Area office at (541) 308-1700.

COYOTE WALL-THE LABYRINTH   04

IN BRIEF

Let's say it's springtime, at least according to the calendar, but Portland is socked-in and wet. Go east, young hiker! To the high and dry lands of the Columbia River Gorge, where flowers bloom, birds croon, and the Coyote Wall looms.

DESCRIPTION

Standing at the trailhead, looking up at Coyote Wall, one might feel a bit intimidated. Fear not, for the way is gradual and the work much rewarding. Just follow the old road around Locke Lake, eventually around the base of the wall itself. Turn left at the first cairn leading uphill, and immediately you're faced with a wealth of trail options. Mountain bikers zip through here in every direction, but our path is always the one to the left and uphill.

Soon, the trail you're on (actually an old Jeep road) is the only one around, and soon you're working your way up the edge of the wall—though rarely too close to be of concern. Just less than a mile up, reach a fence with yet more trail options, and once again stay to the left—and up. Above the fence, the steep road is one option, but so is a switch-backing, more scenic trail.

KEY AT-A-GLANCE INFORMATION

LENGTH: 5.7 miles

CONFIGURATION: Loop

DIFFICULTY: Moderate

SCENERY: Clifftop vistas, wide-open country, spring wildflowers

EXPOSURE: Along a cliff at times and out in the open almost the whole way

TRAFFIC: Moderate on spring weekends

TRAIL SURFACE: Dirt; can be slick when wet

HIKING TIME: 3 hours

DRIVING DISTANCE: 69 miles (1 hour and 15 minutes) from Pioneer Square

SEASON: Year-round, but spring is best

ACCESS: No fee required

WHEELCHAIR ACCESS: The first half-mile is on an old paved road.

MAPS: USGS White Salmon

FACILITIES: None at the trailhead

SPECIAL COMMENTS: This hike can be combined into a big loop with the Catherine Creek hike (page 20). There's an upper and lower connection between the two; the upper will be described here, and the lower is described in the Catherine Creek profile.

Directions ⟶

From Portland on I-84, drive 57 miles east of I-205 and take Exit 64, the third exit for Hood River, Oregon. Turn left at the end of the ramp, following signs for White Salmon, Washington. Pay a 75¢ toll to cross the Columbia River, then turn right onto WA 14. Go 4.6 miles, turn left onto Courtney Road, and look for parking 100 yards ahead on the left.

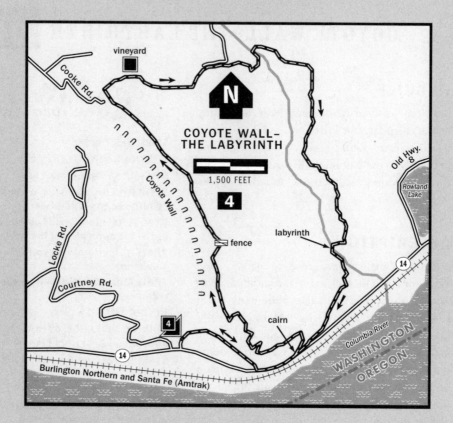

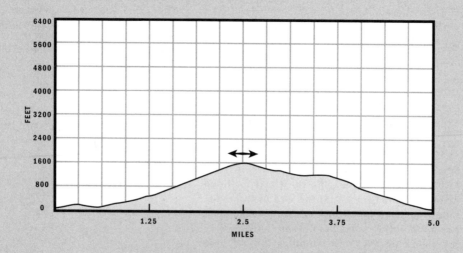

Looking up the Coyote Wall from the trail

After 1.2 miles of steady climbing, generally through a sea of flowers with views behind you to the Columbia and Mount Hood beyond, you reach a junction with several old roads at the head of the wall, close to an area with plenty of big logs to rest on. You could simply turn back here, but more interesting things await. Take the old road into the trees and bear right through a few intersections until you reach the corner of a large, fenced vineyard.

From here, look for a trail dropping downhill though a gap in the trees, and take it as it heads back toward the river and then swings left (east). Stick with this trail as it winds in and out of the trees and then emerges into open country at the top of a broad, open ridge leading down to the right. A trail along this ridge (one of several you will have seen by now) leads down into the Labyrinth. More on that later.

Now, if you're looking for the "upper" connection to Catherine Creek, keep going east until you reach a gravel road, and follow it to the right. The trail ducks back into the woods on the left after 100 yards or so on the road, and soon after this, there's a piece of road that goes right to a nice view and a couple of magnificent oak trees. Keep taking trails to the left, into the woods—and beware the massive amounts of poisonous oak in here.

You'll pass a potential right turn in some woods, just before a creek (don't take it) and then, in a patch of evergreen forest, a left turn leads onto old road—and an old dishwasher! This is your right turn; follow another road into the woods, cross under massive power lines, then stay east and head down a steep, rocky road into Catherine Creek canyon. You'll wind up at the crossing of the creek about a quarter mile up from the trailhead.

Now, if you don't want to deal with all that and just do this loop, follow the trail down the ridge and into the Labyrinth. True to its name, this area can get confusing. The bottom line, though, is that if you keep heading downhill and to the right, you will emerge on the abandoned highway very near where you first left it. The Labyrinth is filled with hidden wonders: waterfalls, a small cave, small buttes to climb, and hidden meadows filled with flowers. So take your time, have faith, and enjoy yourself.

NEARBY ACTIVITIES

Bingen is worth a stop on the way home, especially the slightly bizarre combination coffee–antiques shop called Antiques and Oddities.

DOG MOUNTAIN 05

IN BRIEF

This is probably the most popular of the real hiking trails in the Columbia River Gorge—"real" meaning it requires some real effort. But with an easy-access trailhead, great views of the river, and sunshine and wildflowers at a time when it's still raining in Portland, it's no wonder everybody on Earth comes here.

DESCRIPTION

It seems that everyone around Portland who hikes has been up Dog Mountain. Climbers use it as an early-season conditioner. Wildflower enthusiasts flock to it in early summer. In spring, when it's still raining in Portland, it tends to be sunny here. But most people take the main Dog Mountain Trail, which is therefore crowded, and which was also designed, it seems, to punish the legs and lungs of those who would hike it. This thing is steep! You can come down this way, if you want, but it's no bargain then, either.

Instead, from the parking lot, take the trail on the left, the Augsperger Mountain Trail. It's 0.6 miles longer, but whoever designed it had a much better grasp of the concept of "grade." That's not to say it's easy—it's 3.7 uphill miles, gaining 2,700 feet in elevation. But it's steady, whereas parts of the other trail are insane, and

KEY AT-A-GLANCE INFORMATION

LENGTH: 6.9 miles

CONFIGURATION: Loop

DIFFICULTY: Strenuous

SCENERY: Second-growth forest, wildflowers, and a panoramic view of the Columbia River Gorge

EXPOSURE: Alternates between shady and open

TRAFFIC: Use is very heavy on weekends but moderate otherwise.

TRAIL SURFACE: Packed dirt with rocks, some gravel

HIKING TIME: 4 hours

DRIVING DISTANCE: 56 miles (1 hour and 30 minutes) from Pioneer Square

SEASON: Year-round, but it occasionally gets snowfall on top.

ACCESS: Northwest Forest Pass required.

WHEELCHAIR ACCESS: None

MAPS: Trails of the Columbia Gorge; Green Trails #430 (Hood River)

FACILITIES: Toilets at the trailhead, but no water

Directions

From Portland on I-84, drive 37 miles east of I-205 and take Exit 44/Cascade Locks. As soon as you enter the town, take your first right to get on the Bridge of the Gods, following a sign for Stevenson, Washington. Pay a $1 toll on the bridge, and at the far end turn right onto WA 14. Proceed 12 miles to the trailhead on the left. Start early in the day on this one, if only to make sure you get a parking place.

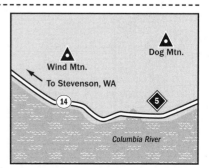

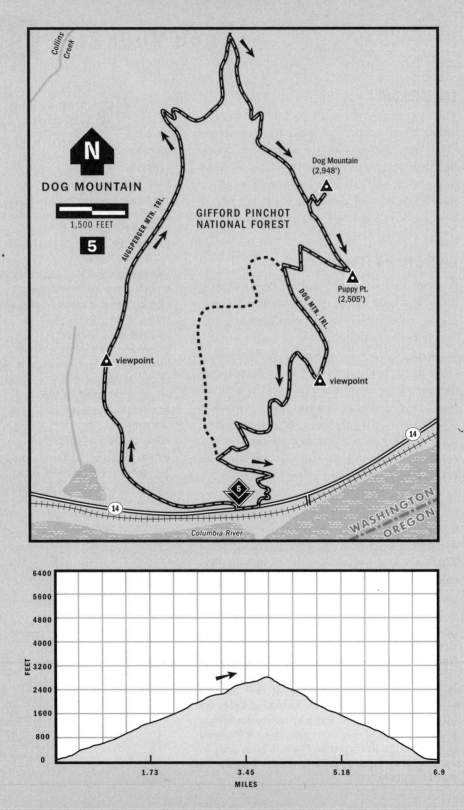

Wind Mountain and the Columbia River from the Augsperger Mountain Trail on Dog Mountain

you'll spend more time in the meadows up top. So take this one as it contours left, with ever-improving views of the river and Wind Mountain. When you turn right and away from the river, you will have gone 0.9 miles and gained 600 feet. Not so bad, right? In the next 1.3 miles you'll gain 1,000 feet. That's when the switchbacks start—and remember, this is the "easier" way. The next half mile gains some 600 feet. Then you'll turn right at a junction toward Dog Mountain.

I'd like to take this moment to explain why Dog Mountain is called Dog Mountain. It's not because of all the dogs on the trail. It's because some pioneers in the area were forced to eat their dogs to avoid starvation. The town of Hood River, Oregon, was in fact first called Dog River, but the name was changed because nobody liked it. Imagine that.

With this knowledge in your head, enjoy a few minutes of flat trail before you climb again and pop out into the sun. Now it's time to claim your reward for all that climbing. In May and June, the open slopes of Dog Mountain are awash in flowers, especially big yellow balsamroot; but year-round, the views here of the river and other mountains—including Mount Hood, which peeks its head over the far side—are sublime. Stroll through this area and know that virtually all your climbing is done. You'll intersect the Dog Mountain Trail after 0.9 miles; turn left and, just 0.1 mile up, you'll be at the top of a sloped meadow with everybody and their dogs.

The view here stretches from the high desert of eastern Oregon to Beacon Rock in the west—look how small it is! Way to the right is Mount St. Helens.

Directly across the way is 4,960-foot Mount Defiance, the one with radio towers on top—look how big it is! The highest point in the gorge, it seems to taunt, "Yeah right, you've climbed barely half of me."

To hike down Dog Mountain, take the scenic loop. From the summit, go left on a trail that soon ducks into the trees, some of which are surprisingly large. Keep an eye out for Mount Adams to the north. This trail rejoins the other branch of the Dog Mountain Trail at a lookout that's actually called Puppy Point (2,505 feet in elevation). Then the bottom drops out, and you lose 600 feet in the next half mile before a junction. You'll save 0.2 miles by going right, but it's worth it to go left for one last view of the river 0.6 miles down. Stay left at another junction 1 mile later, and after a final 0.5 miles you can finally rest your throbbing feet.

For more information, contact the Columbia River Gorge National Scenic Area office at (541) 386-2333.

NEARBY ACTIVITIES

When you get back across to Cascade Locks, take a ride on the sternwheeler *Columbia Gorge,* which has several scenic trips per day from mid-June through September.

EAGLE CREEK 06

IN BRIEF

One of the classic and most popular hikes in Oregon, seemingly everybody has done part of Eagle Creek. That's because this hike's easy to get to, easy to hike, and several kinds of beautiful. So start early, or go on a weekday, so you won't have to share it with everybody in the state.

DESCRIPTION

The magic of this hike, at certain times of the year, begins before you even hit the trail itself. Eagle Creek has a small run of fall chinook salmon—fish that spend their adult lives in the ocean, come more than 70 miles up the Columbia, swim through the fish ladder at Bonneville Dam, and then come here to spawn. A small dam blocks their further progress up Eagle Creek, but in October and November they spawn in little round pools cleared by volunteers to simulate conditions in a wild mountain stream.

The trail was built before 1920 to coincide with the opening of the Columbia River Highway. Although that historic roadway has mostly been gobbled up by I-84, the section from Bonneville Dam to Cascade Locks (which passes right by Eagle Creek) has been converted into a hiking and biking trail, as have a few other sections.

The work that went into the Eagle Creek Trail is a heroic feat. They chipped the trail

KEY AT-A-GLANCE INFORMATION

LENGTH: 4 miles round-trip to Punchbowl Falls; 12.5 miles round-trip to Tunnel Falls

CONFIGURATION: Out-and-back

DIFFICULTY: Easy–moderate

SCENERY: Waterfalls, old-growth forest, spawning salmon in the fall

EXPOSURE: Mostly shady, but some walking (with cables) along cliffs

TRAFFIC: Use is heavy throughout the summer but moderate in the spring and fall.

TRAIL SURFACE: Packed dirt and rocks

HIKING TIME: 2 hours to Punchbowl Falls; 5.5 hours to Tunnel Falls

DRIVING DISTANCE: 41 miles (45 minutes) from Pioneer Square

SEASON: Year-round, but it will be muddy in the winter and spring.

ACCESS: Northwest Forest Pass required.

WHEELCHAIR ACCESS: There's a road along, and a bridge over, Eagle Creek near the trailhead.

MAPS: Trails of the Columbia Gorge

FACILITIES: Toilets at the trailhead, but no water

Directions

From Portland on I-84, drive 34 miles east of I-205 and take Exit 41/Eagle Creek. Go 0.2 miles and turn right, then 0.6 miles to the end of the road. If it's crowded, you might need to park closer to the highway and hike that much farther.

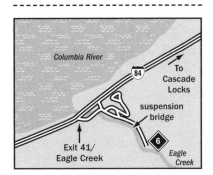

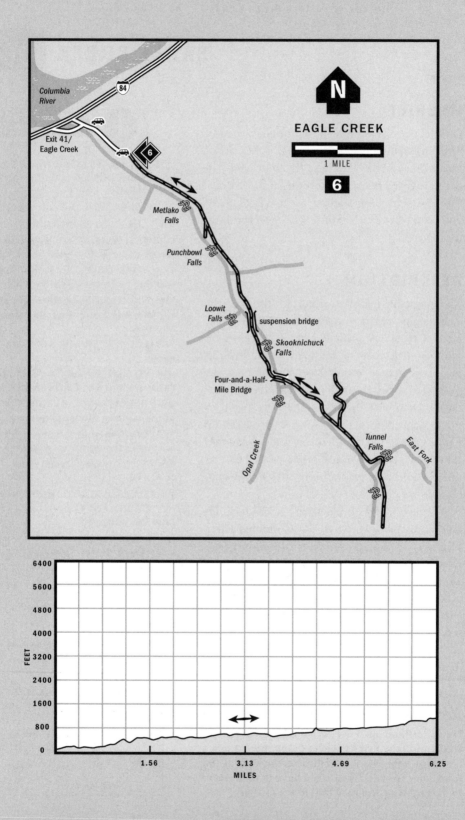

Columbia
River

84

Exit 41/
Eagle Creek

6

N

EAGLE CREEK

1 MILE

6

Metlako
Falls

Punchbowl
Falls

Loowit
Falls

suspension bridge

Skooknichuck
Falls

Four-and-a-Half-
Mile Bridge

Opal Creek

Tunnel
Falls

East Fork

FEET

6400
5600
4800
4000
3200
2400
1600
800
0

1.56   3.13   4.69   6.25

MILES

Punchbowl Falls is just a couple of miles up the Eagle Creek Trail.

into cliff faces, built High Bridge over the gorge, and put a tunnel behind a falls 6 miles up. It's work like this that inspired my dedication for this book.

At just under a mile, you'll come to the first place where you walk a ledge with a cable to hang on to. If it's a summer weekend, things can get interesting here while you are trying to negotiate for cable space with dozens of other hikers. At 1.5 miles, you'll come to a viewpoint of Metlako Falls (named for a native goddess of salmon), the first of many such sights of your day. Just past the viewpoint is a bench for resting. At 1.8 miles, and another bench, a side trail leads down to Punchbowl Falls, a must-see trip and the end of the line for a lot of people. Go 0.2 miles down this trail to an unnamed falls; just above that is a large clearing that's often filled with people swimming and sunbathing. At the upstream end of the clearing is a lovely (and often photographed) view of Punchbowl Falls (see photo above).

If you turn back here, you will have done 4 miles, but it's not much more work to go at least as far as High Bridge, another 1.2 miles up. If you head up, in 0.3 miles you'll get a bird's-eye view of Punchbowl Falls; then the gorge narrows considerably. You'll see Loowit Falls on the right just before High Bridge; if you turn around at the bridge, you'll have a 7-mile day. But even if you are turning back, put in another 0.3 miles to a great picnic spot on the left and, 100 yards later, a rare chance for access to the creek itself, in this case at the top of Skooknichuck Falls. Just past that are some very impressive Douglas firs right on the trail.

Continuing up the trail, you'll soon cross what is officially known as Four-and-a-Half Mile Bridge. Now, even the map acknowledges that this is exactly 4 miles from the trailhead, so what gives? Well, the fish hatchery back at the trailhead wasn't there when the trail was built (there was no need for it, because Bonneville Dam didn't exist yet), so the trailhead used to be half a mile farther north, at the edge of the Columbia River Highway.

Just past the bridge, look on the right for a double waterfall; that's Opal Creek, but it shouldn't be confused with the world-famous Opal Creek described elsewhere in this book (see page 122). About half a mile above that, a sign explains that the area you're now entering was burned in a 1902 fire; there are still some charred stumps around. So all the trees you'll see in this area are less than 100 years old.

After 1.5 more miles, bringing your total to 6, you'll come into a deep gorge where Tunnel Falls plunges 130 feet and the trail goes behind it through a 35-foot tunnel. Tunnel Falls is actually on East Fork Creek, which flows from Wahtum Lake. You could get to Wahtum Lake by hiking another 8 miles up this trail (and several thousand feet) or by following the directions in our Chinidere Mountain profile on the following pages.

To return to Eagle Creek and see one final, dramatic falls, go about 0.2 miles farther. This falls doesn't have an official name, but it does have an interesting criss-cross feature in its upper section, leading many people to call it Crisscross Falls.

You can keep going if you want, but if you head back at this point you'll wind up putting in 12 miles. That should be enough for a day, and besides, you get to see everything again on your way back.

For more information, contact the Columbia River Gorge National Scenic Area office at (541) 308-1700.

NEARBY ACTIVITIES

Stop at the fish hatchery at Bonneville Dam on the way home. They have a fish ladder where at certain times of year you can see salmon and steelhead swimming up past the dam to spawn, and year-round ponds where you can view big trout and sturgeon. It's 1 mile west on I-84, and there's no charge for admission.

CHINIDERE MOUNTAIN 07

IN BRIEF

You might spend more time in the car than on the trail for this one. But the view from the top of Chinidere is more than worth it, and Wahtum Lake is a fine destination, as well. Still, consider making this a part of a longer trip to Lost Lake or the Hood River Valley.

DESCRIPTION

If you're measuring hikes with a view-for-effort scale, Chinidere Mountain would rank an 11 out of 10—once you get there. It's a two-hour drive from Portland, but the roads are all paved, and you'll be rewarded with a fairly easy hike, a beautiful mountain lake with camping and fishing, and a view that stretches over hundreds of miles.

   If you're wondering, *Chinidere* is pronounced "SHI-na-dere," and it's named for the last reigning chief of the local Wasco tribe. And *Wahtum* is a local native word meaning "pond" or "body of water." So you're looking through the trees here at Wahtum Lake.

   From the trailhead, head through the campground (not down the road near the outhouse) and follow a trail called the Wahtum Express—so called because it includes 250 steps. (You can skip this by following a parallel horse trail to the right, if you wish.) At the

KEY AT-A-GLANCE INFORMATION

LENGTH: 4 miles

CONFIGURATION: Loop

DIFFICULTY: Easy, then moderate right at the end

SCENERY: Old-growth forest, a deep mountain lake, and a panoramic view

EXPOSURE: Shady–sunny

TRAFFIC: Light

TRAIL SURFACE: Packed dirt, roots, rocks

HIKING TIME: 2.5 hours

DRIVING DISTANCE: 87 miles (2 hours) from Pioneer Square

SEASON: July–mid-October

ACCESS: Northwest Forest Pass required.

WHEELCHAIR ACCESS: None

MAPS: Green Trails #429 (Bonneville Dam)

FACILITIES: Outhouse at the trailhead

SPECIAL COMMENTS: Wahtum Lake is at the very top of the Eagle Creek Trail, so consider doing a fantastic, one-way, downhill, 14-miler with a car shuttle.

Directions

From I-84, take Exit 62, then turn right onto Country Club Road. After 3 miles, turn left at a stop sign onto Barrett Drive. After 1.3 miles, turn right onto Tucker Road, which turns into Dee Highway. Go 8.5 miles to Dee and turn right onto Lost Lake Road. After 4.8 miles, turn right onto Forest Service Road 13. After 4.4 more miles, turn right again onto FS 1310. Stay on the pavement for 6 miles to find parking on the right. If you leave the pavement, you just missed it.

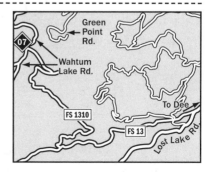

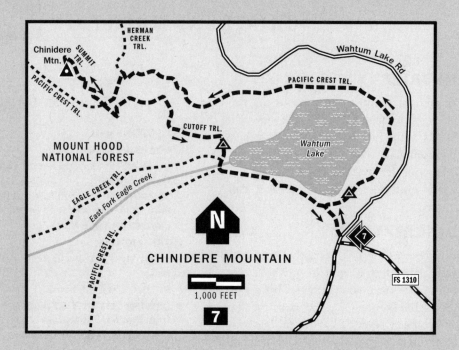

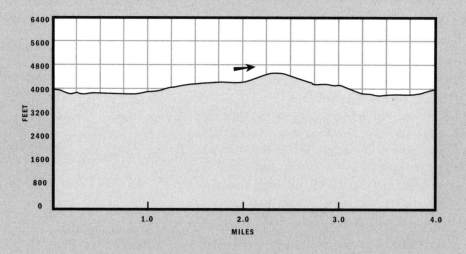

Wahtum Lake from the top of Chinidere Mountain

bottom of the Express, turn left and walk 100 feet down to a big tree with two Pacific Crest Trail signs on it. You'll be right by the lake, with a picnic area in front of you—and also in the middle of several nice lakeshore campsites. Turn right here, onto the PCT headed north.

The trail meanders along at first, near the lake, weaving through a lovely forest of hemlocks with bunchberry, thimbleberry, vanilla leaf, columbine, huckleberries, and salmonberry. Look along the near shore for a small island with about four trees on it. There's also, around half a mile up, some impressive trail construction to let water pass. Tiny springs and other mossy, flower-covered babbling brooks will keep you entertained and charmed.

After about a flat mile, you'll come into more open forest with beargrass that blooms in July, and you'll start climbing gradually on some classic Oregon PCT: wide tread, soft ground, pine needles, and thick forest. At a total of 1.75 miles you'll cross a creek that dries up by midsummer, and at 1.9 miles (now having climbed only 400 feet) you'll intersect the Herman Creek Trail, which leads all the way down to the outskirts of Cascade Locks.

A tenth of a mile later, you'll see the Chinidere Cutoff Trail (#406M) plunging down to the left; we'll take that one back. For now, go another 100 feet and leave the PCT on the Chinidere Mountain Trail. Now you'll put in the climbing you've been warming up for, picking up 400 feet in a third of a mile, eventually rounding out onto the rocky summit. You might want to watch for a side trail from one of the first switchbacks, heading out into the open; it leads to a rocky

Taking in the awesome view from the top of Chinidere Mountain

scramble up the west side of the mountain, including some interesting rock benches made by industrious hikers.

After you've caught your breath, please allow a little view tour. Start by looking at Mount Hood, looming to the south. To the right of that is Mount Jefferson, and just to the left of "Jeff" is Olallie Butte.

To the east, beyond "Lake Lake," you can see the upper parts of Hood River Valley, and to left of that is Dalles Mountain and the desert of Central Oregon. The big peak with all the radio towers is Mount Defiance, highest spot in the Gorge, and Mount Adams is to the left of that. The bald ridge directly between you and Adams is Tomlike Mountain (named for Chief Chinidere's son), and left of that is the Herman Creek drainage. Off in the distance are Mounts Rainier and St. Helens, and right in line with the latter is the broad, flat Benson Plateau. Right below you, to the west, is the Eagle Creek Canyon (the East Fork drains Wahtum Lake straight away from your feet) and in the distance beyond that is Tanner Butte. On a really clear day on Chinidere, I once saw Saddle Mountain, which is about 10 miles this side of the coast!

While we're up here, how about a little introduction to the PCT, a 2,600-mile trail from Mexico to Canada? The northbound PCT, which stretches some 460 miles across Oregon, comes up the right (west) side of Jefferson, around the same side of the butte, then past the right side of Hood, mostly in the trees. In its approach to Wahtum Lake, the PCT rounds an open ridge between you and

Hood called Indian Mountain, and from Chinidere it heads north across the Benson Plateau and down, heinously, into Cascade Locks. But most thru-hikers take the Eagle Creek Trail, since it's well-graded and has about a dozen waterfalls, then walk a few miles along the road into Cascade Locks. After crossing the Bridge of the Gods, the trail then goes past the west side of Table Mountain (which looks like a big gash from Chinidere), then around the north side of it before making a swing east toward Adams, the Goat Rocks, and Rainier. So, from Mount Jefferson to Mount Rainier, you're effectively looking at about 280 miles of PCT—slightly more than ten percent of it!

And by the way, the rusty cables on top of Chinidere are from an old forest service fire lookout, and the pits are tent sites, not Indian vision quest sites. Sorry it's nothing more romantic than that.

Head back down to the PCT, turn left, and take the Chinidere Cutoff Trail, which will seem more like the Chinidere Dropoff Trail for its steep descent to the lake. You'll cross a creek or two along the way, depending on the season, and you'll even see a pipe along the trail that used to carry water down to some camp-sites on the north shore of the lake. When you come to these campsites, stay on the main trail to where it crosses the East Fork of Eagle Creek on an impressive (and fun) logjam.

Cross the creek, and in 200 yards you'll hit the top of the Eagle Creek National Recreation Trail, which was built before 1920 and connects Wahtum Lake with the Columbia River Highway, 14 miles below. (A 12-mile round-trip hike is described on page 33.) Turn left onto this trail and follow it a couple hundred yards back to the PCT, which leads a quarter mile past campsites and swimming holes and even the occasional beach, back to the bottom of the Wahtum Express—whose 250 steps will seem much less appealing to you now, no doubt.

LARCH MOUNTAIN

KEY AT-A-GLANCE INFORMATION

LENGTH: 8.6-mile one-way with a car shuttle; otherwise, 17.2 miles out-and-back. Optional upper loop is 6 miles.

CONFIGURATION: Out-and-back or one-way

DIFFICULTY: Moderate–strenuous

SCENERY: Waterfalls, creeks in wooded canyons, colossal trees, big view on the top

EXPOSURE: Mostly shady until the summit

TRAFFIC: Always heavy on lower stretches

TRAIL SURFACE: Pavement, packed dirt, some gravel

HIKING TIME: 4 hours one-way; 7 for the round-trip; 3 for the upper loop

DRIVING DISTANCE: 31 miles (40 minutes) to lower trailhead, 36 miles (1 hour) to upper trailheads from Pioneer Square

SEASON: June–October

ACCESS: No fees or permits needed.

WHEELCHAIR ACCESS: Only first 0.2 miles to Benson Bridge

MAPS: Trails of the Columbia Gorge; USGS Multnomah Falls

FACILITIES: Full services at Multnomah Falls trailhead; restrooms only at top of Larch Mountain

IN BRIEF

Sure, you can drive to the top of Larch Mountain, but the trail between there and Multnomah Falls is one of the classic walks in Oregon—from the shores of the Columbia River to a high lookout in the Cascades, with old-growth forest on the way up and a view from Portland to several volcanoes on top. There's even a shorter loop hike that takes in the upper parts of the mountain only.

DESCRIPTION

Pick a clear day to take in the view; or think about timing your arrival on top just as the sun is setting—you'll get to see Mount Hood bathed in pink light, and the lights of Portland are spectacular from there. Consider this one in late August, when the upper parts of the hill are awash in huckleberries.

You can actually see Larch Mountain as you drive out I-84; it's just to the left of Mount Hood and has a notch in the top. The top of that notch is where you're headed.

As for the hike, I confess a bias in favor of walking up hills as opposed to walking down them. It seems easier to recover from losing

Directions

To start at Multnomah Falls, take I-84 24 miles east of I-205 to Exit 31/Multnomah Falls, which leads to a parking lot. Park and walk under the expressway to the historic lodge. For the upper trailheads, take I-84 15 miles east of I-205 and take Exit 22/Corbett. At the intersection with the Historic Columbia River Highway, turn left. After 2 miles, veer right onto Larch Mountain Road. The uppermost trailhead is in the parking lot at the end of the road, 14 miles up. The middle trailhead is 11.5 miles on the left, where Larch Mountain Road makes a big turn to the right and a gravel road takes off to the left.

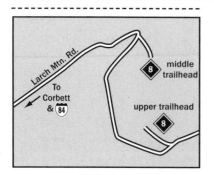

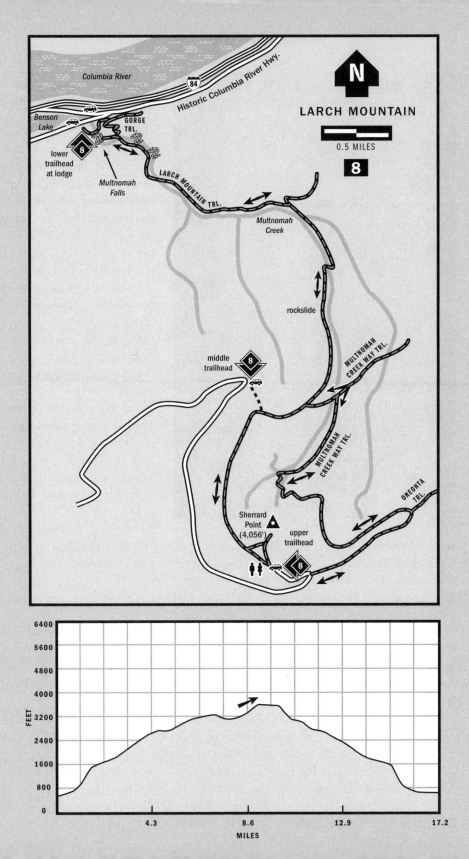

your breath while climbing than from pounding your knees and feet while you descend. Still, you've got three options here, all quite worthwhile. You can start at the top or at the bottom and put in 6.8 miles (assuming you have a second car for a shuttle), or you can start in the middle and do a loop that takes in the view with less work. Or you can combine these.

For our purposes, let's assume you put a second car at the top parking lot, and we'll start at the bottom, then include the upper loop on the way. From the Multnomah Falls Lodge, walk with the masses up the paved trail that leads over the Benson Bridge and a mile (climbing 600 feet) to a junction with a side trail leading to the viewing platform at the top of the falls. When you continue past this point, you'll leave 90 percent of the masses behind; for the next several miles you may well have the Larch Mountain Trail (#441) to yourself. You will also enter one of the few areas of old-growth forest in the Columbia River Gorge.

The trail was built in the early 1900s to coincide with the opening of the Columbia River Highway—and one thing we should get straight is that there are no larch trees on Larch Mountain. The name stuck when old-time loggers confused the noble fir with the larch, which only grows east of the Cascade Range (although they have a few in the Washington Park–Hoyt Arboretum; see page 250).

Staying on this trail, you'll cross Multnomah Creek and pass two lovely waterfalls. At 1.6 miles, ignore the Wahkeena Trail (#420) on the right. At 2 miles you'll cross Multnomah Creek again, then at 3 miles traverse the East Fork of Multnomah Creek. Just 0.6 miles later you'll cross a one-log footbridge, which, by pure coincidence, my friend Christie and I were the first people to cross in 2000. (The workers had just set the log in place and allowed the crossing before they started on the handrails.)

At 3.9 miles you'll cross a rockslide and then start climbing through an old-growth forest of western hemlock and Douglas fir trees that get as thick as five and six feet. In late summer, this area abounds with huckleberries, and in autumn the red/yellow/orange vine maple is astounding.

At 4.8 miles you'll come to a junction with the Multnomah Creek Way Trail (#444), and you'll have an option as to which way to go. Your first option is to simply stay on the Larch Mountain Trail (#441), and in 2 miles you'll come to the top. The second option, (#444) to the left, is a more scenic route to the top but is also 0.7 miles longer. If that sounds OK, take it for 0.2 miles until it crosses Multnomah Creek, then turn right and go 2.8 miles through a marsh and up the ridge of Larch Mountain. When you come to the Oneonta Trail (#424) at the top of the ridge, turn right and follow it 0.9 miles to the parking area atop Larch Mountain. You'll have to follow the road for the last little bit. Then follow a signed, paved trail to Sherrard Point for the big view. It's 0.7 miles from where you enter the road to Sherrard Point—a total 9.5 from the trailhead at Multnomah Falls.

Now, as for your other hiking options on Larch Mountain, you can either start at the top and go down to Multnomah Falls (following either the Larch Mountain Trail all the way down or the loop described above via the Multnomah Creek Way Trail) or you can park at the middle trailhead described above. This accesses the upper part of Larch Mountain without 3,000 feet of climbing from the Columbia. From that trailhead, either walk up the Larch Mountain Trail 1.5 miles to the top, or go down it half a mile, take the Multnomah Creek Way Trail (#444), and take the loop described above.

Any way you go, make sure when on top that you go out the paved trail to Sherrard Point and have a look around. You'll see (if it's clear) Portland, Mount Hood, Mount Jefferson, Mount Adams, Mount St. Helens, and Mount Rainier. You'll also notice that you're at the top of a cliff on a semicircular ridge. That's because Larch Mountain is what remains of an ancient volcano, and what you're looking down into is its former crater.

Millions of years ago lava flows from volcanoes like this used to periodically dam the Columbia River, forming lakes that stretched back into Montana and occasionally broke through in catastrophic floods. At times like this there would have been some 400 feet of water where Portland is now—just a little something to think about as you walk back to your car. For more information, call the Columbia River Gorge National Scenic Area office at (541) 308-1700.

NEARBY ACTIVITIES

If you did the one-way car shuttle, stop on the way to or from Multnomah Falls at the Portland Women's Forum Viewpoint on the Historic Columbia River Highway. It's a little farther west than the more famous Vista House, and it is therefore a less-visited view of the Columbia River Gorge.

09 McCALL NATURE PRESERVE

KEY AT-A-GLANCE INFORMATION

LENGTH: McCall Point Trail is 3 miles long; Plateau Loop is 2 miles.

CONFIGURATION: Out-and-back to McCall Point; balloon to Plateau

DIFFICULTY: McCall Point is moderate due to the climb; Plateau is easy.

SCENERY: Wildflowers, the Columbia River below, 2 volcanoes, old oak trees

EXPOSURE: Wide open most of the time

TRAFFIC: Moderate when the flowers are out, light otherwise

TRAIL SURFACE: Packed dirt

HIKING TIME: 1.5 hours to McCall Point; 1 hour for Plateau Loop

DRIVING DISTANCE: 76 miles (1 hour and 30 minutes) from Pioneer Square

SEASON: McCall Point open May–November; Plateau Loop open year-round

ACCESS: No fees or permits needed.

WHEELCHAIR ACCESS: None

MAPS: USGS Lyle; map at the trailhead

FACILITIES: None

SPECIAL COMMENTS: Dogs not allowed

IN BRIEF

McCall Nature Preserve is in a different world from most of the hikes in this book. It's a glimpse into eastern Oregon, a land of wide-open vistas, grass blowing in the nearly constant wind, and semiarid forests of oaks and ponderosa pine. It also has views of the Columbia, panoramic vistas of Mounts Adams and Hood, and more than 300 species of plants, some of them unique to the Columbia River Gorge.

DESCRIPTION

OK, so this one is more than 60 miles from Portland, even as the crow flies. But it's truly worth the extra bit of driving, especially in the spring and early summer. At those times of the year, there is a kind of rain shroud that exists somewhere between Cascade Locks and Hood River; while it's still pouring in Portland, places like the McCall Preserve are bathed in sunlight and draped in a few dozen different kinds of wildflowers all blooming at once.

Consider wearing long pants; there are ticks, poison oak, and rattlesnakes in the area.

Start with the McCall Point Trail first and get your exercise out of the way. The trail, which climbs about 1,000 feet in 1.5 miles, starts out nearly flat and on an old Jeep road,

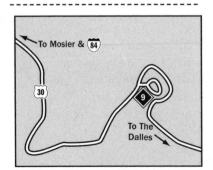

Directions

From Portland on I-84, drive 62 miles east of I-205 and take Exit 69/Mosier. Turn right and follow the Historic Columbia River Highway (US 30) through Mosier for 6.5 miles to the Rowena Crest Viewpoint. The McCall Point Trail begins at a sign at the end of the stone wall. The Plateau Loop begins across the highway with a set of steps leading over a fence.

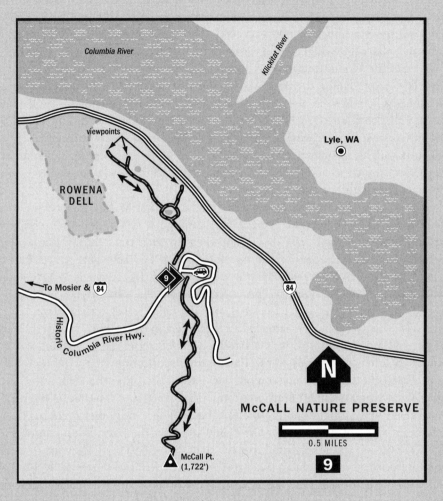

Columbia River

Klickitat River

viewpoints

Lyle, WA

ROWENA
DELL

To Mosier & 84

Historic Columbia River Hwy.

84

N

McCALL NATURE PRESERVE

0.5 MILES

9

McCall Pt.
(1,722')

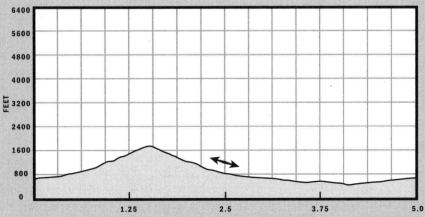

winding through the kind of open space that is so rare in western parts of the state. The trees you eventually encounter are oaks, most of them Oregon white oak, and some as much as 800 years old. The trail turns slightly uphill when it gains the edge of the ridge, with ever more impressive views out to the east. Keep an eye out for Mount Adams as its summit comes into view across the river.

The second half of the trail is a little steeper, and after a rain it might be slick and muddy, so add solid boots to your clothing list. But soon enough you'll come to McCall Point, an open hilltop with a sprawling view from Mount Hood to Mount Adams; you're actually about halfway between the two peaks, each of which is roughly 35 miles away. Looking west, you can see into the Columbia River Gorge; just to the left of it, the high peak with the towers on top is Mount Defiance, the highest point in the gorge.

Now, you summit hounds out there might stand at McCall Point and notice there's still some more trail going south, through a notch, and then climbing again. I walked about a mile down (and then up) that trail, through some very peaceful oak stands, but technically speaking it didn't go anywhere special before it got pinched between a fence and the edge of a cliff. My advice is to have yourself a picnic at McCall Point and don't worry about that other trail.

Back at the highway, use the steps over the fence to begin the Plateau Loop. This wide, easy path (which actually drops 100 feet in elevation) goes out through flower and grass country to loop around a pond. Early in the year, there will be numerous other little ponds and wet areas, each supporting their own microhabitats. The small canyon below you on your left is called Rowena Dell.

When a sign reading "Trail" indicates a right turn, you'll notice another trail that keeps going straight out into the grasslands. There is another pond out there among the trees, as well as other viewpoints out over the river. But the most dramatic view is on the official trail to your right. After that trail has gone past the pond it turns right again, but a small trail to the left leads to the top of a cliff that is not for the acrophobes among us. It's a sheer drop of 500 feet from where you stand (without a railing, so keep an eye on the kids) down to the railroad tracks and the river. The town across the river is Lyle, Washington, which lies on a gravel bar left behind by catastrophic floods more than 10,000 years ago.

To return to the trailhead, follow the trail back around the pond and turn left (uphill) at the sign. Or wander farther to your right here to keep exploring.

For more information, contact the Columbia River Gorge National Scenic Area office at (541) 308-1700 or the Nature Conservancy at (503) 230-1221.

NEARBY ACTIVITIES

As long as you're this far east, keep going to The Dalles and visit the Columbia Gorge Discovery Center. Its displays range from a working model of the Columbia before and after the Dalles Dam to a Living History Center with presentations on the life of Oregon Trail pioneers.

TABLE MOUNTAIN 10

IN BRIEF

This tough climb has a great reward on top: one of the best panoramas in the whole Columbia River Gorge, including a bird's-eye view of the Bonneville Dam, from a lunch spot atop 800-foot cliffs. And there are hot springs nearby.

DESCRIPTION

You have two options for where to start this hike. Using the "official" trailhead on Washington Highway 14 at North Bonneville makes it about a 16-mile tromp, though it does visit a lake and an additional viewpoint along the way. If that's what you're after, take the trail from WA 14 up 0.6 miles to the PCT and turn left, following it 1.9 miles to Gillette Lake, then 1.3 miles to Greenleaf Overlook, then 1.7 miles to the top of the road where the other route comes in.

As for that other route, which is the highly recommended one, it's 6 round-trip miles shorter and starts at a hot-springs resort. The only qualifier to that is that the resort has major construction planned for 2007, and they

---

Directions ⟶

From Portland on I-84, take Exit 44/Cascade Locks. As soon as you enter the town, take the first right to get on the Bridge of the Gods, following a sign for Stevenson, Washington. Pay a $1 toll on the bridge, and at the far end, turn left onto WA 14. The North Bonneville Trailhead is 2 miles ahead on the right—this is the starting point for the longer hike and also has the only public toilet in the area. To go for the shorter hike, continue another 1.1 mile on WA 14 and turn right, crossing under the railroad tracks. Just beyond the tracks, turn right onto Hot Springs Way. The entrance to the resort is 0.9 miles ahead.

KEY AT-A-GLANCE INFORMATION

LENGTH: 9.3 miles

CONFIGURATION: Out-and-back

DIFFICULTY: Strenuous

SCENERY: A tumbling stream, 5 volcanoes, and a bird's-eye view of the Columbia River Gorge

EXPOSURE: Shady, then open rock at the top

TRAFFIC: Use is moderate on summer weekends but light otherwise.

TRAIL SURFACE: Grass, packed dirt with rocks, then just rocks

HIKING TIME: 5 hours

DRIVING DISTANCE: 45 miles (50 minutes) from Pioneer Square

SEASON: Spring–fall

ACCESS: No fee

WHEELCHAIR ACCESS: None

MAPS: USGS Bonneville Dam or Green Trails #429 (Bonneville Dam), though only the PCT appears on either map.

FACILITIES: Trailhead for longer hike has toilets; the other one has no facilities other than those at the resort.

SPECIAL COMMENTS: The trails to the summit were being reconstructed at press time (work was to be finished in May 2007). For more information, call the Columbia River Gorge Visitors Association at (800) 984-6743.

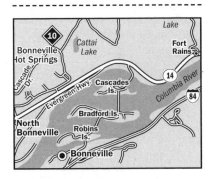

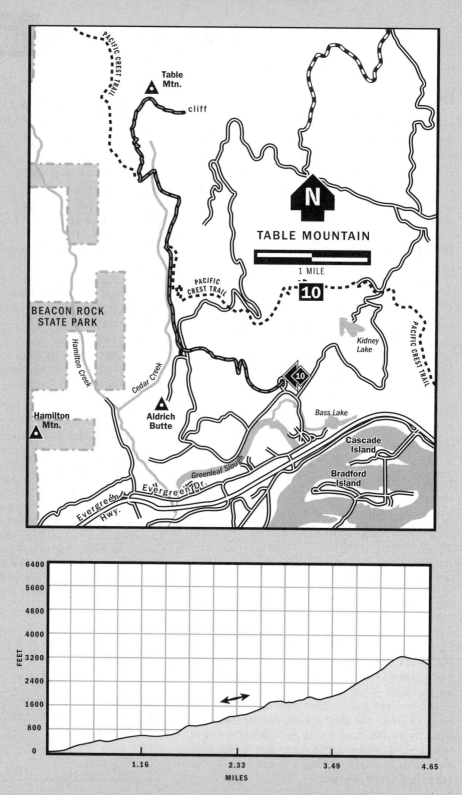

have also become weary of hikers stomping around with their muddy boots. So call them ahead of time to see if their lot is available, and please treat the place with respect so they'll let us keep parking there. (See Nearby Activities on next page.)

With all the preliminaries aside, let's start hiking. From the parking lot, head for the far west end of the pavement, beyond the rock wall surrounding the bath area, and look for an old road heading up the hill. Follow it up 100 yards to a T intersection, then take a little trail heading for a tree with a sign that says "PCT" and "Table Mountain."

Follow that trail as it winds up, steeply at times, through a young forest choked with vine maple, and pass a tiny lake on the right after half a mile. Just under a mile, top out over a ridge, and 0.2 miles later cross a tiny creek where logs are generally in place.

Two minutes later, turn right onto a road, and take a moment to look up toward Table Mountain and Sacajawea Rocks beyond the meadow. Yes, that's where we're headed. One minute past this, turn left at another road junction, and after a swooping switchback to the right, stay straight at yet another junction. Now climb along the edge of the meadow, in which lies tough-to-spot Carpenters Lake, and just past 1.5 miles after the trailhead, cross over the ridge to climb along Cedar Creek, which is lined mostly by alder and Douglas fir.

When you've gone a total of 2.4 miles—about a mile since the meadow— arrive in what looks like a campground area at an intersection with the PCT. (This is the spot that's 5.5 miles from the North Bonneville trailhead.) Turn left on the PCT, which goes left from the road and climbs moderately through a more interesting forest. There are a few Douglas firs of decent size, but this whole area has been logged, much of it more than once. After 0.3 miles, a side trail leads left to a campsite; stay right on the PCT. About 0.4 miles later, an old summit trail enters from the right. If it's open, it's very steep and you're better off continuing.

Around 0.3 miles later, reach the ridgeline at a large, moss-covered rock on the right. Turn right and start climbing through the woods. And I do mean climbing: Right now you're just below 2,000 feet elevation; in 1.2 miles you'll be at 3,417 feet. You'll start in the woods but soon pop out onto the sometimes-loose rock, where you'll have to scramble at times. If it gets confusing, just stick to the ridgeline.

When you get to the top and catch your breath, you'll find that trails actually crisscross the broad summit. Stay to the left for views of Mounts St. Helens, Rainier, and Adams. Go right (toward the Columbia River) for 0.4 miles to a spectacular view that ranges from Dog Mountain and Mount Defiance to Mount Hood, looking right up the Eagle Creek drainage. Beware that the final portions of this trail literally take you a foot away from a drop of hundreds of feet, and there's no protection.

Those cliffs are part of Table Mountain's fascinating geological history. As you look out toward the Columbia, you can start to make out the fact that the southern half of Table Mountain actually slid into the river, leaving behind the cliffs and narrowing the Columbia to just a couple hundred yards at the most (at the point where the Bridge of the Gods crosses). This slide, encompassing an area of more than 10 square miles, occurred about 550 years ago—basically yesterday in geologic time. It created first a natural dam that blocked the river, then the Cascades of the Columbia, which were submerged when the Bonneville Dam went in.

Now look up at Mount Hood. On the left skyline you can see a ridge leading up to a bump just below the snow line. That's Cooper Spur (see page 134). For a real adventure, hike up that one and look for Table Mountain.

You may notice a trail descending the south side of Table Mountain via an open steep section called Heartbreak Ridge. That trail was closed for years but was being considered for a 2007 reconstruction.

NEARBY ACTIVITIES

Now, about those hot springs. It's a giant, lush place with a restaurant, overnight rooms ($139 and up), and a day spa with hot tubs, massage and skin treatments, and so on. Your basic soak starts at $15 for 25 minutes. For more information, call (509) 427-7767 or visit **www.bonnevilleresort.com**.

TRIPLE FALLS 11

IN BRIEF

A unique waterfall lies at the end of this moderate hike, but you don't have to go that far to see some fine Columbia River Gorge scenery. You can, in fact, just drive by the trailhead and admire Horsetail Falls.

DESCRIPTION

If all you do is slow down while driving by Horsetail Falls, you'll be pleased. If that's all you want to see, you should at least cross the parking area and pick some blackberries over by the railroad tracks; they're ripe in late summer. But the great thing about this trail is that the farther you go, the better it gets, and you never have to work very hard at all.

From Horsetail Falls, follow the gravel trail behind the sign describing some of the animals that live in the area. At 0.2 miles, stay right at a trail junction. A few hundred yards later you'll come around a bend and see Upper Horsetail Falls. A popular turn-around spot because it's so near the car, these falls are also a hit with kids because, with supervision, they can get under them and catch some spray. The falls seem to shoot out of a basalt cliff face, and the area behind them is a grotto through which the trail passes. If you get under them, some smaller streams trickle down onto the heads of hikers and dogs. Just don't get directly under the main stream of water; even this relatively small waterfall is extremely powerful.

Directions ⟶

From Portland on I-84, drive 21 miles east of I-205 to Exit 28/Bridal Veil. Turn left onto the Historic Columbia River Highway and proceed 5.2 miles to the signed parking area at Horsetail Falls.

KEY AT-A-GLANCE INFORMATION

LENGTH: 4.5 miles

CONFIGURATION: Out-and-back or loop

DIFFICULTY: Moderate

SCENERY: Four waterfalls, a spectacular gorge, a view of the Columbia River

EXPOSURE: In the forest all the way, with some clifftop walking

TRAFFIC: Moderate use on summer weekends, light otherwise

TRAIL SURFACE: Gravel and packed dirt, roots, rocks

HIKING TIME: 2.5 hours to Triple Falls

DRIVING DISTANCE: 33 miles (40 minutes) from Pioneer Square

SEASON: Year-round, though it gets muddy during winter and spring

ACCESS: No fees or permits needed.

WHEELCHAIR ACCESS: None

MAPS: Trails of the Columbia Gorge; Green Trails #428 (Bridal Veil); USGS Multnomah Falls

FACILITIES: None at the trailhead; water and restrooms are available half a mile east at Ainsworth State Park.

SPECIAL COMMENTS: For more information, call the Columbia River Gorge Visitors Association at (800) 984-6743.

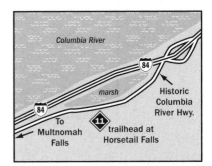

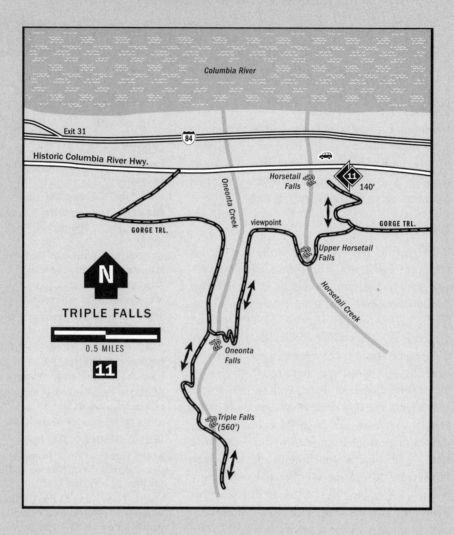

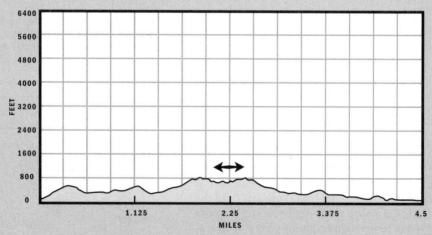

Be sure to visit Oneonta Gorge at the end of the Triple Falls hike.

To keep going, simply follow the trail as it contours around the gorge wall. It soon comes to a brushy area on the right, through which several trails lead out to clifftop viewpoints of the Columbia River. You can make a side loop out there and work your way back to the main trail as it turns away from the river. There's a network of trails in this tiny area, but they all lead to the same place, so you won't get lost.

A mile past Upper Horsetail Falls, after passing underneath a mossy "weeping" rock face, you'll drop down to a bridge over the top of spectacular Oneonta Gorge. A geologic and biological wonder, Oneonta is worth a visit on its own; from here, you're looking down into it from the bridge, with waterfalls above and below you. Just across the bridge (and after a little climbing) is another junction; you can loop back to the highway by going right (you'll have to walk along the road, however, to get back to your car) or you can turn left and head up toward Triple Falls. The trail is rocky in places, and there's a little more elevation gain, but nice views across the way will help keep you moving.

About a mile up you'll see Triple Falls. It's actually just one creek (Oneonta), but it divides into three just before it goes over the edge. So take your pictures from here, and then walk another minute or two to a wooden bridge across the wide stream just above the falls. Across the bridge are some nice rocks for picnicking, and just upstream are some pools the kids can jump in, if you've managed to get them this far.

The trail to Triple Falls passes behind Upper Horsetail Falls.

NEARBY ACTIVITIES

Oneonta Gorge is one of the truly amazing sights in the Columbia River Gorge. You can get about a quarter of a mile into it, but not without getting wet. Even in late summer, adults will find themselves wading in waist-high water or climbing rocks to avoid it. (I saw one gallant gent carry his girlfriend through this section.) So put on your swimsuit, along with some shoes you don't mind soaking, and explore this official U.S. Forest Service Botanical Area.

WAHKEENA FALLS TO MULTNOMAH FALLS

IN BRIEF

Just off I-84 and bookmarked by two beautiful waterfalls, this is the ideal introduction to all that the Columbia River Gorge has to offer, including great scenery, big crowds, and nice steep climbs.

DESCRIPTION

When hiking friends come to visit Oregon, this is where I take them first. They get to see the scenic spectacle that is the Columbia River Gorge, they get to view the highest waterfall in Oregon, they get to see old-growth Douglas firs, and they get their hearts pumping—from excitement and, at times, from effort.

You can hike either way on this trail and park at either falls; my preference is to park at Multnomah Falls (either on the Historic Columbia River Highway or at the I-84 exit) and begin at Wahkeena Falls. I'll tell you why later.

To do this, walk 100 yards down the historic highway to the west of Multnomah Falls Lodge and take the Return Trail (#442), which parallels the road for 0.6 miles to Wahkeena Falls. Along the way you'll pass under an overhanging rock and be cooled off by a mossy, "weeping" rock wall.

Actually several falls in one, Wahkeena Falls encompasses sheer drops to cascades to

KEY AT-A-GLANCE INFORMATION

LENGTH: 5.2 miles

CONFIGURATION: Loop

DIFFICULTY: Moderate

SCENERY: Waterfalls, canyons, river views, flowers, a spring, big trees

EXPOSURE: In the forest all the way

TRAFFIC: Heavy, especially on weekends; moderate on weekdays and on the trail away from Multnomah Falls

TRAIL SURFACE: Pavement, gravel, packed dirt with some rocky sections

HIKING TIME: 3 hours

DRIVING DISTANCE: 31 miles (35 minutes) from Pioneer Square

SEASON: Year-round (muddy in spots during winter and spring)

ACCESS: No fees or permits required.

WHEELCHAIR ACCESS: The first section of trail heading up from either falls is paved.

MAPS: Trails of the Columbia Gorge, Green Trails #428 (Bridal Veil)

FACILITIES: Full service at Multnomah Falls

Directions

To park at Multnomah Falls, take I-84 for 24 miles east of I-205 to Exit 31/Multnomah Falls. Park and walk under the expressway and railroad tracks to the historic lodge. To park at Wahkeena Falls, go 21 miles east on I-84 to Exit 28/Bridal Veil. Turn left onto the Historic Columbia River Highway and proceed 2 miles to the signed parking area at the falls.

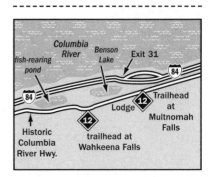

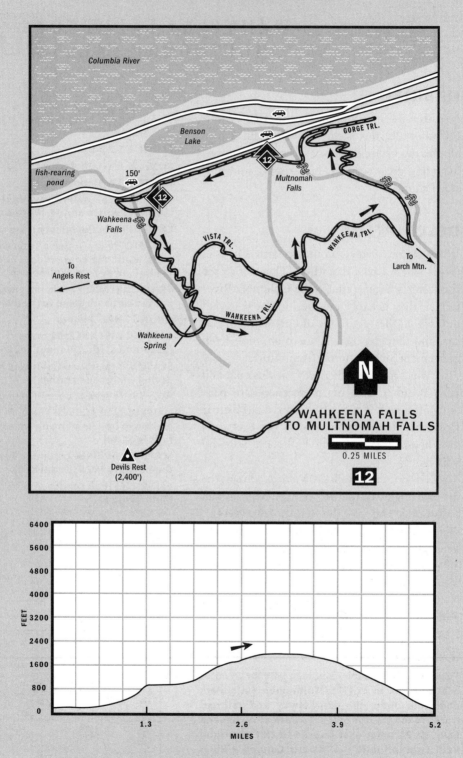

Columbia River

Benson Lake

fish-rearing pond

150'

Wahkeena Falls

VISTA TRL.

WAHKEENA TRL.

To Angels Rest

Wahkeena Spring

Multnomah Falls

GORGE TRL.

WAHKEENA TRL.

To Larch Mtn.

Devils Rest (2,400')

N

WAHKEENA FALLS
TO MULTNOMAH FALLS

0.25 MILES

12

Descending alongside Multnomah Falls at the end of the Wahkeena-Multnomah loop

misty sprays. This creek, by the way, comes primarily from a spring up on the ridge that you'll see later. To start the loop, follow the paved trail across the creek and the 0.2 miles up to a footbridge at the base of the upper falls. Take a nice deep breath of that cool, moist air; your workout is about to begin.

In the next 0.4 miles of paved switchbacks, you'll gain about 400 feet in elevation; such quick climbs are the trademark of gorge hikes. When you get to a lookout point on the right with a great view of the Columbia, the worst is over. You can rest a few minutes later on a bench at lovely Fairy Falls, sort of a miniature version of Ramona Falls (hike 35 in this book).

There's still come climbing to do; it's just that now it's more gradual and you have the creek and some lovely old forest of ferns, cedars, hemlocks, and firs to take your mind off it. Fairly recent fires took out smaller growth, blackened the trunks of bigger trees, and opened the forest floor for berries and wildflowers to move in. Just above lovely Fairy Falls, you'll encounter the Vista Point Trail; turn right here, staying on the Wahkeena Trail (#420). In 0.4 miles you'll come to an intersection with the Angels Rest Trail (#415). The sign here has an interesting quirk: It lacked the word "trail" after Vista Point, Devils Rest, and Larch Mountain (the distances listed are to those trails, not to the destinations), so somebody came by later and scratched "trail" after each one. At any rate, you should at least take a detour here on the Angels Rest Trail for about 100 yards to see Wahkeena Spring.

At the intersection of the Wahkeena and Angels Rest trails, back near the spring, take the Wahkeena Trail up the hill 0.4 miles to a four-way intersection. Coming up the hill from your left is the Vista Point Trail; ignore it. Going up the hill to your right is the Devils Rest Trail. Straight ahead is the Wahkeena Trail.

Continuing east on the Wahkeena Trail, you'll soon start downhill and, in 0.9 miles, intersect the Larch Mountain Trail (#441), which connects Multnomah Falls with Larch Mountain (see hike profile, page 42). For our purposes here, turn left and head down rock-filled Multnomah Creek. In the next mile, you'll pass several waterfalls in a gorge filled with ferns and large, old-growth Douglas firs.

A well-marked (and well-traveled) paved trail to the left leads 0.1 mile to the top of Multnomah Falls, where a wooden platform offers an ego-building view of the camera-toting throngs below. "Yeah," you can say later at the bottom, "I've been up there." This brings me to why I like to do the hike this way. From this point on, especially on a weekend, you'll be among hundreds of people. From my perspective, it's better to move downhill (hence, more quickly) through this scene, arriving at Multnomah Falls and the Benson Bridge a mile later.

The highest falls in Oregon at 542 feet, upper Multnomah Falls is indeed quite a sight. Be sure to stop in the information office at the lodge to see the pictures of various floods and a massive rockfall that occurred there in years gone by. Now for the final reason I like to start this hike at Wahkeena Falls but park at Multnomah Falls: When you're all done, you can get yourself an ice-cream cone or an espresso, or cruise the gift shop if you're into that, and your car is right there waiting for you.

NEARBY ACTIVITIES

The 1925 Multnomah Falls Lodge is well worth checking out, with its skylights and fireplace in the restaurant and old-style stone-and-wood construction. The food is not as good as the setting, but the Sunday brunch is massive.

AROUND MOUNT ST. HELENS

13 APE CANYON

KEY AT-A-GLANCE INFORMATION

LENGTH: 11.6 miles

CONFIGURATION: Out-and-back

DIFFICULTY: Moderate

SCENERY: Old-growth forest, a volcanic mudflow, a narrow canyon

EXPOSURE: Alternating shady and open on the way up, then wide open at the top

TRAFFIC: Moderate on summer weekends, light otherwise

TRAIL SURFACE: Packed dirt with roots and rocks, rock at the top

HIKING TIME: 5.5 hours

DRIVING DISTANCE: 66 miles (1 hour and 35 minutes) from Pioneer Square

SEASON: Late June to October

ACCESS: Northwest Forest Pass required.

WHEELCHAIR ACCESS: None, but some of the nearby Lava Canyon trail is traversable.

MAPS: USFS Mount St. Helens National Volcanic Monument

FACILITIES: None at trailhead; toilets at Lava Canyon trailhead. There's no water at the trailhead or on the trail.

SPECIAL COMMENTS: In June, call the monument at (360) 247-3900 to make sure FS 83 is open and snow-free.

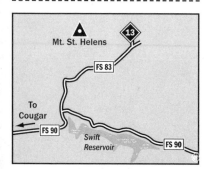

IN BRIEF

This trail visits two worlds not ordinarily seen: the upper reaches of a volcano and the edge of what they call the "blast zone." Without too much climbing, you can stand in a wonderful old-growth forest and be about 20 feet from an area that was completely obliterated in 1980. At the top, you'll have a sweeping view highlighted by an amazing geological oddity.

DESCRIPTION

You'll get your first glimpse of the contrasts ahead when you have only walked 500 feet on this trail. You'll be at the top of a little bluff, looking out over a wide area of rocks. Those rocks used to be on the upper slopes of the volcano Mount St. Helens, but on May 18, 1980, they came down the hill at about 45 miles per hour, part of a landslide triggered when most of the Shoestring Glacier melted a moment after the volcano erupted. But the mudslide stayed within the boundaries of the Muddy River, so the forest you're standing in—even though it was within feet of the slide—was spared. You'll spend the next 5 miles climbing this ridge, but don't worry: You'll only gain a little more than 1,300 feet along the way.

Before you leave this viewpoint, look down. You're standing on an example of stratigraphy; that's a fancy word for the fact

Directions

From Portland on Interstate 5, drive 21 miles north of the Columbia River and take Exit 21/Woodland. Turn right onto WA 503 (Lewis River Road), which after 31 miles (2 miles past Cougar) turns into Forest Service 90. Follow FS 90 for 3.3 miles and turn left onto FS 83. The trailhead is 11.2 miles ahead on the left, just before the Lava Canyon trailhead.

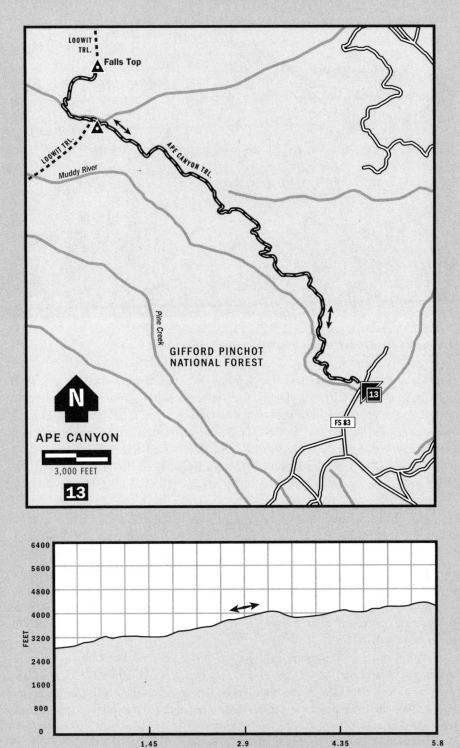

LOOWIT TRL.

▲ Falls Top

LOOWIT TRL.

Muddy River

APE CANYON TRL.

Pine Creek

GIFFORD PINCHOT
NATIONAL FOREST

N

APE CANYON

3,000 FEET

13

13

FS 83

The south side of Mount St. Helens, from the lower Ape Canyon Trail

that when the 1980 mudflow came through, it exposed several underlying layers of rock, which give scientists clues to the previous eruption history of the volcano.

If you're on this trail in September or October, you'll be in the world of the vine maple, and its red and orange explosion contrasts beautifully with the ever-green canopy. Keep an eye out for deer and elk, both of which are in the area. At a quarter mile, look for an island of trees on the edge of the mudflow, and after a half mile, enjoy your first view south to Mount Hood. Ahead, on the slopes of St. Helens, the canyon left behind by the Shoestring Glacier is apparent.

At 1.2 miles, reach a little ridge, and soon after make a switchback to the right and climb a bit more; you'll also notice some social trails heading out to brushy viewpoints facing east to Mount Adams. Around 2 miles, enter a series of switchbacks, now well within the old-growth forest of towering hemlocks and thick vine maple. Just past 3 miles, you'll actually lose some elevation before a viewpoint that takes in two-humped Mount Rainier off to your right. From here, you can also make out a large waterfall on an eastern ridge of St. Helens; we'll be at the top of that soon!

At 4.4 miles you'll be out in the open at the head of Ape Canyon proper—and in the "blast zone" itself. You'll see trees that were killed by the super-heated gases produced when the mountain blew in 1980, and to the north (ahead of you) you will see the utter desolation the eruption created. (The explosion was actually "aimed" that way.)

The spectacular top of
Ape Canyon

When you come to a lookout point on the right, you can scramble down a bit (be very careful) and look into the 300-foot slot at the head of Ape Canyon, which now stretches away to your right. If you work it right, it makes a heck of a foreground for a picture of Mount Adams. It's also visible from a little farther up the trail.

Just 0.2 miles father up is an intersection with the Loowit Trail, which goes all the way around Mount St. Helens. Stay to the right here, wind through another lahar, and half a mile later climb out of it to the east to where a series of rock cairns marks the trail's path across the Plains of Abraham. When the trail dips down to the cliff edge, you'll be at the top of that waterfall with a sweeping view south.

If you're wondering about the name of this hike, it comes from a 1920s incident in which an apelike "Bigfoot" (decades later found to be a kid playing a prank) threw rocks at some miners in the area. The only connection between Ape Canyon and Ape Cave is in the name. Ape Cave (see below) was discovered by the Mount St. Helens Apes, who took their name from the Ape Canyon legend.

For more information, contact the Mount St. Helens National Volcanic Monument office at (360) 247-3900.

NEARBY ACTIVITIES

On the way back down FS 83, you'll pass a sign for Ape Cave, actually a long lava tube divided by an access ladder. The lower trip is a 1.6-mile round-trip walk through a large cavern. The upper, 2.3-mile cave is trickier, with some rock scrambling here and there. Take two flashlights to either cave.

14   BLUFF MOUNTAIN

 **KEY AT-A-GLANCE
INFORMATION**

LENGTH: 13.2 miles

CONFIGURATION: Out-and-back

DIFFICULTY: Strenuous

SCENERY: Wide open, flower-covered ridges; exposed mountainsides; waterfalls; a panoramic vista

EXPOSURE: Exposed almost the whole way, occasionally on knife-edge ridges

TRAFFIC: Light

TRAIL SURFACE: Rocky

HIKING TIME: 7.5 hours

DRIVING DISTANCE: 55 miles (1 hour and 45 minutes) from Pioneer Square

SEASON: Late June–October

ACCESS: No fee required

WHEELCHAIR ACCESS: None

MAPS: Green Trails #396 (Lookout Mountain, WA) and #428 (Bridal Veil, OR)

FACILITIES: None at the trailhead; restrooms and water available in Sunset Falls Campground on the way.

SPECIAL COMMENTS: FS 41, while passable to all vehicles, does get tedious with all the potholes. Also, the last parts of this trail will retain snow well into July. And finally, avoid this hike on a hot day, as you'll be in the open about 95 percent of the time.

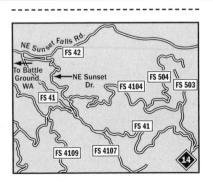

IN BRIEF

There are several ways to reach the summit of Silver Star Mountain; this is the longest and toughest one, and possibly the roughest to reach. But it is without question the most entertaining, with constant views, extensive flowers, few hikers, and an almost expeditionary feel to it.

DESCRIPTION

Epic. That's the word that always comes to mind when I think of this hike. By the end of the (long, often hot) day, you feel like you've been on an adventure, and as you sit on the summit of Silver Star, with all the other slackers who came up one of the easy ways, you can tell them you ain't done nothin' if you ain't done the Bluff Mountain Trail.

Speaking of those "easy" ways, one of them, Ed's Trail, is described in this book's Silver Star Mountain profile (page 83). It's also a tedious drive, but the hike is easier than this one.

Directions ⟶

From Portland on I-205, drive 5 miles north of the Columbia River and take Exit 30/Orchards. Turn right onto WA 500, which turns into WA 503 in 0.9 miles (follow signs for Battle Ground). Stay on WA 503 for 9 miles to its intersection with WA 502 in the middle of Battle Ground. From here, travel 5.7 miles north on WA 503, then turn right onto NE Rock Creek Road, which turns into Lucia Falls Road. After 8.5 miles on this road, take a right onto NE Sunset Falls Road and follow it 7.4 miles to Sunset Campground. Turn right to go through the campground and across a bridge over the East Fork Lewis River, then leave the pavement for 9 bumpy miles on FS 41 to a big ridgetop parking area, where the trailhead is on the right.

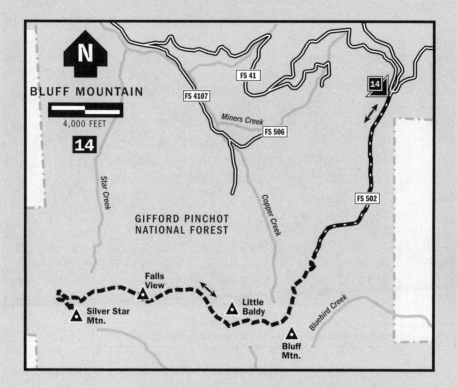

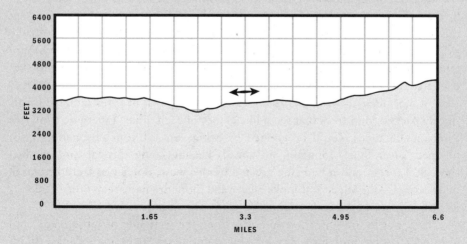

Approaching Silver Star Mountain on the flower-covered Bluff Mountain Trail

From the trailhead, the Bluff Mountain Trail starts on an old Jeep road along a ridge that looks and feels like it's way up in the alpine country of Mount Hood. That's because it's wide open and covered with flowers; but it's open because of a fire, not elevation. The 1902 Yacolt Burn was so intense that very few trees have grown back.

Wander along this ridge, among views of other peaks and ridges swept clean by the fire, for 2.5 sun-baked miles, to where the trail descends into a notch where the road ends. Here, look for the trail taking off for the right (west) side of the ridge and passing under a series of dramatic cliffs (the north side of Bluff Mountain), with views of Little Baldy off to the right. You will probably have to skip over a couple of small creeks, which will be welcome sights on hot summer days.

At 3.5 miles, the trail climbs westward into a patch of forest notable for its thickly packed, thin trees that seem like clones of each other. Emerging from this forest at 3.8 miles, you'll be greeted by a big view of your destination, two-humped Silver Star Mountain, up ahead. Having come this far and climbed through a forest, and now being greeted by this view, don't you feel like you're on an expedition? Silver Star looks bigger and more dramatic than other peaks, as its generally treeless east face looms beyond such an impressive vista.

Back out in the sun, traverse north along the west side of Little Baldy, and just under 5 miles look for a view of a big waterfall on Silver Star's flanks. At 5.3 miles, stay straight at an intersection with Trail 175, and soon climb onto the dramatic (perhaps not for the acrophobic) ridges of Silver Star, which you wind along for almost a mile before dropping into forest again just below the peak.

In these woods, you'll intersect a road coming in from the right; this is the end of the Ed's Trail hike. Turn left on the road for a fairly steep climb (stay left again when the road splits) to a saddle between the two peaks of Silver Star. The higher one is on the left, and the view is as impressive as the 6.6-mile hike you just did. On a clear day, you can see from the Three Sisters to Mount Rainier, and since you're on the highest peak in the immediate vicinity, there's a sense of being on a mountain throne.

For more information, contact the Mount St. Helens National Volcanic Monument office at (360) 247-3900.

15 LAVA CANYON

  KEY AT-A-GLANCE INFORMATION

LENGTH: 1–6 miles

CONFIGURATION: Out-and-back, loop

DIFFICULTY: Easy for the upper section, hard to do the whole thing

SCENERY: Waterfalls, canyon, lava, suspension bridge

EXPOSURE: Mostly open; several sections are quite exposed. In fact, people have fallen to their deaths here: if it's rained or snowed recently, or if you don't like heights, go someplace else.

TRAFFIC: Very heavy on summer weekends, heavy during the week, and moderate the rest of the season

TRAIL SURFACE: Paved, boardwalk, gravel, then packed dirt with rocks

HIKING TIME: 30 minutes to do upper loop, 3 hours to do the whole thing

DRIVING DISTANCE: 85 miles (1 hour and 40 minutes) from Pioneer Square

SEASON: June–October; call the Monument in June to make sure the road is snow-free

ACCESS: Northwest Forest Pass required.

WHEELCHAIR ACCESS: There is a barrier-free trail in the upper section.

MAPS: USFS Mount St. Helens National Monument

FACILITIES: Toilets at the trailhead, but no water

IN BRIEF

An unparalleled look at geological forces at work, Lava Canyon is also a beautiful place to be, with several waterfalls, a dramatic bridge, some challenging hiking, and a short, barrier-free loop trail.

DESCRIPTION

First, a little history, so you'll know what you're looking at here. In ancient times, a forest covered a deep valley. Then, 3,500 years ago, Mount St. Helens erupted, sending a massive mudflow down through the canyon, filling it with volcanic rock. Over the years, the river cut its way through the rock, forming a canyon with waterfalls and deep cuts and towers of harder rock—Lava Canyon. Then other mudflows covered all of that, and eventually forest grew back over the whole thing.

Then on May 18, 1980, Mount St. Helens erupted again, melting 70% of its glaciers in an instant and sending millions of cubic feet of mud and rock blasting down the side of the mountain at about 45 miles an hour. That eruption scoured out the forest and rock, exposing Lava Canyon for the first time in thousands of years. As you drove in, you got a glimpse of this 1980 mudflow (also known

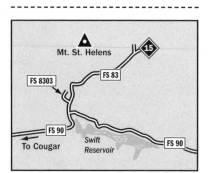

Directions

From Portland on I-5, drive 21 miles north of the Columbia River, take Exit 21/Woodland, and turn right onto WA 503 (Lewis River Road). After 23 miles, stay straight to leave 503 for 503 Spur, and 10 miles farther ahead (3 miles past the town of Cougar), 503 Spur turns into FS 90. Follow FS 90 for 3.5 miles and turn left onto FS 83, following a sign for Ape Cave and Lava Canyon. The Lava Canyon trailhead is at the end of FS 83, 11.5 miles ahead.

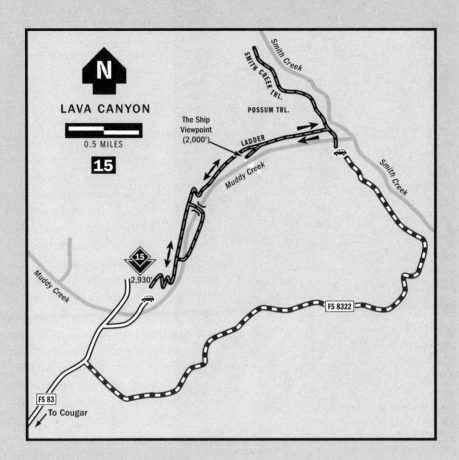

LAVA CANYON

0.5 MILES

15

Smith Creek

SMITH CREEK TRL.

POSSUM TRL.

The Ship
Viewpoint
(2,000')

LADDER

Muddy Creek

Smith Creek

15

2,930'

Muddy Creek

FS 8322

FS 83

To Cougar

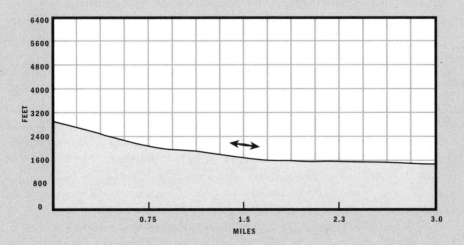

as a lahar); now go see what it gave us.

From the trailhead, you start on a paved path leading left which, though officially barrier-free, would require some work to push a wheelchair through. You can see here that the trees around you survived the 1980 eruption, but everything below was wiped out. Also, look around for trees that have rocks embedded in them—that's how strong the eruption was, and this point is some 5 miles from the crater. The pavement will soon give way to boardwalk, and two viewing platforms give both information and dramatic views of the upper canyon.

After 0.4 miles you'll come to a junction with the loop trail, and by now you've seen perhaps 15 warning signs about the various dangers in the area and imploring you to stay on the trail. Here, at this junction, is my favorite: a sign with "danger" written in seven languages—and you have to get off the trail to read it! Anyway, be careful, and stay on the trail.

For the longer loop, stay straight for now, and in 100 yards pass a nice view of a waterfall and swirling pools above it. In 0.2 miles come to the suspension bridge. It's only 3 feet wide and 100 feet long, and it was also built by the same company that built the suspension bridge at Drift Creek Falls (see hike profile, page 80). Small kids probably shouldn't go below the suspension bridge, and everybody should be careful if it has rained recently. If you'd like to do only a 1.3-mile loop, cross the bridge and follow the trail back up; you'll wind up at the first intersection after crossing another small bridge.

Follow the trail downhill (and I do mean down) from the suspension bridge. In the next section of trail, you'll go down steep slopes, along unguarded ledges, across a couple of bridgeless creeks (one with a cable to hang onto), and down a

40-foot ladder. So if it has been raining, or you have small kids, or you're tired or nervous about heights, think twice before you go past the bridge.

After a steep half mile down, passing several beautiful waterfalls and an area where the river flows through a chute just a few feet wide, the trail mellows somewhat. At 1.1 miles total, climb down a ladder (be careful if your shoes are wet!) and then cross a mossy stream. The rock formation on your right here is known as The Ship; it was one of the formations left standing thousands of years ago when the river cut a new course through the ancient canyon. The top of The Ship was the floor of the valley before 1980. There's a little perspective, eh?

It's worth the effort to get to the top of The Ship. A couple hundred yards past the ladder, an unsigned trail on the right leads 0.2 miles up it; it's pretty steep and includes rock steps and yet another (smaller) ladder, but there are late-summer huckleberries up there, and it's a heck of a place for a picnic, with an excellent view looking back up the canyon.

At this point, you've seen the best of the hike, so it's a good spot to turn around. But if you'd like to keep going, the Lava Canyon Trail continues another 1.3 miles to the Smith Creek trailhead, losing 350 feet in elevation on the way. There's a bridge over the creek just 0.4 miles below The Ship trail that is worth visiting.

Whenever you head back, cross the suspension bridge, and take the loop hike back onto a pre-1980 lava flow. When you cross a small metal bridge, turn left, and you're 0.4 miles from the car. For more information, call the Mount St. Helens National Volcanic Monument office at (360) 247-3900.

16 LEWIS RIVER

KEY AT-A-GLANCE INFORMATION

LENGTH: 5.2 miles

CONFIGURATION: Out-and-back

DIFFICULTY: Easy

SCENERY: Several waterfalls, a wild stream flowing through a wooded canyon, old-growth forest

EXPOSURE: Shady all the way

TRAFFIC: Use is heavy all summer long, especially on weekends.

TRAIL SURFACE: Gravel at first, then packed dirt with some roots

HIKING TIME: 3 hours

DRIVING DISTANCE: 92 miles (2 hours and 10 minutes) from Pioneer Square

SEASON: Year-round, although it might get snow in the winter

ACCESS: Northwest Forest Pass required.

WHEELCHAIR ACCESS: Campsites and restrooms only

MAPS: Green Trails #365 (Lone Butte)

FACILITIES: Toilets at the trailhead; from spring to fall there's drinking water in the campground.

IN BRIEF

Here's a pleasant, mostly flat stroll along a beautiful river with three dramatic waterfalls. Chances are, they're unlike most falls you've seen. The long drive to the trailhead is worth it, especially if you get a campsite at the Lower Falls Recreation Area and make a night of it.

DESCRIPTION

From the trailhead in the picnic area, follow a trail that starts just left of the restrooms. In 100 yards turn right to reach several viewpoints above Lower Falls, one of the most dramatic falls around. The water looks like it's spilling off a shelf, and in fact it is—this is the edge of an ancient lava flow. Over the next stretch of trail, you're walking around the campground, so there are a lot of trails. Turning left will throw you off track and into the campground, but turning right will offer several opportunities to get right down to the river. Once you're safely above the falls, there are some nice opportunities to swim.

Directions ————————————➤

From Portland on I-5, drive 21 miles north of the Columbia River and take Exit 21/Woodland. Turn right onto WA 503 (Lewis River Road), which after 31 miles (2 miles past the town of Cougar) turns into FS 90. Follow FS 90 for 30 more miles (you'll have to turn right just past the Pine Creek Information Center to stay on FS 90) to the Lower Lewis River Falls Recreation Area. Take the first right off the entrance road for the trailhead. You may notice that a mile before the campground on FS 90 there's a Lewis River trailhead, just past a bridge. You can start there if you'd like, but it adds 3 miles to the round-trip hike, and it doesn't add any waterfalls to the view.

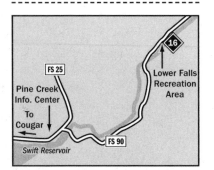

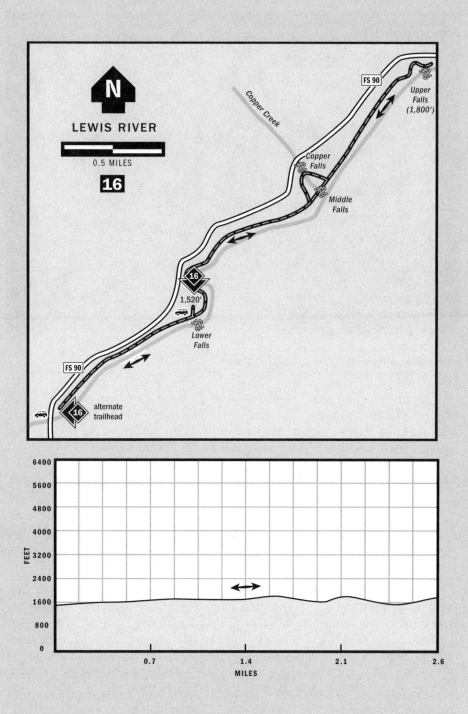

N

LEWIS RIVER

0.5 MILES

16

Copper Creek

FS 90

Upper
Falls
(1,800')

Copper
Falls

Middle
Falls

16

1,520'

Lower
Falls

FS 90

16 alternate
trailhead

FEET

6400
5600
4800
4000
3200
2400
1600
800
0

0.7   1.4   2.1   2.6

MILES

Lower Falls, at the trailhead for the Lewis River Trail

About half a mile after you leave the campground area, look for a bridge (or, rather, half a bridge) across the river. According to the 1965 USGS map of the area, the Lewis River Campground used to be on the far side of the river, so that bridge offered access from that campground to this trail.

Around 0.8 miles from the campground, you'll pass the top of a small waterfall, and then 1.2 miles out you'll cross Copper Creek Falls, which looks like a waterslide into the Lewis River (don't try it). You may notice, on the left, two trails leading up the hill, one just before Copper Creek and one just after. This is a half-mile scenic loop you can do on the way back, if you'd like. Just past the second of these trails, the main trail arrives at Middle Falls, another shelflike falls worth exploring. Just be careful, because the rock here is almost always wet and slippery.

Back on the main trail, you'll soon pass under some enormous cliffs, then drop down into an area with some seriously large trees. There are some Western red cedars here in the neighborhood of six feet thick, and one Douglas fir on the left that must be ten feet thick. Just past this area you'll come to a campsite on the right, then the amphitheater of Upper Falls, an 80-foot plunge. There are good logs and rocks in the sun here for picnicking or just general lounging. A trail to the left leads 0.2 miles up the hill to a platform at the top of Upper Falls, a very worthy side trip. Just a few moments above it, there's a view of yet another falls above Upper Falls.

On the way back, just past Middle Falls, go ahead and take the Copper Creek scenic byway. Just take the first right past Middle Falls, climb briefly to

Another view of Lower Falls through the trees

another waterfall up Copper Creek, then take a left at the fork (the road is to the right) and you'll be back on the main trail, 1.5 miles from the car.

For more information, call the Mount St. Helens National Volcanic Monument office at (360) 449-7800.

17 FALLS CREEK FALLS

KEY AT-A-GLANCE INFORMATION

LENGTH: 3.4 miles
CONFIGURATION: Out-and-back
DIFFICULTY: Easy
SCENERY: Shady forest, a serene stream, and a big-time waterfall
EXPOSURE: Some cliff edges at the end of the trail, easily avoided
TRAFFIC: Moderate on weekends, light otherwise
TRAIL SURFACE: Packed dirt
HIKING TIME: 2 hours
DRIVING DISTANCE: 68 miles (1 hour and 20 minutes) from Pioneer Square
SEASON: April–November; probably snowbound in winter
ACCESS: No fee required
WHEELCHAIR ACCESS: None
MAPS: Green Trails #397 (Wind River)
FACILITIES: None at the trailhead

IN BRIEF

If you're looking for an easy trail to a spectacular destination, this is your choice. This 1.7-mile ramble gains about 700 feet—which you'll hardly notice on the way and quickly forget when you reach one of the area's most impressive waterfalls.

DESCRIPTION

This trail starts out flat through second-growth forest, passing huckleberry, Oregon grape, and Douglas firs. In a quarter mile, pass through meadows with a view of an interesting rock formation to the left. Soon after, cross the creek in a narrow gorge, and look for some cool round water-formed rock faces.

At 0.6 miles, now into an older forest, pass a couple of impressive root balls in an area that might get sketchy when wet; a good slip might send you down toward the creek. At 0.75 miles, pass nearly under a big Douglas fir, and look for another (dead) one with countless woodpecker holes.

Directions ⟶

From Portland on I-84, drive 37 miles east of I-205 and take Exit 44/Cascade Locks. As soon as you enter the town, make your first right to get on the Bridge of the Gods, following a sign for Stevenson, Washington. Pay the $1 toll, cross the river, and turn right onto WA 14. Go 5.8 miles and turn left, following a sign for Carson, Washington. This is Wind River Road. After 14.5 miles on Wind River Road, turn right (staying on Wind River Road) and go 0.8 miles, then turn right onto gravel FS 3062. Go 2 miles on this and turn right onto FS 057, following a sign for Lower Falls Creek Falls Trail. The trailhead is half a mile ahead, at the end of the road.

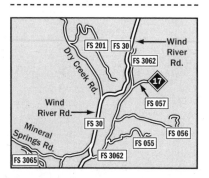

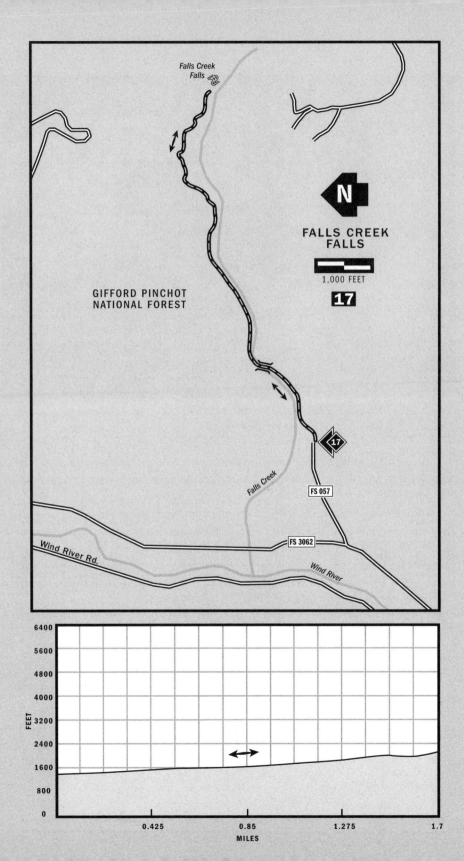

A close-up view of the upper reaches of Falls Creek Falls

Just past 1 mile, after passing a nice creekside picnic area on the right, reach a big rock formation on the left, and ahead to the right catch your first glimpse of the upper falls.

When you arrive at the falls, in an area of large boulders that provide plenty of seating, you'll see it's actually two falls plunging into a mossy bowl filled with maidenhair ferns. (In fact, there's a hidden falls even higher, making for a total drop of 200 feet.) The whole scene seems straight out of *The Lord of the Rings;* one expects to see archers on the hill, guarding their sacred pool. It's particularly impressive in the early afternoon.

SILVER STAR MOUNTAIN 18

IN BRIEF

You may be reading the directions to this one and thinking, What a drive! But when you're on Ed's Trail approaching Silver Star Mountain, you'll be thinking, This is too beautiful and mountainous to be so close to town! This flower-soaked traverse through rocky, alpine country is worth all the hassles of getting there.

DESCRIPTION

Even the trailhead for this one is scenic, and other than a few moments here and there, every foot of the trail is, as well. From the trailhead, look for the path heading to the right, past a brown hiker's sign. Follow this through several brushy switchbacks to an old Jeep road, then go up that for 150 yards to a wide gravel area with a nice view of Mount Hood through a notch in a ridge. Stop here, at the half-mile point, and catch your breath.

Where the road swings back to the right and heads uphill, look for Ed's Trail heading

KEY AT-A-GLANCE INFORMATION

LENGTH: 4.8 miles

CONFIGURATION: Balloon

DIFFICULTY: Moderate

SCENERY: Wildflowers, open ridgetops, rocky crags, a natural arch, several volcanoes

EXPOSURE: In the sun the whole time, with occasional trips along rocky cliff edges

TRAFFIC: Moderate on weekends, light otherwise

TRAIL SURFACE: Dirt, rocks, some scrambling involved

HIKING TIME: 3 hours

DRIVING DISTANCE: 56 miles (1 hour and 30 minutes) from Pioneer Square

SEASON: June–October

ACCESS: No fee required

WHEELCHAIR ACCESS: None

MAPS: Green Trails #396 (Lookout Mountain) and #428 (Bridal Veil), though Ed's Trail isn't on either one

FACILITIES: None at the trailhead.

SPECIAL COMMENTS: The road to this one is not exactly smooth, but it passed my 1992 Nissan Sentra Test.

Directions ➔

From Portland on I-205, drive 5 miles north of the Columbia River and take Exit 30/Orchards. Turn right onto WA 500, which turns into WA 503 in 0.9 miles (follow signs for Battle Ground). Stay on WA 503 for 9 miles to its intersection with WA 502 in the middle of Battle Ground. From here, travel 5.7 miles north on WA 503, then turn right onto NE Rock Creek Road, which turns into Lucia Falls Road. After 8.5 miles on this road, take a right onto NE Sunset Falls Road, follow it for 2 miles, and turn right onto NE Dole Valley Road. Go 2.4 miles on this one and turn left onto Road L 1100, which is marked with "1100" on a tree and a sign for Tarbell Picnic Area. On this road, stay straight at 2.2 miles, bear left (downhill) at 4.3 miles, then turn right (uphill) at 7.7 miles. The trailhead is 2.6 miles up, at the end of this narrow, bumpy road.

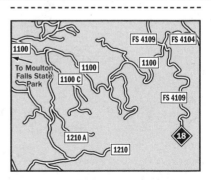

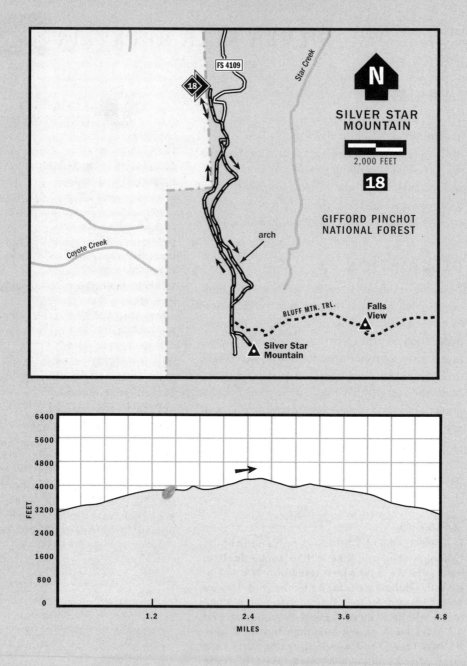

Flowers on the summit of Silver Star Mountain, with Bluff Mountain in the distance

left, along the ridge. We'll come back on the road, but it's better to follow Ed for now. This Ed must have been a lover of flowers and open country, because his trail is a piece of work: an ambling, gentle climb along a ridge that looks as if it's thousands of feet higher than it really is. That's because 100 years ago, fires swept this area clean, and very few trees have grown back—though millions of flowers have. So it's like you're getting a look at the skeletons of the mountains, complete with bony spurs, cliffs, and rock formations normally lost in forest.

Climb toward some of these exposed formations for 0.7 miles before the trail flattens out and starts a tour of the rocky ridgetop. At 1.5 miles, pass through a rock arch and next to a small, overhanging cave that offers just about the only shade around on a hot day. A few moments later the trail takes off up the ridge face, becoming nearly a climb in spots as you scramble up through the rocks to a view of, for the first time, two-humped Silver Star up ahead. Dramatic, huh?

Now the trail drops down through meadows and into the trees, then climbs again to a junction with the road you left behind—so this whole Ed's Trail was just a scenic, adventurous diversion. Follow the road to the left, staying left again at a junction a couple hundred yards up, and after a quarter mile the road comes up to a saddle between the two peaks. Head left for the big (shadeless) view at the official summit, and enjoy views of the Columbia River Gorge, Mount Defiance (with radio towers), the back of Dog Mountain, Larch Mountain, the Portland area, and everything from Mount Jefferson to Mount Rainier. Look, also, for the Bluff Mountain Trail (hike 14) coming along the narrow ridges from the east.

For yet another scenic diversion, keep going along the road, past the summits, for about 300 yards, and turn left at a junction; this trail leads just under a

The upper reaches of Silver Star Mountain with Mount St. Helens in the distance

mile to some Native American vision-quest pits at the end of the ridge. (Don't disturb anything!)

On your way back to the car, enjoy some different scenery while avoiding a treacherous down-climb of Ed's Trail. Simply stay on the Jeep road as it winds along the opposite side of the ridge. This will lead you back to the far end of Ed's Trail, where you started on it, and then to the car.

SIOUXON CREEK 19

IN BRIEF

An easy, pleasant stroll along a mountain stream, with old-growth forest and waterfalls all around, plus options that include stream crossing and rugged climbing. What more could you want? Even the kids will like it; with supervision, they could go for a swim.

DESCRIPTION

The only spectacular thing about this hike is how easy and scenic it is. There are no panoramic viewpoints, no exotic geological features, and no serious hiking challenges. It's just a beautiful river in a peaceful, lush, tree-filled canyon, with waterfalls all over the place and not too many hikers.

In fact, two mysteries have long intrigued me about this hike: One is why more people don't seem to know about it, and the other is why everyone stops at Chinook Falls, when there are numerous beautiful spots farther up the creek, and the most amazing falls of all (Wildcat) just across it.

From the trailhead, there are several trails leading into the woods. Just take any of them and turn right when you reach the main

KEY AT-A-GLANCE INFORMATION

LENGTH: 10.8 miles along the creek, with possible side trips

CONFIGURATION: Out-and-back with an optional loop

DIFFICULTY: Easy–moderate

SCENERY: Old-growth forest, waterfalls, pools in the river

EXPOSURE: Shady all the way, some optional creek wading

TRAFFIC: Use is moderate on summer weekends but light otherwise.

TRAIL SURFACE: Packed dirt with some rocks and roots

HIKING TIME: 3–5 hours

DRIVING DISTANCE: 55 miles (1 hour and 30 minutes) from Pioneer Square

SEASON: Year-round, but muddy in winter and spring with occasional snow

WHEELCHAIR ACCESS: None

MAPS: Green Trails #396 (Lookout Mountain)

FACILITIES: None at the trailhead; the water on the trail must be treated.

SPECIAL COMMENTS: For more information, contact the Mount St. Helens National Volcanic Monument office at (360) 247-3900.

Directions

From Portland on I-205, drive 5 miles north of the Columbia River and take Exit 30B/Orchards. Turn right onto WA 500, which turns into WA 503 in 0.9 miles (follow signs for Battle Ground). Stay on WA 503 for 25 miles, passing through the town of Amboy. Just past the Mount St. Helens National Volcanic Monument headquarters, turn right onto NE Healy Road. Go 9 miles (note that Healy turns into FS 54 at 2.4 miles), then turn left (uphill) on FS 57. After 1.2 miles on FS 57, turn left onto FS 5701. The trailhead is 3.6 miles ahead, at the end of the road.

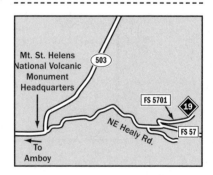

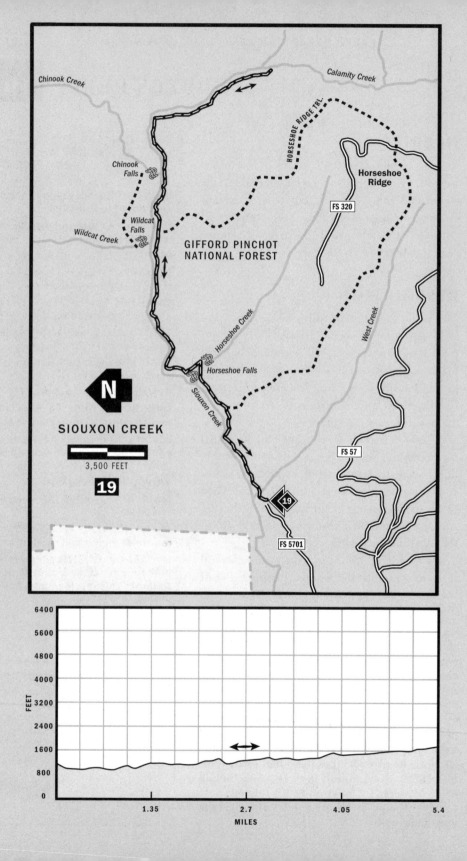

Chinook Creek

Calamity Creek

HORSESHOE RIDGE TRL.

Chinook Falls

Horseshoe Ridge

Wildcat Falls

Wildcat Creek

FS 320

GIFFORD PINCHOT
NATIONAL FOREST

Horseshoe Creek

West Creek

N

SIOUXON CREEK

Horseshoe Falls

3,500 FEET

Siouxon Creek

19

FS 57

19

FS 5701

6400

5600

4800

4000

3200

2400

1600

800

0

FEET

1.35   2.7   4.05   5.4

MILES

Mount St. Helens is just visible from the top of Siouxon Peak, a steep side loop off the Siouxon Creek Trail.

trail. You'll walk downhill briefly, cross West Creek on a log bridge, then stroll over a small ridge to Siouxon Creek. At 0.9 miles you'll see, on the right, the Horseshoe Ridge Trail, which makes a 7-mile, rugged and solitary loop back to this trail. After 1.4 miles, your trail crosses Horseshoe Creek (so named because it drains a horseshoe-shaped ridge, of which you're crossing the open mouth). There will be a waterfall above and below you here; to get a view of the lower one, take a side trail to the left just after the bridge.

Over the next 0.3 miles you'll climb slightly to a viewpoint of Siouxon Falls, which could almost be called a really big rapid as opposed to a classic falls. Then the trail traverses along flat ground for half a mile, some 200 feet above the creek, before dropping to its side for half a mile. This is where some swimming might happen—just know that it would be brief, unless you're part polar bear.

At the 3-mile mark, you'll see two side trails in quick succession. The first, unmarked and on the left, leads down to the creek; this is one way to reach Wildcat Falls, but it involves a tricky crossing of Siouxon Creek that will be sketchy for most people until late summer, at least. There's an easier way a little farther up. The second trail you'll see, heading up and to the right, is the second appearance of the Horseshoe Ridge Trail.

Go another 0.7 miles and you'll come to an unnamed creek on the right; careful here, as the rocks tend to be slick. There's also a nice new bridge over Siouxon Creek, which at this point flows through a narrow gorge. Cross the

bridge and go 0.3 miles to beautiful, 50-foot Chinook Falls.

Here, there are decisions to make. You could head back the way you came and call it a day at just under 8 miles. Or you could go visit Wildcat Falls by wading across Chinook Creek here and following an up-and-down trail for half a mile to Wildcat Creek. Go up that creek from a junction, and in 0.2 miles arrive at the base of the 100-foot beauty. There are even more dramatic views of it farther up the trail. And if you're *really* looking for some exercise, put in 3.5 miles (and about 3,000 feet) up this trail to Siouxon Peak, following a route that's well-marked on the Green Trails map. Go back to Chinook Falls the way you came, or take on the crossing of Siouxon for a shortcut.

At the very least, from the bridge near Chinook Falls, go a little farther up Siouxon Creek. I have no idea why no other guidebook recommends this, because it's just as beautiful up there, requires no more effort, and visits several more waterfalls. There's another 1.7 miles of creekside trail, ending at a bridgeless crossing of Calamity Creek and gaining only another 250 feet. Beyond Calamity Creek the trail climbs away from Siouxon, ending some 2 miles later a road near Observation Peak and Sister Rocks.

SOUTH FORK TOUTLE RIVER

Note: This trail was closed in 2007 due to road damage; it might not re-open. Call (360) 247-3900 for up-to-date information.

IN BRIEF

Without your driving all the way around to the other side of Mount St. Helens, this is the most dramatic view you can get of the results of that mountain's 1980 eruption. A major mudflow went all the way down the Toutle ("toodle") River to the Columbia, where shipping was stopped for days while the debris was dredged out. This hike will show you the South Fork of that river, where the mudflow was half a mile wide, as well as a glimpse of the majesty that the eruption destroyed.

DESCRIPTION

Back in 2003, this hike got a bit longer when the road beyond the Blue Lake Trailhead was washed out, cutting off a trailhead that was only half a mile from Sheep Canyon. Then, in 2006, the Blue Lake Trailhead itself was destroyed (see Special Comments at right). One hopes that all this will be fixed, because this happens to be one of my two or three favorite hikes in this entire book.

We'll assume for now that the road beyond the Blue Lake Trailhead isn't open. From that

KEY AT-A-GLANCE INFORMATION

LENGTH: 10.8 miles

CONFIGURATION: Balloon

DIFFICULTY: Strenuous

SCENERY: Forest, waterfalls, meadows, a close-up view of Mount St. Helens

EXPOSURE: Mostly shady until the end, when you'll be out in the open

TRAFFIC: Use is moderate on summer weekends but light otherwise.

TRAIL SURFACE: Packed dirt with rocks and roots; just rock in some areas

HIKING TIME: 6 hours

DRIVING DISTANCE: 73 miles (1 hour and 30 minutes) from Pioneer Square

SEASON: June–October; in June, call to make sure the road is snow-free

ACCESS: Northwest Forest Pass required.

WHEELCHAIR ACCESS: None

MAPS: USFS Mount St. Helens National Monument; Green Trails #364 (Mount St. Helens) or #364S (Mount St. Helens NW)

FACILITIES: None at trailhead; the water on the trail must be treated.

SPECIAL COMMENTS: Late in 2006, the Blue Lake Trailhead and sections of the road leading to it were wiped out by mudslides. Call (360) 247-3900 for up-to-date information.

Directions ⟶

From Portland on I-5, drive 21 miles north of the Columbia River and take Exit 21/ Woodland. Turn right onto WA 503 (Lewis River Road) and travel 28 miles, then turn left onto FS 8100, between mileposts 35 and 36, following a sign for Kalama Recreation Area. Travel 11.5 miles on FS 8100 to the Blue Lake Trailhead on the right.

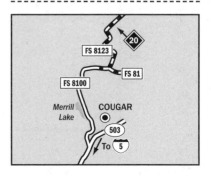

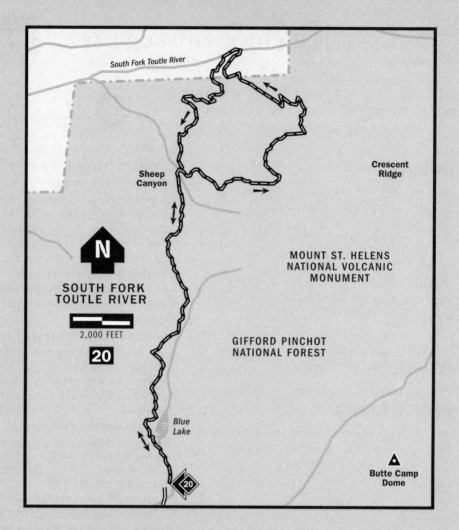

South Fork Toutle River

Sheep
Canyon

Crescent
Ridge

N

**SOUTH FORK
TOULE RIVER**

2,000 FEET

20

MOUNT ST. HELENS
NATIONAL VOLCANIC
MONUMENT

GIFFORD PINCHOT
NATIONAL FOREST

Blue
Lake

20

Butte Camp
Dome

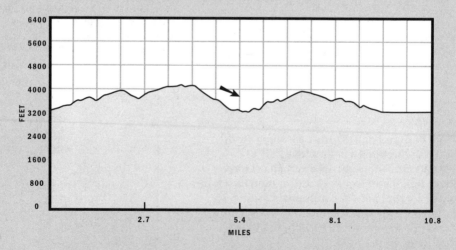

The bridge over Sheep Canyon is a treat towards the end of the loop to South Fork Toutle River.

trailhead, take the trail leading left and across Cold-spring Creek—a bridgeless crossing which often has a rope strung up for assistance. Pass Blue Lake in less than half a mile, then go slowly up and over a low, rounded ridge through a beautiful old forest. After 2.4 miles, arrive at the Sheep Canyon Trail, coming up from the left (from the old road-end trailhead cut off in 2003). For the easiest route to the South Fork of the Toutle, follow this trail straight ahead for 1.5 miles, but for the recommended loop, which will come back that way, turn right and start climbing gradually through a lovely forest. Just after some neat cliffs appear on the right, look for a triple-trunk tree to the right of the trail.

After a total of 4 miles (1.6 miles since the junction), come to an intersection with the Loowit Trail, which goes all the way around Mount St. Helens. Turn left here and climb just a little more, through a wonderful subalpine area of firs and hemlocks. In August the place will be ablaze with flowers, especially blue lupine, and in fall the mountain ash and other plants roar with color. And the views up here, at the foot of the mountain, are fantastic.

Soon you'll drop down and traverse an ash-filled ravine with a pond below you. Keep an eye out among the trees down there for deer or elk. After a little more climbing you'll find yourself at the top of a cliff looking out over the canyon of the South Fork Toutle River. The river, some 800 feet below you, is in the process of recarving its way through the mudflow. The contrast between your side of the canyon and the other side, well within the blast zone, couldn't be more stark.

The trail will now turn downhill, descending Crescent Ridge, for 1.5 miles to a junction with the Toutle Trail. Go to the right here, exploring around the

Indian paintbrush and other wildflowers are reclaiming the mudflow along South Fork Toutle River.

edge of the mini-gorge the river has cut into the mudflow. Then go back to the Toutle Trail and follow it for 1.5 miles through old-growth forest. You'll climb over a small ridge, but the reward is a field of huckleberries at the bridge over Sheep Canyon. Cross that spectacular span, then stay straight at the junction to retrace your steps 2.4 miles back to the car.

NEARBY ACTIVITIES

If you'd like to see what this eruption was all about, go see the award-winning 28-minute film on the giant screen at Castle Rock, Washington. Castle Rock is at Exit 48 on I-5, 27 miles north of Woodland. You can't miss the theater.

TRAPPER CREEK WILDERNESS 21

IN BRIEF

This is like a secret hike. Most people have never heard of it, but everybody who goes there loves it. It's quiet and woodsy with lots of creeks, two waterfalls, and—if you're up for some elevation—a great view from Observation Peak.

DESCRIPTION

I can't explain why so few people have heard of Trapper Creek. It's barely an hour from Portland, it's loaded with trails, and it couldn't be any prettier. If you're a fan of the forest and don't mind climbing, this is the place to be. One section of the wilderness was actually set aside in the 1950s as a research area for old-growth Pacific Silver Firs. And up on the ridge, there are huckleberries—the big, blue, juicy kind—everywhere.

The wilderness covers a little more than 6,000 acres, and it's basically one U-shaped watershed, drained by Trapper Creek and its many tributaries. It's heavily forested with firs, hemlocks, cedars, and pines. Wildflowers are abundant in the spring and early summer, and the animals here include owls, black bears,

KEY AT-A-GLANCE INFORMATION

LENGTH: This loop is 13 miles, but options abound.

CONFIGURATION: Loop

DIFFICULTY: Easy–strenuous

TRAFFIC: Moderate on summer weekends, light otherwise

SCENERY: Magnificent forest, two waterfalls, a sweeping mountaintop view

EXPOSURE: A couple of lookouts, otherwise in the woods

TRAFFIC: Light

TRAIL SURFACE: Packed dirt and rocks

HIKING TIME: 8 hours to do the big loop

DRIVING DISTANCE: 66 miles (1 hour and 30 minutes) from Pioneer Square

SEASON: July–October to climb the ridge; lower elevations are essentially year-round but could get snow.

WHEELCHAIR ACCESS: None

MAPS: USFS Trapper Creek Wilderness

FACILITIES: None at the trailhead; there's water everywhere, but it must be treated.

Directions ————————→

From Portland on I-84, drive 37 miles east of I-205 and take Exit 44/Cascade Locks. As soon as you enter the town, make your first right to get on the Bridge of the Gods, following a sign for Stevenson, Washington. Pay the $1 toll, cross the river, and turn right onto WA 14. Go 5.8 miles and turn left, following a sign for Carson, Washington. This is Wind River Road. After 14.5 miles on this road, stay straight, leaving Wind River Road and following a sign for Government Mineral Springs. Half a mile later, turn right on FS 5401; the trailhead is 0.4 miles ahead, at the end of the road.

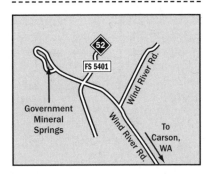

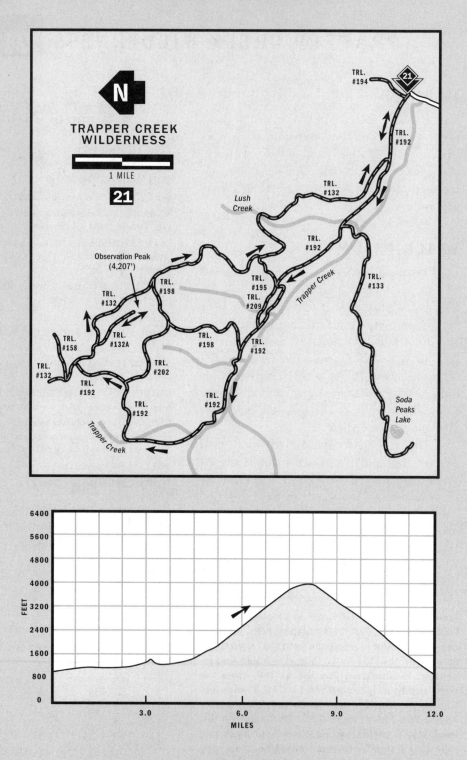

cougars, and bobcats—though the only sign I've seen of any of those was the sound of an owl and some very fresh, berry-filled bear scat on the trail. You have virtually nothing to fear from a black bear; if you see one, you'll likely see its rump disappearing into the woods.

To explore this area, you have numerous options; let this challenging 13-mile loop serve as an introduction. From the trailhead, start into the woods on the Trapper Creek Trail, #192, which you'll follow for 6 miles to its end. Right off the bat you'll intersect the Dry Creek Trail (#194), which runs about 4 miles north along Dry Creek. Half a mile out on 192, look for a rotting stump in the shape of an hourglass. Look, also, for such forest features as woodpecker holes in snags and new trees growing out of old stumps. In 1 mile, you'll see the Observation Trail (#132) on the right; we'll be coming down this one later. For now, stay straight on 192, and the forest gets even better as you get deeper into the canyon.

Just less than a mile later, you'll cross Lush Creek and encounter trail #133, the Soda Peaks Trail, on the left. This leads to the one lake in the wilderness, Soda Peaks Lake; it's a climb of 2,500 feet in about 3 miles, and the trail doesn't loop back to this one. So unless you're looking for another hill to climb, stay on #192, Trapper Creek Trail.

About a mile later, barely climbing, you'll come to two trails at once: the Big Slide Trail (#195) and the Deer Way Trail (#209). Each of these, and several other trails in the wilderness, were built and are maintained by the Mazamas, a Portland-based mountaineering club that has adopted this wilderness area. But before you go off on one of their trails, you should know a few things about Mazamas and their trails. For one thing—and I say this as a Mazama—there is an element in that crowd that uses the phrase "get your butt kicked" to mean "have a good time." Some of these trails were designed with that attitude: They're steep scrambles, without such niceties as switchbacks, and they can be tough to follow. And when a log falls across them, rather than cut the log away (like the Forest Service does), the Mazamas might cut a little notch in the top of it, to help you swing your leg over. So these trails are fun—and the Mazamas' signs are really cool—but they aren't necessarily casual.

The Deer Way Trail is basically an easy cutoff that avoids some elevation for those traveling the Trapper Creek Trail, so if that's your bag, take it. Otherwise, the Trapper Creek Trail dips down, for the first time, to Trapper Creek, then crosses Slump Creek before climbing back up the hill to the west end of the Deer Way Trail. Next, you'll cross the Sunshine Trail (#198), a Mazama masterpiece that goes straight up about 2,000 feet in less than 2 miles. I've done it; it's a "wonderful" butt-kicking.

There's no need to climb that hill, though, because right after this, the Trapper Creek Trail gets pretty serious about climbing as well. You'll have it easy for another half mile, then put in 1,200 feet in just over a mile. It is broken up for you by a side trip to see Hidden Creek Falls, marked by a Mazama sign, and also by a view from the main trail of 100-foot Trapper Creek Falls.

When you get to a wonderful viewpoint looking back down the forested canyon, you're at 3,200 feet, with the last 1,000 feet spread over 2 miles to Observation Peak. You'll also be in a dreamland forest. To my mind, there's nothing lovelier than a Northwest forest around 3,000 to 4,000 feet above sea level. And the crossing, at 3,300 feet, of Trapper Creek in a berry-filled basin is about as nice as it gets.

You'll cross one more Mazama trail, the Rim Trail (#202), before a trail to the right cuts off some distance to the Observation Trail (#132). Turn right here, then take another right onto #132A in half a mile, and after just over a half mile of climbing you'll be at Observation Peak. My hiking friend and I encountered two other folks up there—the only people we saw on an August Saturday—and we struggled to come up with the right word for the view. Look for Mount St. Helens and its blast zone to the north; from there around to the right, we have Mount Rainier, the Goat Rocks off on the horizon, and then Mount Adams, bigger than life. See if you can spot, well to the right of that, the meadow on top of Dog Mountain—it's rare to see it from this direction—and across from that the radio towers atop Mount Defiance, the highest point in the Columbia River Gorge. Right of that are Mounts Hood and Jefferson, and closer in are the two Soda Peaks, host to the aforementioned lake. Nice, huh?

Getting down from here is simple; just go back down the #132A trail you came up and turn right on the Observation Trail, #132. You can follow this trail 5 miles to its end at the #192, a mile up from the parking lot, or you can test your knees going down a Mazama trail. Just turn right on either the Sunshine Trail (#198) or the much shorter Big Slide Trail (#195), and don't blame me if you have a hard time walking the next day. Either way you go, you'll come to the Trapper Creek Trail, and your car is to the left.

NEARBY ACTIVITIES

It's all about springs in this area. When you drive back down FS 5401 on your way out, take a right for Government Mineral Springs and follow signs to Iron Mike Well, which puts out mineral water from an iron pump. Or, when you get back to Carson, go to the Carson Hot Springs Resort, with its 1901 hotel and 1923 bathhouse and cabins. You can soak, get a massage, and then they wrap you in hot towels. A new hotel and golf course were in the works as this book went to press. And in the fall, their restaurant makes a mean apple crisp. Call (800) 607-3678 for details.

UP THE CLACKAMAS RIVER

22 BAGBY HOT SPRINGS

KEY AT-A-GLANCE INFORMATION

LENGTH: 3 miles round-trip to the springs; 3.6 miles to Shower Creek

CONFIGURATION: Out-and-back

DIFFICULTY: Easy

SCENERY: Old-growth forest, a mountain stream, and tubs of hot water

EXPOSURE: Shady all the way

TRAFFIC: Use is quite heavy.

TRAIL SURFACE: Packed dirt with some muddy spots in winter and spring

HIKING TIME: 1 hour round-trip (with hot soak)

DRIVING DISTANCE: 74 miles (1 hour and 35 minutes) from Pioneer Square

SEASON: Year-round, but it does get some snow, so call ahead for conditions.

ACCESS: Northwest Forest Pass required.

WHEELCHAIR ACCESS: None

MAPS: USGS Bagby Hot Springs; USFS Bull of the Woods Wilderness

FACILITIES: Toilets at the trailhead and at the springs, but no water. The water in streams along the hike must be treated.

SPECIAL COMMENTS: Don't leave any valuables in your car at this trailhead.

IN BRIEF

Unless you've got issues about being among naked people, this is one place you should positively visit. The hike isn't much of a challenge, but the destination is sublime: historic hot springs with cedar-log tubs, some of them private, surrounded by ancient-growth forest. It can get rowdy on weekends (though alcohol is now banned at the springs), and there have been many reports of car break-ins at the trailhead.

DESCRIPTION

It seems everybody in the area knows about Bagby, even the folks who haven't actually been there. Just the word seems to stand for something about life in the Pacific Northwest: soothing, relaxing, a retreat from the hustle-and-bustle world, back into the days of the ancient forest and natural elements.

Well, it's not just that. A nonprofit group called Friends of Bagby built two bathhouses on the property, and the chances you'll be the only people there are slim. On weekends you might have to wait to soak, unless you start early.

One note on parking in the area: in 2005, while a new bridge was being constructed on the trail, an alternative parking area developed at a bend in the road near the trailhead. Some folks continued using this

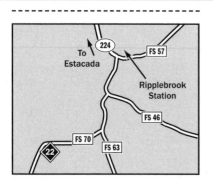

Directions

From Portland on OR 224, travel 44 miles southeast of Interstate 205, through the town of Estacada, to the Ranger Station at Ripplebrook. Turn right onto Forest Service Road 46 and, 3.6 miles later, right again onto FS 63. Travel 3.5 miles and turn right onto FS 70. The trailhead is 6 miles ahead on the left.

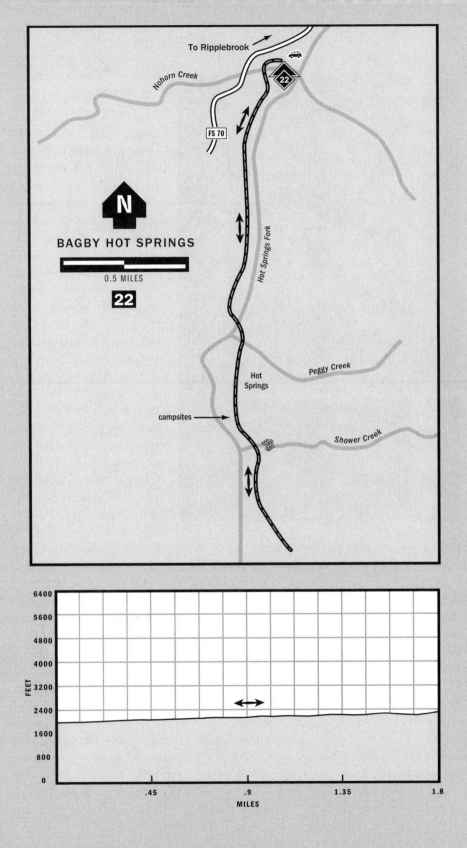

area, even after the bridge went in, but the Forest Service will ticket you if you park here.

From the trailhead parking lot, start up the wide trail and cross the new, $200,000, 119-foot bridge over Nohorn Creek, named after the nickname of an early pioneer in the area. The hiking is pleasant, the pools in the river inviting, and the forest inspiring. If you happen to notice some old metal loops tacked high into the trees, those once held telephone wires that connected fire lookouts back in the 1930s. Cross a bridge over Hot Springs Fork, and you're almost to the springs.

When you come to the springs area, the first thing you'll notice is the 1913 ranger cabin, which is listed on the National Register of Historic Places. It was a central communications station for those fire lookouts. I should mention that this cabin of 16-inch cedar logs was hand-built by one ranger, a certain Phil Putz, who first visited the area after walking 39 miles in one day. You think he was happy to find the springs? The path behind the cabin leads to a monumental downed tree; check out the inside, which was rotted away long before the giant was cut to keep it from squashing the bathhouses.

The bathhouse on the right has one big tub, with room for five or six adults. The one on the left has an open area with several tubs and five private rooms, each with a two-person log tub. The water comes out of the springs at 136 degrees and runs through a system of log flumes. To fill a tub, you just open up the valve and let the hot water in, then grab a bucket, fill it with cold water from a nearby tub, and get the temperature where you want it. Typically, a full tub needs four or five buckets of cold water to make it tolerable. As it cools off, just open up the valve and let some more hot stuff in. It's fantastic. About 50 percent of bathers don't wear swimsuits, but in areas other than the tubs you are requested to wear clothing. It's also requested that if people are waiting you limit your soaking to one hour.

Even if there's nobody around when you get to the springs, consider taking some time to explore farther up the trail before you soak. It's old growth all the way, up the Hot Springs Fork of the Collawash River, past Shower Creek and Spray Creek, and eventually into the Bull of the Woods Wilderness. You should go at least as far as Shower Creek (0.3 miles past the springs and just 0.1 mile past a camping area on the right) to enjoy the 50-foot falls and a little wooden platform somebody built underneath it for folks to shower on.

Bagby is best avoided on weekend nights, when partiers sometimes take over the place. So unless you too are a yahoo, go on a weekday or early on the weekends. For more information, call the Clackamas Ranger District office at (503) 630-6861.

23 BULL OF THE WOODS

IN BRIEF

This is like two great hikes in one: an easy stroll through old-growth forest and rhododendrons to two beautiful lakes, and a more challenging climb to a fire lookout tower with a panoramic view.

DESCRIPTION

This trail has it all. Come in late June, as soon as the snow has cleared, and let your mind be boggled by the rhododendron show among the old-growth towers on the way to Pansy Lake. (But bring bug repellent!)

Come in late summer and pick huckleberries up on the ridge. Or come in fall, when the ridge will be awash in color and the mountains might have their first coat of snow. Just make sure you get here.

The peak is the second-highest point in the 27,000-acre Bull of the Woods Wilderness, which boasts more than a dozen lakes bigger than an acre, 68 miles of hiking trails, and even the world-famous northern spotted owl, which you almost certainly won't see.

From the trailhead, you start right out through a beautiful forest, walking basically flat for 0.8 miles, across some nice little creeks

----

Directions ⟶

From Portland on OR 224, travel 44 miles southeast of I-205, through the town of Estacada, to the Ranger Station at Ripplebrook. Bear right onto FS 46 and, 3.6 miles later, right again onto FS 63. After 5.7 miles, turn right onto FS 6340, following a sign for Bull of the Woods and Pansy Basin. At a junction 3.5 miles later, stay straight, still on FS 6340. Then, 4.4 miles past that junction (7.9 miles after FS 63), turn right on FS 6341, ignoring a sign to the left saying Bull of the Woods Trail. The parking area is 3.6 miles ahead on the right.

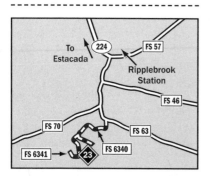

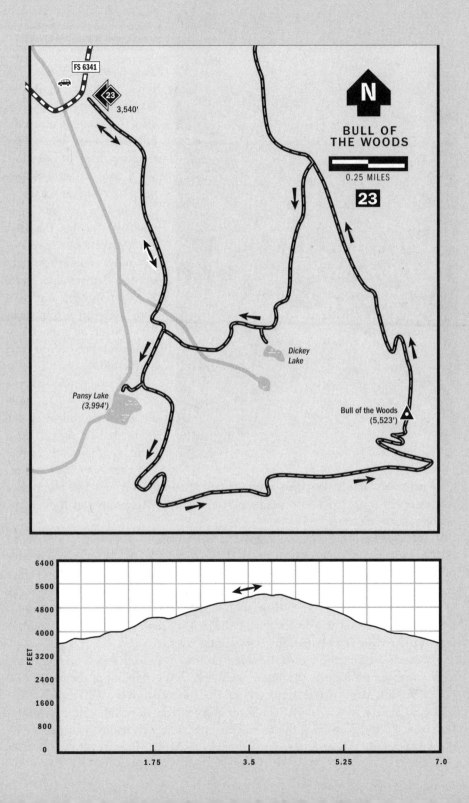

and through gauntlets of rhododendrons, until you reach a signed trail junction. Trail 549, coming down the hill from your left, is the return portion of our loop. We'll go right here, following a sign for Pansy Lake.

Just before the lake, you'll pass a sign that says Twin Lakes, but ignore it (for now) and keep straight to visit Pansy Lake. There is a campsite on the right with excellent sitting rocks for a picnic or a quick rest and snack before you start up the hill.

Now, return to the trail and take what's now a right turn, following the Twin Lakes sign. You'll climb gradually for a while and then start into a series of switchbacks. In just less than a mile from the lake, you'll gain 500 feet before you intersect trail #558 in a saddle between Pansy Mountain and Bull of the Woods. Turn left onto #558.

While the switchbacks you just did were obviously steep, this trail is what I call "sneaky steep," which means that it doesn't look like much, but you'll be able to feel the elevation gain. You're gaining about 700 feet in 1.1 miles, and since you're now going over 5,000 feet, you're probably starting to feel the relative lack of oxygen. The forest in here is beautiful, though, and should take your mind off the climb. And if you're wondering why the moss doesn't grow on the bottom ten feet of the trunks, it's because that's where the average snow depth is.

When you gain the top of the ridge and intersect trail #554, turn left, and with one more push through some switchbacks you'll pop out at the top of Bull of the Woods, with its old forest service fire lookout tower. Walk up onto the deck and have a look around. You'll see Big Slide Lake below you, but Mount Jefferson, 20 miles away, is the dominant sight. On a clear day, you can see all the way from the Three Sisters on your right to Mount Rainier on your left. As the crow flies, it's about 175 miles from the Sisters to Rainier. Rest here and feel proud.

To continue the loop, find a trail junction in the trees on the opposite side of the watchtower from Mount Jefferson. This is the Bull of the Woods Trail (#550). Follow it to your right, along the ridge. You'll see occasional great views and many, many flowers for 1.1 miles, at which point you'll intersect Trail #549. Take #549 down and to the left, and your elevation loss will quickly get serious. Just past half a mile, keep an eye out through the trees on your left for Dickey Lake—a lake seen through trees is always a magical sight—and also for a trail that leads down to the lake itself. That trail is just past a meadow on Trail #549.

After another half mile, most of it through a sea of rhododendrons, you'll get back to the trail where this whole thing started, the Pansy Lake Trail (#551). Turn right there, and you'll be back to the car in no time.

24 CLACKAMAS RIVER

KEY AT-A-GLANCE INFORMATION

LENGTH: 7.8 miles one-way with a car shuttle or 7.2 miles round-trip to Pup Creek Falls

CONFIGURATION: Out-and-back

DIFFICULTY: Moderate

SCENERY: Old-growth forest, a white-water river, and a few waterfalls

EXPOSURE: Shady all the way

TRAFFIC: Use is heavy on summer weekends but light to moderate otherwise.

TRAIL SURFACE: Packed dirt with roots and rocks

HIKING TIME: 4 hours for either option

DRIVING DISTANCE: 50 miles (1 hour) from Pioneer Square

SEASON: Year-round; muddy and possibly snowy in winter and spring

ACCESS: Northwest Forest Pass required.

WHEELCHAIR ACCESS: None

MAPS: Green Trails #492 (Fish Creek Mountain)

FACILITIES: Toilets at the trailhead; the water along the way must be treated.

IN BRIEF

Convenient, not too tough, and not terribly long, the Clackamas River Trail is a great way to stretch your legs and enjoy the scenery among old trees and along a beautiful river.

DESCRIPTION

It's that rare nice day in winter or early spring—"nice" meaning it's not pouring—and you want to get out and do some hiking. Or it's blazing hot in summer and you want to visit a cool, shady place. Or it's autumn and you want to see the fall colors. Whatever the time, it's always a nice day to go out and hike the Clackamas River Trail. If you can work it out to bring a second car to be stashed at Indian Henry, it'll be that much better. Otherwise, you can do essentially the same distance and make a fine day of it.

From the trailhead, you'll start out in a flat section with the river a short distance to your left. After a half mile you'll come to a river-access point with moss-covered rocks and a sandy beach—perfect for chilling out or, if you've brought small kids, perhaps for turning around. Soon after, you'll come into the first exceptional old-growth forest, featuring

Directions

From Portland on OR 224, travel 33 miles southeast of I-205. Fifteen miles past the town of Estacada, just after crossing two bridges in quick succession, turn right onto Fish Creek Road. Go past the Fish Creek Campground, cross another bridge, and park in the parking lot on the right. The trail starts across the road on your left. To leave a car at the other end, stay on OR 224 for 7 more miles and turn right into the Indian Henry Campground. The trailhead is a half a mile up on the right.

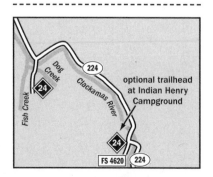

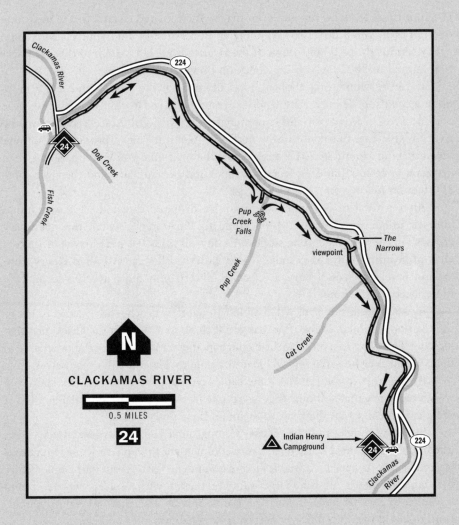

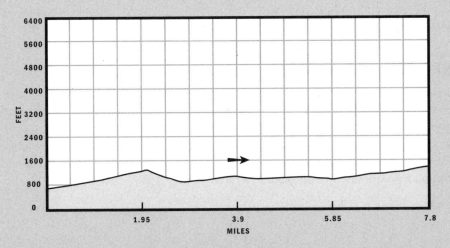

five-foot-thick Douglas firs and even bigger Western red cedars. In the next mile or so of trail, you'll do a little climbing and occasionally find yourself with some pretty serious drops to and views of the river to your left. Much of this early section burned in 2002, so you can check on how it's recovering.

If you're wondering about a good place to picnic, you'll find it 2.5 miles up in a campsite. There's a stupendous western red cedar right by the water here and plenty of places to sit and contemplate the river. OR 224 is right across the river, by the way, but you'll rarely notice it. Again, if you've brought kids, think about turning around here, because during the next mile you'll go up, down, then up again (a couple hundred feet each time) and occasionally find the river some 200 feet far below you.

After a total of 3.5 miles, after you've dropped down the hill and found yourself under power lines, you'll come to Pup Creek, which the main trail crosses on a series of stepping stones. A side trail leads 0.1 mile up the creek to a view of beautiful Pup Creek Falls. If you didn't stash a car at Indian Henry, turn around here, and you'll have a 7.2-mile hike. If you did leave the second car there, keep on trucking.

In 0.9 miles a side trail will lead left to another beach—last chance to get to the river on this hike. Right after that you'll climb to a view up the Clackamas that includes The Narrows, a spectacular gouge in ancient lava. Down the other side of this hill, another side trail left will lead 0.1 mile to The Narrows themselves.

By the way, if you've seen some cables crossing the river in a few spots and wondered what that's about, they were put in by Portland General Electric for cable-car access across the river to maintain their power lines.

In the last 3 miles to Indian Henry Campground you'll cross several side creeks (the biggest one named Cat Creek, a nice complement to Pup Creek), see numerous big cedars, get sprayed by a waterfall, and go under a cliff. About half a mile before the end, keep an eye out for a large stump on the left with a cable wrapped around it leading to another large stump. The Forest Service does that to keep big stumps from rolling down into the river and squashing fishermen or boaters.

For more information, contact the Clackamas Ranger District office at (503) 630-4256.

NEARBY ACTIVITIES

If you haven't had enough riverside fun, stop by Promontory Park and its 350-acre North Fork Reservoir. The park has a marina, campground with showers, and store where you can get all your fishing supplies and licenses, rent boats, and get ice cream when you're done fishing. Small Fry Lake is designed for kiddie fishing. Campsites are $16 per night and can be reserved at (503) 622-7229; for more info on the park and marina, call (503) 630-5152.

SERENE LAKE 25

IN BRIEF

Several lakes, a flower-filled meadow, late-summer huckleberries, and dramatic views await on this remote and little-known loop hike, which is just one of several options in the area. You can visit mountain lakes here with just over a mile of walking.

DESCRIPTION

The recommended loop here is just one of several options from the trailhead. You could, for example, take Trail #700 down 1.3 miles to Shellrock Lake, and then another mile to Hideaway Lake. To get to that trail, walk to the uphill end of the parking area and follow an old road 0.1 mile, then follow #700 down to the lake.

But our loop is the most popular one in the area, because it takes in several lakes and a variety of scenery. Just bring mosquito repellent if you're here in the early summer.

From the trailhead, take the Serene Lake Trail (#512) gently downhill, and arrive at the first trail junction in 0.8 miles. From this junction, go left a quarter mile to Middle Rock Lake. From the campsite there, turn right,

KEY AT-A-GLANCE INFORMATION

LENGTH: 8.9 miles to do the whole thing, 7.7 if you skip the Rock Lakes

CONFIGURATION: Loop

DIFFICULTY: Moderate

SCENERY: Lakes, a meadow, forest, panoramic views

EXPOSURE: Shady most of the way, with a few open spots

TRAFFIC: Use is moderate on summer weekends, light otherwise.

TRAIL SURFACE: Packed dirt with roots and rocks

HIKING TIME: 5 hours

DRIVING DISTANCE: 82 miles (2 hours and 10 minutes) from Pioneer Square

SEASON: June–October

WHEELCHAIR ACCESS: None

MAPS: Green Trails #492 (Fish Creek Mountain) and #493 (High Rock)

FACILITIES: None at the trailhead; water on the trail should be treated.

SPECIAL COMMENTS: For more information, call Clackamas Ranger District, (503) 630-6861.

Directions ⟶

From Portland on OR 224, travel 44 miles southeast of I-205, through the town of Estacada, to the Ranger Station at Rippplebrook. Half a mile past the Ranger Station, turn left onto FS 57. Follow FS 57 for 7.6 miles, and turn left onto FS 58. After 7 miles, turn left, following a sign for High Rock, then 0.1 mile later, turn left onto FS 4610. Take that 1.3 miles and a left onto FS 4610-240, which is marked simply "240." The last 4.4 miles of the drive to this trailhead are narrow and very rough, so if your car is low to the ground, go someplace else. The trailhead is at the end of the road.

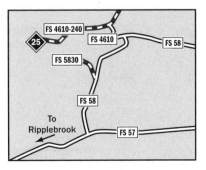

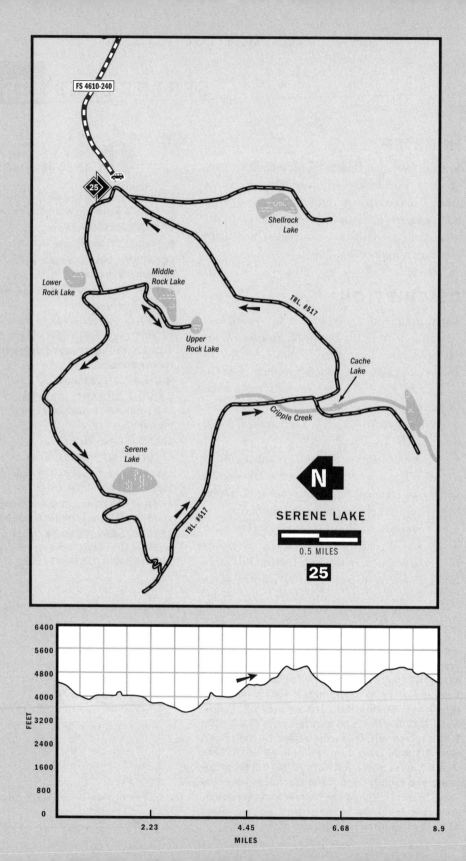

FS 4610-240

25

Shellrock
Lake

Lower
Rock Lake

Middle
Rock Lake

Upper
Rock Lake

TRL. #517

Cache
Lake

Cripple Creek

Serene
Lake

TRL. #517

N

SERENE LAKE

0.5 MILES

25

cross the creek, walk to the far end of the lake, then up the hill a short ways to Upper Rock Lake, the smallest of the three. That trail gets a little brushy and can be tough to follow in early summer; if you lose it, aim a little left toward a notch in the ridge. If you keep going around Middle Rock Lake to the left, you'll get to a nice rock where the water is deep just off shore—an excellent place to jump in. The loop to Upper Rock Lake adds just over a mile to your day.

Back at the main trail (in other words, had you not turned left for Middle Rock Lake) go another couple hundred yards and you'll come to a trail leading right to Lower Rock Lake. All these lakes are stocked with trout, by the way, so if you're into fishing, get a license and bring your rod. If you've got small kids, or you feel done for the day, go back to the car now, and you will have done around 2 miles. But for an even nicer lake, and then some, keep going.

You'll put in another 0.7 miles going downhill, then turn up (steeply at times) for most of a mile to gain the top of a ridge, thick with bear grass. Just over the top of the hill (and 2.5 miles from the trailhead) you'll come to Serene Lake and several side trails leading left to campsites. Serene Lake is just what its name implies; fishermen pull 15-inch trout from its deep, cold, green water, and the same boulders, grassy shallows, downed trees, and thickly vegetated shoreline that hide the fish also make for outstanding scenery for humans. Swing around toward the right side of the lake to continue our loop.

If you're camping, there are several excellent spots, one at the trail junction that actually has a picnic table (who put *that* there?), one at the far end on a point that sticks out into the lake, and another on the left side. There's also a huge boulder about 100 yards along the shoreline from the trail junction—it's an awesome spot to jump into the (very cold) lake. There's a decent trail all the way around the lake, but you'll have to cross a couple of rockslides to make the circuit.

Beyond Serene Lake, the trail climbs about 600 feet in 1 mile to the top of a ridge and a junction with the Grouse Point Trail (#517). Turn left here, top a small hill, and in 0.7 miles reach a clear cut, which was put in for helicopters to drop off firefighters. Not a romantic history, but there's a cliff with a sublime view back down to Serene Lake, as well as of Mounts St. Helens, Rainier, Adams, and Hood. The two bare peaks to the right are the Signal Buttes. Also, as you look north toward Hood, you're seeing an area of about 8 miles as the crow flies with only one road and two trails to break it up.

The trail now drops 700 feet in a mile, and when you get to flower-filled Cache Meadow, you'll find an intersection. The trail to the right leads out into the meadow, where you can see lily-filled Cache Lake to the left. To continue the loop, turn left and go 200 yards to the remains of an old shelter, and a minute past it, turn left onto Trail #517, and take it uphill 1 mile (you'll get all of that 700 feet back!) until you come to an abandoned road. Turn right here, and in a mile you'll be back at the car. Just keep an eye out, in the clear areas along the road, for a view back to Mount Jefferson. That makes this a five-volcano day!

UP THE SANTIAM RIVER

26 BREITENBUSH HOT SPRINGS AREA

KEY AT-A-GLANCE INFORMATION

LENGTH: 1–8 miles

CONFIGURATION: Out-and-back or one-way with a car shuttle

DIFFICULTY: Easy–strenuous

SCENERY: Ancient forest, a beautiful river, a narrow gorge, a mountain viewpoint

EXPOSURE: Shady all the way

TRAFFIC: Moderate–light

TRAIL SURFACE: Packed dirt with a few roots

HIKING TIME: 30 minutes–5 hours

DRIVING DISTANCE: 103 miles (2 hours) from Pioneer Square

SEASON: Year-round, but even lower elevations could be snowy in winter

ACCESS: Northwest Forest Pass required to park on FS 4685; day-use fee required to park at the hot springs.

WHEELCHAIR ACCESS: None

MAPS: USGS Breitenbush Hot Springs; free maps available at resort office

FACILITIES: None at the trailhead; all are available at the hot springs.

SPECIAL COMMENTS: The hot springs resort requests that if you're not using their facilities you park at a parking area just outside their gate. But why *wouldn't* you use their facilities?

IN BRIEF

With its combination of old-growth majesty and New Age spirituality and wellness, the area around Breitenbush Hot Springs is one of the most peaceful and inspiring places in Oregon. The trails are easy and plentiful, the surroundings are sublime, and the water is hot.

DESCRIPTION

Like a bay of tranquility amid a sea of logging operations, the area along the South Fork of the Breitenbush River is often described with words like peaceful, magical, and special. The resort is a draw unto itself—with its pools, tubs, well-being programs, massage, and other healing arts—but the forest and the river beckon for easy, pleasant walks.

One option is to simply go to the hot springs resort, register as a day user, and start your hike on the Spotted Owl Trail, which starts across from the resort parking lot. After 1.1 miles on that trail, you'll come to a junction with the Cliff Trail. Turn right on the Cliff Trail for 0.7 fairly steep miles, including some exposed sections on a cliff, to an intersection with the Devils Ridge Trail, which

----

Directions ⟶

From Portland on Interstate 5, drive 35 miles south of I-205 and take Exit 253/Stayton/Detroit Lake. Turn left (east) onto OR 22 and follow it 49 miles to Detroit. Turn left onto Forest Service Road 46. For the trailheads on FS 4685, travel 12.2 miles, turn right onto FS 4685, and go a half mile to the trailhead on the right. The trailhead nearest the gorge is another 1.6 miles up the road. For the hot springs, from Detroit go 10 miles on FS 46 and turn right onto a one-lane bridge just past the Cleator Bend Campground. Over the next 1.5 miles, stay left at three junctions and you're there.

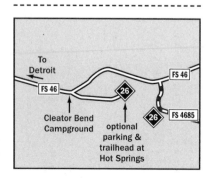

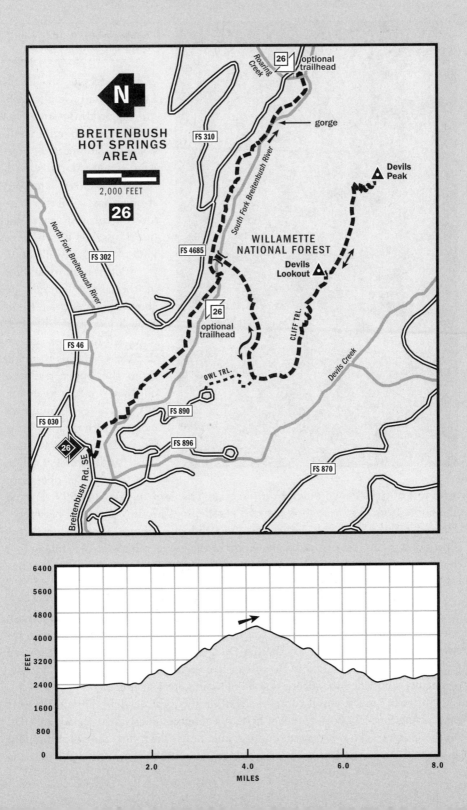

climbs steeply to Devils Lookout and Devils Peak. Staying on the Spotted Owl Trail, in a half mile you'll come to the Emerald Forest Trail at a junction that we'll describe below. The hot springs has a hiking map. Or you can just ignore the directions and go on some kind of spiritual walkabout.

For the shortest hike in the area, you can go about a mile and see Breitenbush Gorge, a 100-yard-long, 40-foot-deep chasm that the river rips through. From the upper trailhead on Road 4685, start downhill and, after a couple of minutes, turn right onto the Gorge Trail. Cross Roaring Creek and, after 0.4 miles, pass through an open area with lots of trees blown down by a storm on Thanksgiving Day in 1999. To find the gorge from this area, look for two parallel logs heading downhill between a big cedar and a root ball with ferns and hemlock saplings. This unsigned trail drops down 100 feet or so to a viewpoint of the gorge, which has several big logs lying across it. A little trail leading left and under some logs leads to another view of the upper part of gorge.

Our most recommended hike starts at the lower parking area on FS 4685. From there, walk 0.1 mile downhill and turn left onto the South Breitenbush Gorge National Recreation Trail. You will only hear the river at this point, so for views you'll have to settle for the big Douglas firs, hemlocks, and Western red cedars towering over you and the clover-like oxalis and early-summer wildflowers below you. Rhododendrons will be blooming here in June.

After 0.7 miles, you'll come to a trail on the right, leading downhill, with a sign saying Emerald Forest. (From here, it's about a mile straight ahead, and flat, to the Gorge) Take this trail and go 0.1 mile down the hill to the South Breitenbush, which you used to cross on a bridge. The 1999 storm rolled this one-log bridge over on its side, officially closing it. But subsequent storms blew several trees down over the river, and someone added a helpful handrail to one of these logs. Cross it, and on the other side climb for half a mile on the Emerald Forest Trail through as pretty a forest as you'll ever see.

When you've gone 0.8 miles past the bridge, intersect the Tree Trail and the Devils Ridge Trail. Along the way, you may notice a sign referring to the Neotropical Migratory Bird Conservation Program, which was a program of small grants that improved habitat for birds in Central and South America; many of those birds come here for the summer. Turning right toward the Spotted Owl Trail leads you back to the hot springs, but if you're looking for some serious exercise and a serious view, turn left onto the Devils Ridge Trail, which soon becomes heinously steep in its quarter-mile climb to the Cliff Trail. From this intersection, you can turn right and loop back, again toward the Spotted Owl Trail, passing under steep cliffs about 0.2 miles out. Or you can turn left and keep doing the "heinously steep" thing. It's 700 feet (in half a mile!) to Devils Lookout and 1,500 feet (in 1.5 miles) to Devils Peak.

Like I said, there are a lot of options around here, but all of them are beautiful, and all of them are close to the hot springs.

NEARBY ACTIVITIES

Breitenbush Hot Springs is open from 9 a.m. to 6 p.m. to day-use visitors, but advance reservations are required. You'll have access to the pools, steam room, and daily well-being programs. The cost is on a sliding scale (based on your ability to pay) and ranges from $12 to $25. Lunch and dinner (all vegetarian) are $10 each. Overnight rates, depending on time of year, range from $46 for a tent site to $105 for a cabin with bathroom. For more information, visit their Web site at **www.breitenbush.com** or call (503) 854-3320. The Detroit Ranger District is at (503) 854-3366.

27 OPAL CREEK WILDERNESS

KEY AT-A-GLANCE INFORMATION

LENGTH: 7 miles round-trip to Opal Pool; 10 miles round-trip to Cedar Flats; 13 miles to see it all

CONFIGURATION: Out-and-back

DIFFICULTY: Easy–moderate

SCENERY: Virgin forest, clear-water pools and historic mining structures

EXPOSURE: Shady

TRAFFIC: Use is heavy on summer weekends, moderate otherwise.

TRAIL SURFACE: Gravel road for 3.2 miles; otherwise packed dirt, roots, rocks

HIKING TIME: 2.5 hours to Opal Pool; 5 hours to Cedar Flats; 6 hours to see it all

DRIVING DISTANCE: 92 miles (2 hours) from Pioneer Square

SEASON: March–mid-November

ACCESS: Northwest Forest Pass required; they can be purchased at the trailhead.

WHEELCHAIR ACCESS: None

MAPS: USGS Battle Ax; USFS Opal Creek Wilderness

FACILITIES: Outhouses at the trailhead; outhouses along the trail and at Jawbone Flats

SPECIAL COMMENTS: For information, call (503) 897-2921, or go to www.opalcreek.org.

IN BRIEF

Opal Creek's history can be traced from ancient times to early-20th-century mining to modern-day legislative showdown, but its value can hardly be measured. It is an almost completely preserved sample of what the Northwest used to be, a place that hasn't been logged and where the water runs clear. It's the largest such area in the state that's at a low elevation. And you don't even have to work hard to see most of it.

DESCRIPTION

For thousands of years, the Santiam Indians had their summer camp at the confluence of what we now call Opal Creek and Battle Ax Creek. Other tribes would come here to trade such items as fish from the Pacific Ocean and obsidian from east of the Cascades. In the 1850s, pioneers arrived and started mining for silver and gold. Not much of either was found, but there were enough other minerals to keep mining alive here until the early 1980s. A mining town was built at the confluence in the 1920s, and it came to be known as Jawbone Flats; according to legend, while the men were out mining, the women were back there "jawboning." A sawmill was also built nearby, but it burned in the 1940s. In 1992 the mining

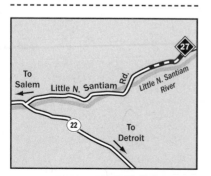

Directions

From Portland on I-5, drive 35 miles south of I-205 and take Exit 253/Stayton/Detroit Lake. Turn left (east) onto OR 22 and follow it 22.5 miles, and then turn left onto Little North Santiam Road, following a sign for Elkhorn. In just over 15 miles, the pavement will end; beware that beyond this there are some serious potholes. Stay left at two junctions; the trailhead is at the end of the road, 5.6 miles after you leave the pavement.

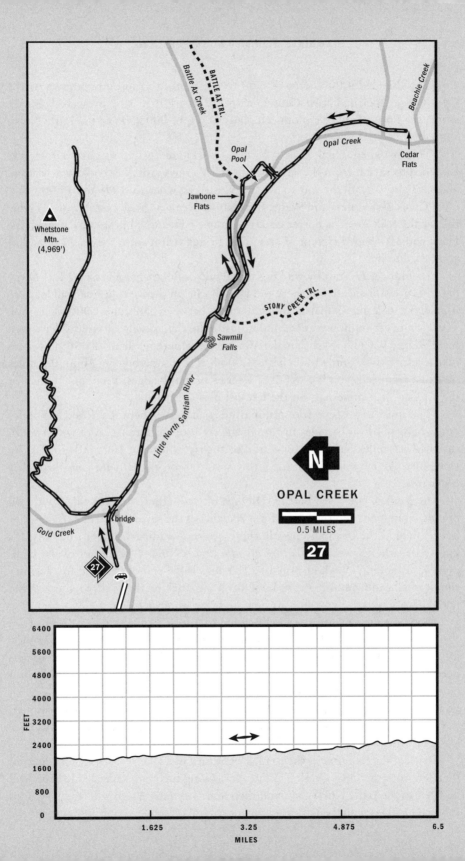

company donated 4,000 acres of land to a nonprofit group now known as the Opal Creek Ancient Forest Center, with the desire that it be preserved. Meanwhile, the Forest Service announced plans to log 15,000 acres of the Little North Santiam Valley.

This is when Opal Creek became world-famous; a massive effort was launched to save it from the saw. National TV crews visited, a book was written, and the fight went all the way to the U.S. Congress, where in 1998 the 35,000-acre Opal Creek Wilderness and Scenic Recreation Area was finally established. Today the Opal Creek Ancient Forest center operates educational programs at Jawbone Flats, and a Y-shaped system of easy trails brings visitors into the magical land of what used to be.

From the gate, start by walking slightly downhill on an old road. Most of the big trees are still ahead, but there is a Douglas fir on the right (a side trail leads to it at about 0.2 miles) that is thought to be between 700 and 1,000 years old. There's a rustic outhouse at 0.3 miles, just before a crossing of Gold Creek on a high bridge; 0.1 mile past that the Whetstone Mountain Trail (#3369) appears on the left. This 3.5-mile trail climbs 3,000 feet to a superb view. About 0.2 miles past that trailhead, you'll cross over a series of half bridges; keep an eye out for the Golden Bear mineshaft on the left just past them.

The most impressive forest along the road occurs between 1 and 1.5 miles out, where a host of Douglas firs are in the six-foot-thick range. At a wide spot in the road 1.5 miles out, look for a trail to the right, leading 100 yards to a rocky viewpoint. At 1.9 miles, look for a tiny waterfall on the left, flowing through a cedar tree.

At 2 miles, you'll see on the right a trail leading into an area filled with old mining equipment and the burned-out remains of the sawmill's steel and masonry boiler. Behind the one building still there is a trail leading 100 feet to a falls; it's known as either Sawmill Falls or *Cascadia de los Niños* ("Waterfall of the Children"), depending on whom you ask. This falls is the end of the road for a winter run of steelhead from the ocean. Look for a log stuck on the rocks high up on the left. That should give you an idea how high the water gets here.

Just past the sawmill site, you'll come to a fork. Straight ahead on the road there's a river access point on the right at 0.2 miles, then Jawbone Flats in 1.2 miles. Here, you'll find several cabins from the 1920s and 1930s (some can be rented overnight!), and two new ones built after a fire in 1999. (They were both built largely from wood cut and milled right on the site.) To reach local highlight Opal Pool from here, go straight through the camp on the road, following signs through a right-hand turn and past a collection of old vehicles that includes a U.S. Navy fire truck. The pool is 0.1 mile past the cars.

Back at the first fork in the road, a right turn will take you across a bridge and then left onto the Opal Creek Trail proper. Along this trail, several side trails will lead left to the Little North Santiam; then after 1.4 miles a sign will lead to you to sublime Opal Pool on the left. In summer you will often see people jumping off the

The road to Jawbone Flats, in Opal Creek Wilderness, after a fall snow

rocks into the amazingly clear, cold water. You're now looking at Opal Creek itself, probably the clearest water you could ever see, and the best bet in Oregon for a stream you can drink out of. I have ingested several gallons of Opal Creek and never gotten sick; take that for what it's worth and make your own decisions.

A quarter mile up the trail, a bridge offers a glimpse into the crystal-clear waters; there's also a great little rock pool on the far side that is a safe place for a quick dip. Another mile up—a total of 5 miles from the gate, whichever way you go—the trail more or less ends at Cedar Flats, where Beachie Creek flows into Opal Creek from the left, and three 1,000-year-old cedars frame the trail.

I say "more or less ends" because the trail beyond there is not maintained, but it is possible, even recommended, to go off exploring. Look for a big log over Beachie Creek and then just go with it. Sometimes there's a trail, sometimes there are logs to walk on. Sometimes there are logs to climb over. If a trail dead ends near a log, hop up on it, walk a ways, and look around; you just might find some more trail. I can't give any specifics (not that I'm not willing; I just can't explain it) but there is at least one more waterfall and one more pool like Opal Pool up there. Some folks just wander off up the creek itself.

There are long-term plans to relocate the trail and build a new 4-mile section up to Opal Lake. There are also plans to connect the Opal Creek Trail with the Little North Santiam Trail, which currently ends several miles down that river. None of that work had begun when this book was written, but one day you'll be able to hike from the Elkhorn recreation area (back on Little North Santiam Road) to Opal Lake, some 17 miles one-way.

Sawmill Falls, aka *Cascadia de los Niños*, in Opal Creek Wilderness

Even with all this hiking, Opal Creek has more to offer. From Jawbone Flats, look for an old road that goes up Battle Ax Creek; follow it a ways and look for a trail heading down toward the creek, and you might be able to locate some old train tracks related to the mining operations. From the start of the Opal Creek Trail, near the bridge, another trail leads up Stony Creek to a hidden waterfall. There's even a trail that branches off the Whetstone Mountain Trail, heading up Gold Creek, and beyond Whetstone Mountain it's 14 miles down to Bagby Hot Springs. The Ancient Forest Center has an excellent map that covers all of this.

Basically, it's hiker heaven. Get some friends together, rent a cabin in Jawbone Flats for the weekend, and go for it.

NEARBY ACTIVITIES

A mile back on OR 22, you may have noticed the Gingerbread House. It will be on your left as you head home. Stop in there for some fresh, warm gingerbread after the hike, and your day will be complete.

AROUND MOUNT HOOD

28 BARLOW PASS

KEY AT-A-GLANCE INFORMATION

LENGTH: Up to 10 miles, or 5 miles with car shuttle

CONFIGURATION: Out-and-back or one-way with shuttle

DIFFICULTY: Moderate

SCENERY: Forest, meadows, view of Mount Hood, and two river canyons

EXPOSURE: Forest on the way up, open on top

TRAFFIC: Use is light.

TRAIL SURFACE: Packed dirt with some roots

HIKING TIME: 3.5 hours

DRIVING DISTANCE: 62 miles (1 hour and 30 minutes) from Pioneer Square

SEASON: Late June–October

ACCESS: Northwest Forest Pass required.

WHEELCHAIR ACCESS: None

MAPS: USGS Mount Hood South; Mount Hood Wilderness; Green Trails #462 (Mount Hood)

FACILITIES: None; water on the hike must be treated.

SPECIAL COMMENTS: Consider doing this hike as a one-way, 5-mile trek with a second car parked at Timberline Lodge.

IN BRIEF

There's a great view of Mount Hood at the top, and a one-way car-shuttle option that ends at Timberline Lodge, but this convenient, not-too-tough hike is all about the forest. It goes through some of the finest high-elevation old-growth around and winds up at an Oregon landmark.

DESCRIPTION

There are more-spectacular hikes in the Mount Hood area, but none has the combination of solitude and old-growth beauty that this one has. It's also perfect for a picnic, or just a dose of sunshine, in a high altitude meadow with Mount Hood looming over you. And if you do the one-way option with a shuttle, you can wind up at Timberline Lodge.

From the trailhead, walk across Forest Service 3531 and into the woods on the Pacific Crest Trail (#2000). Stop to admire the relief map of the PCT in Oregon, and contemplate some of the distances on there. People who hike the whole PCT in five or six months average about 20 miles a day! You'll get in 4 to 5 miles on the PCT today; note that on the USGS Mount Hood South map, which was created in 1962, this trail is still labeled as the Oregon Skyline Trail, an old path that mostly got swallowed up when the PCT was created.

Directions ————————————→

From Portland on US 26, drive 51 miles east of Interstate 205 and turn north on OR 35, following signs for Hood River. After 2.5 miles on OR 35, turn right onto FS 3531, following signs for Barlow Pass and the Pacific Crest Trail (PCT). The trailhead is 0.2 miles ahead on FS 3531.

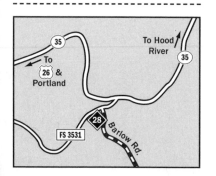

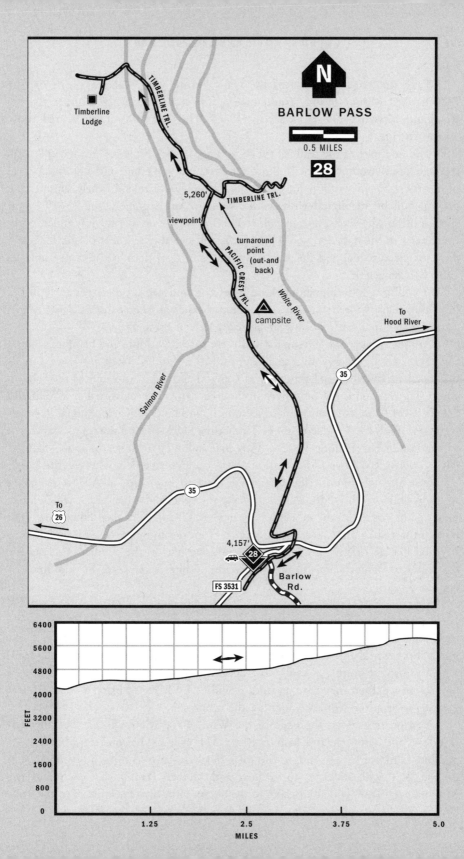

N

BARLOW PASS

0.5 MILES

28

Timberline Lodge

TIMBERLINE TRL.

5,260'

viewpoint

TIMBERLINE TRL.

turnaround
point
(out-and
back)

PACIFIC CREST TRL.

△
campsite

White River

To
Hood River

Salmon River

35

To
26

35

4,157'

28

FS 3531

Barlow
Rd.

FEET

6400
5600
4800
4000
3200
2400
1600
800
0

1.25   2.5   3.75   5.0

MILES

Take the left-most fork of the trails before you, walking north on the PCT toward Mount Hood. You'll take a few steps across the historic Barlow Road and, after 0.1 mile, walk across OR 35. The trail continues in a small draw on the far side.

The first part of the trail isn't too exciting; in fact, after 0.5 miles you'll walk through a fairly recent clear-cut. But right after that you come into a glorious stand of mostly noble fir, with its long, straight, branchless trunks. In early summer the ground will be blanketed with wildflowers. In late summer, you'll see several species of huckleberries, and in fall, red-and-orange vine maple. Stay quiet, especially early in the day, and you'll hear birds and possibly see deer or elk. It's just a pleasant place to be, and the trail's altitude gain (less than 400 feet per mile) is entirely manageable.

If you're wondering about those blue diamonds up on the trees early in the hike, they mark winter trails for cross-country skiers and snowshoers. Their height should give you a sense of how much snow falls in these parts.

At the 2-mile mark, enter a more diverse forest, with firs and hemlocks mixed together. Cross a creek with a small campsite at 2.7 miles. Then, just over 3 miles out, reach an overlook of Salmon River Canyon and the headwaters of the Salmon River. The Salmon is the only river in the lower 48 states classified as a Wild and Scenic River from its headwaters to its mouth, and here you're looking at its headwaters. It flows from a glacier above Timberline Ski Area, and snakes its way down to the Sandy River along US 26. Two hikes along the lower Salmon—Salmon River Trail and Wildwood Recreation Area—are described elsewhere in this book.

Just after this point, the forest will start to open up, in August revealing meadows filled with wildflowers, especially the spectacular beargrass, which looks like a giant cotton swab. In a few minutes, you'll intersect the Timberline Trail that's in just such a meadow, with Mount Hood looming above you. Relax here if you'd like and then turn around, or continue left on the Timberline Trail for 0.3 miles to a spectacular lookout onto the White River Canyon, hundreds of feet deep.

If you've opted to park a car up at Timberline and are doing a one-way hike, keep going up the Timberline Trail (which at this point is also the PCT) toward the mountain. It's 1.25 more miles to the lodge—700 feet up—so it's not too much more work. However, most of the climbing is in the first part of the trail, which is also, at points, as sandy as a beach. So it can get tedious. And if there's any rough weather anywhere around, it will be up here, so bring a coat. There's nothing to stop the wind this high on the mountain.

You go first along the edge of the White River Canyon and then through meadows and across the tiny Salmon River. This crossing has no bridge but is manageable. Look for views south to Mount Jefferson, some 45 miles away, and a sign on the PCT with mileages to Canada and Mexico. You'll also encounter the Mountaineer Trail, which loops up to the Silcox Hut, then back down to the Timberline Trail west of the lodge, in a section that's part of the Timberline Lodge hike profile (see page 172). When you get close to the lodge, trails will go every which way, so just aim for the hot chocolate and finish the hike with style. It's possible to hike just the upper part of this walk starting at Timberline Lodge—especially recommended if you have kids with you. This shorter option creates an easy, scenic alternative with very little elevation gain; if you go over to the White River Canyon overlook, it's about a mile round-trip.

NEARBY ACTIVITIES

If you've got some clearance on your vehicle, you can drive the Barlow Road for miles, eventually making your way to The Dalles—though the road improves dramatically a long way before The Dalles.

29 COOPER SPUR

KEY AT-A-GLANCE INFORMATION

LENGTH: 7.5 miles

CONFIGURATION: Balloon

DIFFICULTY: Strenuous

SCENERY: Old-growth forest, glaciers, wide panoramas, the upper reaches of Mount Hood

EXPOSURE: Shady–sunny; plenty of wind

TRAFFIC: Use is moderate on summer weekends but light otherwise.

TRAIL SURFACE: Packed dirt, roots, sand, rocks

HIKING TIME: 4.5 hours

DRIVING DISTANCE: 88 miles (2 hours and 15 minutes) from Pioneer Square

SEASON: July–mid-October

WHEELCHAIR ACCESS: None

MAPS: USGS Mount Hood North; USFS Mount Hood Wilderness; Green Trails #462 (Mount Hood)

FACILITIES: Outhouse and water at the trailhead

SPECIAL COMMENTS: No matter the forecast, bring warm clothing. Weather at this altitude can change quickly.

IN BRIEF

Though it's not the toughest, this is the highest hiking trail in this book—right up into the realm of the mountain climber. You'll be in the world of rock and snow, and you won't even wear yourself out getting there—well, not completely. You'll also get to see the oldest buildings on Mount Hood and the results of a massive landslide.

DESCRIPTION

If you want to get way, way up there, this is your hike. In the days before Timberline Lodge and the road to it were built, Cooper Spur was the standard climbing route to Mount Hood's 11,239-foot summit, and people still climb it that way today.

The whole area, in fact, is historically significant. Just up a hill from the trailhead, and at the end of the road, is the Cloud Cap Inn, built in 1889 by two prominent Portland families as a recreation destination. It's the oldest building on Mount Hood. The hotel venture never took off, and by World War II the property was given to the Forest Service. In 1956 the Crag Rats, a Hood River–based climbing and rescue organization, took it over, and they maintain it to this day. Although the public

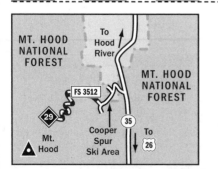

Directions

From Portland on US 26, drive 51 miles east of I-205 and turn north on OR 35, following signs for Hood River. After 17 miles on OR 35, turn left at a sign for Cooper Spur Ski Area. After 2.4 miles, turn left, again following a sign for Cooper Spur Ski Area. In 1.4 miles, stay straight and leave the pavement. Go 8.3 winding miles to a T junction and turn right. The trailhead is half a mile ahead on the right, in the Cloud Cap Saddle campground.

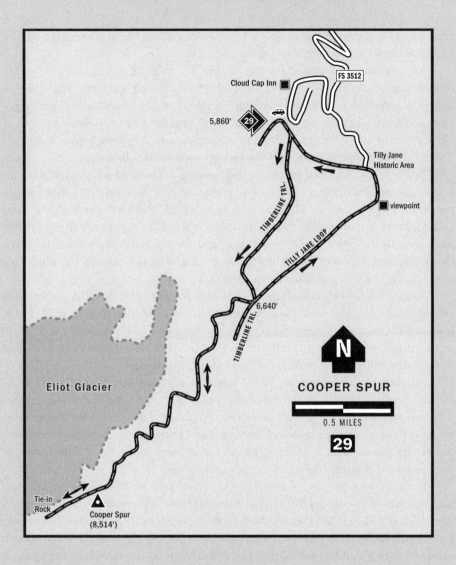

Cloud Cap Inn

FS 3512

5,860'

29

Tilly Jane
Historic Area

■ viewpoint

TIMBERLINE TRL.

TILLY JANE LOOP

6,640'

TIMBERLINE TRL.

N

COOPER SPUR

0.5 MILES

29

Eliot Glacier

Tie-in
Rock

Cooper Spur
(8,514')

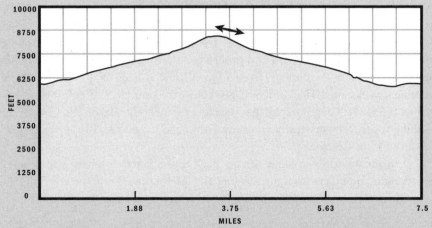

can't officially go in, if you're nice to some folks you see there, they might let you stick your head in for a bit.

More history later; now, for the hiking. The trail starts at the far end of the campground. Take the Timberline Trail (#600) to the left and enter a rare, snow-zone, old-growth forest, where mountain hemlock and Pacific silver firs get bigger than you'd think possible in an area that usually has ten feet of snow by the end of November. In 1.2 miles you'll come to a junction just above the forest; following a sign for Cooper Spur, turn uphill—and get used to the climbing.

Just a couple hundred yards up, back among the twisted white bark pines on your right, sits the Cooper Spur shelter at the end of a small side trail. But for our purposes, keep going up. The trail will switch back and forth through the sand and rocks on a manageable grade, and slowly the Eliot Glacier will start to fill your view to the right. You'll hear it pop and rumble as it carves the side of the mountain, and if you're lucky, especially on late summer afternoons, you'll see big pieces of it calving and tumbling downhill.

After 2 miles of this climbing, you'll come to the top of the ridge, where you should look for a rock with some impressive carvings and the date July 17, 1910. It commemorates a Japanese climbing party. Since you've climbed all the altitude at this point, you might as well go another 0.2 miles along the ridgetop—just beware that this ridge is thin, rocky, and usually wind-swept.

Just before the snow line, you'll come to a plaque attached to the side of what they call Tie-In Rock; it's called that because it's here that climbers tie themselves to one another to venture out onto the glacier. Do not, under any circumstances (short of having ropes and crampons and relevant experience) go out onto the glacier. Be satisfied with being at the top of your local hiking world, and sit back among the sheltering rocks to take in the view.

From left to right, with Mount Hood behind you, we have the Eliot Glacier, and way off in the distance the bare face of Table Mountain in the Columbia River Gorge, Mount St. Helens, Mount Rainier, Mount Adams, Elk Meadows, and Gnarl Ridge down at your feet. Lookout Mountain is on a ridge to the east, and then a building below you on a Mount Hood ridge, which is the top of a ski lift at Mount Hood Meadows Ski Area. Now do you feel like you're way up there?

Now look up at Mount Hood. The Cooper Spur climbing route begins on the snowfield right in front of you and proceeds up through the rocks above, tending slightly to your left. As climbers like to say, it's not as steep as it looks. Look for a prominent rock called The Chimney, just below the summit, and Pulpit Rock more to your right. The Crag Rats say that whenever somebody falls on the Cooper Spur climbing route, they generally wind up within about 200 feet of the same spot at the top of Eliot Glacier.

On your way down, when you get back to the junction where you originally turned right, now stay straight, leaving the Timberline Trail for the Tilly Jane Loop. After 0.6 miles, you'll come to an overlook of a large, bare bowl on your right. That's what was left behind by the Polallie Slide, a massive debris flow and flood in December 1980 that wiped out parts of OR 35.

A short while later you'll find yourself looking at some old buildings. This is part of the 1,400-acre Tilly Jane Historic Area. This area, by the way, is immensely popular with cross-country skiers and snowshoers, who come up a 2.7-mile trail from Cooper Spur Ski Area and spend the night in some of these buildings. And if you're wondering about that name, Tilly Jane was the nickname of the matriarch of the Ladd family, one of the builders of Cloud Cap Inn.

Now, to get back to your car, just put Mount Hood on your left and follow the trail half a mile back to the trailhead.

NEARBY ACTIVITIES

When you get back to OR 35, go north (left) and indulge yourself at some of the berry and fruit stands in the Hood River Valley. Some let you pick your own.

30 ELK MEADOWS

KEY AT-A-GLANCE INFORMATION

LENGTH: 6 miles round-trip to Elk Meadows, 11 miles to see it all

CONFIGURATION: Out-and-back with optional loops

DIFFICULTY: Moderate to Elk Meadows; strenuous to Gnarl Ridge

SCENERY: Meadows, mountain streams, close-ups of Mount Hood

EXPOSURE: Shady most of the way

TRAFFIC: Moderate use on weekends, light otherwise

TRAIL SURFACE: Dirt, some roots

HIKING TIME: 3.5 hours to Elk Meadows, 6 hours for the whole loop

DRIVING DISTANCE: 69 miles (1 hour and 30 minutes) from Pioneer Square

SEASON: July–October

ACCESS: Northwest Forest Pass needed

WHEELCHAIR ACCESS: None

MAPS: Mount Hood Wilderness; Green Trails #462 (Mount Hood)

FACILITIES: Outhouse at trailhead; the water on the trail must be treated.

SPECIAL COMMENTS: Call (503) 622-4822 for up-to-date conditions.

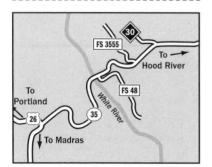

IN BRIEF

One of the most spectacular sights in the Mount Hood area, sprawling and flower-filled Elk Meadows is relatively easy to reach. Beyond that, several side trips in the area invite you to soaring viewpoints.

DESCRIPTION

If all you're doing is going to Elk Meadows, there's only one hill between you and your destination. But while you're at it, there are some other options worth checking out.

From the trailhead, you'll follow a flat trail through moss-draped forest, pocket meadows with wildflowers, and huckleberries that are ripe in late August. Ignore two trails on the left, the first (#667) to Umbrella Falls and the second (#646) up Newton Creek. After 0.6 miles you'll cross Clark Creek on a bridge, and after another 0.7 miles you'll cross Newton Creek on logs. This crossing might be too challenging for some folks, especially early in the season. There are often logs in place, but many folks will turn around here. If you do, consider exploring up trail #667 or #646 instead.

Now you are at the hill. In 1 mile, you'll gain almost 700 feet in a series of long switchbacks; consider it your price of admission to Elk Meadows. Just over the top, you'll come to a four-way intersection. For Elk Meadows,

Directions ⟶

From Portland on US 26, drive 51 miles east of I-205 and turn north on OR 35, following signs for Hood River. After 7 miles on OR 35, turn left at the second entrance for the Mount Hood Meadows Ski Area (the one for the Nordic Center). The trailhead is half a mile ahead on the right.

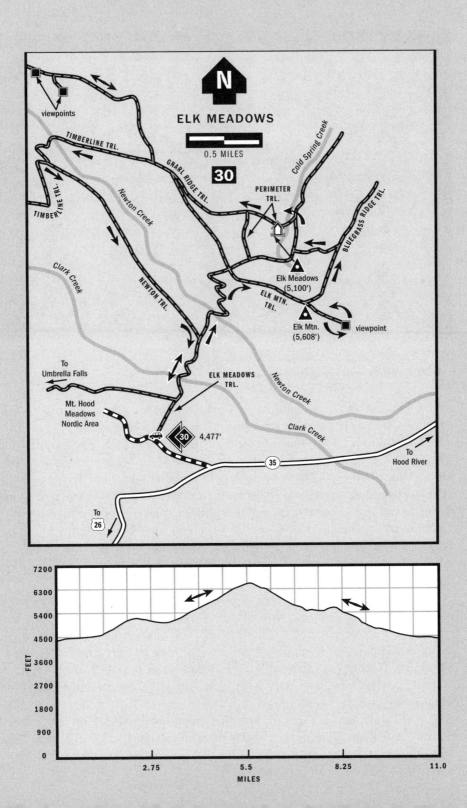

ELK MEADOWS

0.5 MILES

30

viewpoints

TIMBERLINE TRL.

TIMBERLINE TRL.

GNARL RIDGE TRL.

Newton Creek

Clark Creek

NEWTON TRL.

Cold Spring Creek

PERIMETER TRL.

BLUEGRASS RIDGE TRL.

Elk Meadows (5,100')

ELK MTN. TRL.

Elk Mtn. (5,608')

viewpoint

To Umbrella Falls

ELK MEADOWS TRL.

Newton Creek

Clark Creek

Mt. Hood Meadows Nordic Area

30   4,477'

35

To Hood River

To 26

Mount Hood looms over expansive Elk Meadows.

go straight and you'll be there in about three minutes. For a side trip to Elk Mountain, turn right—and into the area that burned in 2006.

The trail to Elk Mountain is not spectacular in and of itself, but it's quiet and woodsy and leads to a nice view east across OR 35 to Mount Jefferson to the south. Also, while staying quiet on an August morning hike, I briefly saw two elk up there, bounding through the forest away from me. To get to the lookout, go up 0.6 miles and stay straight at the junction with the Bluegrass Ridge Trail (#647). The lookout is 0.3 miles straight ahead. When you come back, take the Bluegrass Ridge Trail (it would now be a right turn) and follow it half a mile along the ridgetop before turning left, at a large stone cairn, and plunging 0.4 miles down the Bluegrass Tie Trail (#647B) to Elk Meadows.

Elk Meadows is almost unbelievable. It's basically a circular area of meadows about half a mile in diameter, with islands of trees throughout and streams criss-crossing it. For the good of the flowers and grass, resist the temptation to go meadow stomping, but by all means find a log or rock on the perimeter and have a sit-down. To complete a loop around the meadows or to explore the other loop available on this hike, turn right when you get to the meadows (regardless of whether you went to Elk Mountain or not).

When you come to a sign for Polallie Campground, stay left on the perimeter trail, and about 30 steps later you'll come to an unmarked trail leading left. That is the trail out into the middle of the meadows, where a stone shelter hosts

Mount Hood and the upper crossing of Newton Creek, on the Elk Meadows–Timberline Trail loop

backpackers most summer nights. It's worth a side trip, if only to be surrounded by the meadows.

Continuing on the perimeter trail, you'll cross Cold Spring Creek, and in about half a mile you'll come to a junction with the Gnarl Ridge Trail (#652). To go back to your car, turn left here, finish the loop around the meadows, and then turn right at the junction with the Elk Meadows Trail. But to go a little higher up toward Mount Hood, stay straight here on the Gnarl Ridge Trail.

After just less than a mile of gradual climbing, you'll come to a trail on the left; ignore it. Just past that you'll get to the Timberline Trail (#600). Here, you can turn right and climb 800 feet in 1.5 miles to a fantastic viewpoint atop Gnarl Ridge; or, you can turn left, stay at the same level, and make a loop back to the car. This way will take you along the west side of Gnarl Ridge (6,540 feet elevation) to a bridgeless crossing of Newton Creek. You can even explore up the creek by walking through the boulder field to your right; just be careful, as even the largest of the rocks can roll when you step on them.

To get back to the car, cross the creek, climb about a quarter mile, then turn left at the ridgetop onto the Newton Trail (#646). Two miles down that heavily huckleberried trail, you'll intersect with the trail you started all this wandering on—the Elk Meadows Trail. Turn right and you'll be back at the trailhead in just over a mile.

NEARBY ACTIVITIES

For a little piece of Oregon history, pay your respects at the Pioneer Woman's Grave, off OR 35 just north of its intersection with US 26. Workers building the old Mount Hood Loop Highway found the woman buried beneath a crude marker; her remains have since been moved twice, and to this day people lay crosses or flowers on the pile of rocks marking her grave.

LOOKOUT MOUNTAIN 31

IN BRIEF

One of the easternmost points in this book, Lookout Mountain is also one of the widest and most wonderful viewpoints, stretching from south of the Three Sisters all the way to Mount Rainier, and including desert, lake, and river.

DESCRIPTION

First, for the "studly" route, which is a whole lot more work but comes with a lot of benefits. From the Gumjuwac Trailhead on OR 35, the first couple of miles are relentlessly uphill. You'll gain 1,400 feet in 2 miles, then catch a little break over the last half mile to Gumjuwac Saddle. There's also, at the top of the real climbing around 2 miles up, a wonderful rocky viewpoint back toward Mount Hood—basically the first thing you'll see other than trees.

At Gumjuwac Saddle, you'll encounter several trails. The Gumjuwac Trail crosses FS 3550 and drops down the other side of the ridge into Badger Creek Wilderness. Coming in from the right is the Gunsight Trail, popular

KEY AT-A-GLANCE INFORMATION

LENGTH: 2.2 or 9.2 miles

CONFIGURATION: Out-and-back or loop

DIFFICULTY: Easy or strenuous

SCENERY: Meadows, forest, and one of the great vista points in Oregon

EXPOSURE: Shady, exposed rock at the top

TRAFFIC: Moderate use on weekends, light otherwise

TRAIL SURFACE: Packed dirt and rock

HIKING TIME: 1 hour or 5 hours

DRIVING DISTANCE: 60 miles (1 hour and 30 minutes) from Pioneer Square

SEASON: July–October

ACCESS: Northwest Forest Pass required at High Prairie only.

WHEELCHAIR ACCESS: None

MAPS: Green Trails #462 (Mount Hood); USGS Badger Lake

FACILITIES: Outhouse at High Prairie; there are two springs on the way up from Gumjuwac and one more near the summit.

Directions ⟶

From Portland on US 26, drive 51 miles east of I-205 and turn north on OR 35, following signs for Hood River. For the longer hike on the Gumjuwac Trail, go 10.5 miles on OR 35 and park on the right just after the road crosses the East Fork of Hood River. To drive to High Prairie for the shorter loop, go 2.5 more miles on OR 35 and turn right onto FS 44. After 3.7 miles, turn right (following a sign for High Prairie) onto gravel FS 4410. Over the next 4.6 miles, during which the road occasionally rides like a washboard, take the larger, more uphill road at all the junctions. At a sign for Badger Lake on the right, follow FS 4410 around to the left; the parking area is 100 yards ahead.

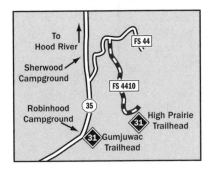

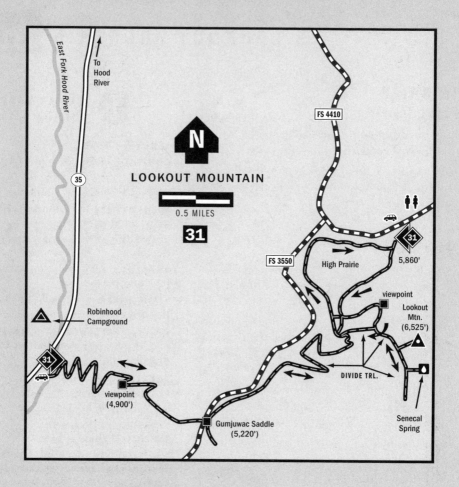

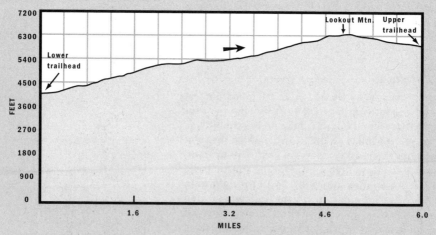

with mountain bikers because it's 4.5 miles along the ridge with very little elevation change. In case you're thinking of driving FS 3550 to this point, you'd better have some clearance. But if you insist, turn right at the Badger Lake sign
mentioned in the directions to High Prairie (see previous page) and then bounce
about 3 miles to the saddle.

And if you're wondering about the name Gumjuwac, it comes from a sheep-
herder, Jack. Apparently Jack liked gum shoes, hence Gum Shoe Jack. Somehow
that became "Gumjuwac" over the years. This is explained in what's left of the sign
at the Saddle; that sign also refers to the Mount Hood Loop Highway, which has-
n't existed for decades.

To keep going to Lookout Mountain, simply walk across FS 3550 and start
to your left on the Divide Trail (#458), following a sign for Lookout Mountain.
You'll encounter a lovely spring half a mile up, and during this time you'll also
have a view straight ahead of Lookout Mountain. And see why this trail is called
the Divide Trail. Technically, it splits two watersheds—Hood River from The
Dalles—but it's also an amazing sample of east versus west. Coming up the
Gumjuwac Trail, it was all shady, with a view of glacier-covered Mount Hood;
but on this side you'll encounter meadows and flowers and views of the desert. As
you climb with Hood on your left, look for views over your right shoulder to
Badger Lake. Watch out for wildlife, too; I once saw two falcons chasing each
other around here, and I scared up an owl in the woods.

Keep climbing, and just below the summit, stay straight (and uphill) when
the High Prairie Loop (#493) cuts down to the left. This will put you on a rocky
outcrop with an amazing view; this is where many people stop, but it's not the
top of Lookout Mountain. To get there, put Mount Hood behind you and keep
going, still on the Divide Trail. You'll walk along a rocky ridge looking down into
the Badger Creek drainage, stay right where an old road goes left, then climb
briefly to a trail leading left to the wide-open summit, with the foundation of an
old fire lookout. For a description of the view, see below.

There's one more spring up here that's worth visiting. To reach Senecal
Spring (named for a forest service ranger from the turn of the 20th century) take
the Divide Trail 0.2 miles past the summit and turn left on a trail that's barely
visible and whose sign is often lying on the ground. The (very cold) spring is
a quarter mile below the Divide Trail.

Now, if you're more into driving up long hills than walking up them, here's
the High Prairie Loop. There are many trails on Lookout Mountain, some of
which are not on maps. So take our map with you and remember that just about
all these trails go to the same two places: Lookout Mountain and the trailhead.

From the parking area on FS 4410, walk straight across 4410 and up the
wide path, so well worn it's practically paved, into the meadows. The fields of
daisies and lupine might make you want to stop there, but it's worth it to keep
going. The trail you see immediately on your right, labeled for horses to follow,
is the High Prairie Loop (#493) coming back to the trailhead. Ignore it for now.

Follow the wide trail ahead for 0.7 miles until, in an area of reddish rock, it splits into three. The faint one through the trees on the right is a cutoff to the return portion of the Loop Trail; ignore it. The one straight ahead (and up the hill) is a cutoff to the Divide Trail. If you stay on the wide trail, you'll loop around to the left to a point with a fine view east of the Cascades, out into the Oregon High Desert. The road then loops back around to the right and intersects the Divide Trail (#458). Turn left on the Divide Trail, climb briefly, and follow a small trail to the left to reach the summit. This approach is listed on our elevation profile, as well as the Gumjuwac trail.

The view from Lookout Mountain's 6,500-foot summit is one that you just can't get from the western side of the Cascades, or for that matter from most points in the Cascades. From left to right, on a clear day, you can see Diamond Peak, the Three Sisters, Jefferson, Hood (absolutely huge just 7 miles across the way), St. Helens, Rainier, and Adams. From Diamond Peak to Rainier, as the crow flies, it is about 225 miles. You can also see, if you look closely, a stretch of the Columbia River to the northeast.

If you came up from Gumjuwac, you might as well see some new country on the way back by completing the High Prairie Loop. To do this, when you're on Lookout Mountain walk toward Mount Hood on the Divide Trail. At 0.3 miles down, take the signed Loop Trail to your right and follow it as it crosses the face of Lookout Mountain and dives into the woods. After 0.7 miles, turn right at a sign and walk back through the meadows to rejoin the wide, packed trail you started on just above FS 4410.

For more information, call the Barlow Ranger District office at (541) 467-2291.

LOST LAKE 32

IN BRIEF

This is like a resort area, with boats for rent, picnic tables with grills, a campground, and a beautiful lake stocked with trout. It's also a lovely walk around the natural, 240-acre lake, including an interpretive, barrier-free old-growth trail and one of the most photographed views of Mount Hood. All this, and there's an optional climb to a fine lookout point.

DESCRIPTION

Whether you're looking for a pleasant family campout or a good day of hiking, Lost Lake has what you need; that's why there are often so many people there. But, as is always the case, their number decreases in direct proportion to how far you walk.

For the 3.3-mile trail around the lake, start in front of the newly renovated general store. Walk to the boat dock and turn right. The first quarter mile of this trail, which parallels the road, is dotted with picnic tables tucked by the lakeshore. Soon you'll come to a platform with the killer view of Mount Hood.

Directions ⟶

From Portland on I-84, drive 55 miles east of I-205 and take Exit 62/W Hood River. Turn right at the end of the off-ramp, then take an immediate right onto Country Club Road, following signs for several wineries. At the end of Country Club Road, 3 miles later, turn left at a stop sign onto Barrett Drive. After 1.3 miles, turn right onto Tucker Road, the second stop sign you'll come to on Barrett Drive. Go 2 miles up Tucker and turn right onto Dee Highway. After 6.5 miles on Dee Highway, turn right onto FS 13, following signs for Lost Lake. The resort is 14 miles ahead at the end of the road. Just keep following the Lost Lake signs.

KEY AT-A-GLANCE INFORMATION

LENGTH: 3.3 miles around the lake; 4 more miles to Lost Lake Butte

CONFIGURATION: Loop with an out-and-back option

DIFFICULTY: Easy around the lake, moderate to the butte

SCENERY: Lake beaches, views of Mount Hood, huge trees, ice cream

EXPOSURE: Shady except for the lake and the top of the butte

TRAFFIC: Heavy on summer days, very heavy on weekends

TRAIL SURFACE: Packed dirt and boardwalk; Lakeshore Trail is wheelchair traversable.

HIKING TIME: 1.5 hours around the lake; 2 more hours to Lost Lake Butte

DRIVING DISTANCE: 88 miles (1 hour and 45 minutes) from Pioneer Square

SEASON: May–October; call the resort to make sure the road is snow-free before June.

ACCESS: $6 day-use fee per vehicle

WHEELCHAIR ACCESS: 2 miles of lakeside trails, including the old-growth boardwalk

MAPS: USGS Bull Run Lake; free maps at Lost Lake General Store

FACILITIES: Full-service camping resort

SPECIAL COMMENTS: A one-day fishing license costs $12.50.

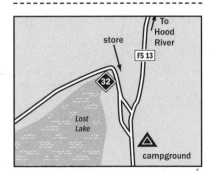

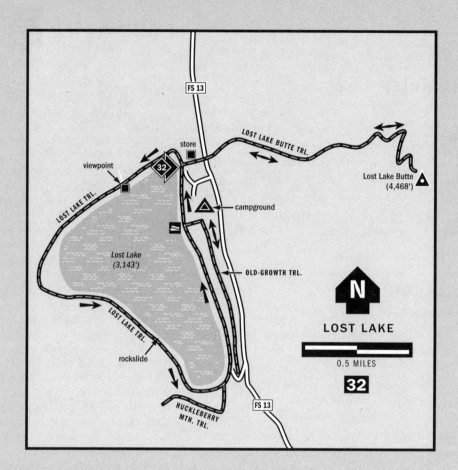

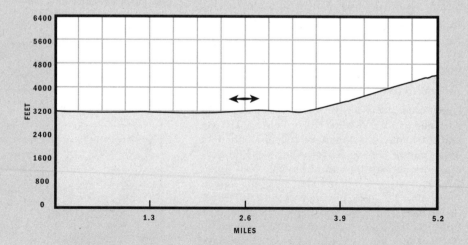

Beyond the platform, the trail leaves the road, and you start to feel like you're actually out in the woods. In late summer, your progress will be reduced by plump, ripe huckleberries; you can pick a handful or two to go along with your lunch, then choose a little beach off the trail to sit on a log and find some peace while you eat. Keep an eye out for signs identifying tree species.

After just less than a mile, you'll come to a marshy area where the trail becomes a boardwalk. At 1.6 miles there's a rockslide with excellent swimming. After another mile, the Huckleberry Mountain Trail (#617) leads right 2.5 miles to an intersection with the Pacific Crest Trail. During its 900-foot climb, this trail passes between Devils Pulpit and Preachers Peak—but nowhere near Huckleberry Mountain. Go figure. If you're really looking for some exercise, put in about 4.5 miles south on the PCT to Buck Peak.

Just past the Huckleberry Mountain Trail, veer right from the Lakeshore Trail onto the Old Growth Trail (#657). To reach it, after you veer right the first time, stay left as you approach a group of buildings. This will put you onto a road; the Old Growth Trail begins 100 yards ahead on a boardwalk and immediately passes between two of the largest cedars you are ever likely to see. They're both in the neighborhood of 12 feet thick.

This trail is a great one for the kids because it's not too long and includes educational signs explaining the roles in a forest's life of nurse logs, the forest canopy, the weather, pileated woodpeckers, and other animals. Some of these trees are hundreds of years old and more than 200 feet tall. When the boardwalk runs out, go another 0.3 miles, follow a trail through the campground down to the lake, and turn right to get back to your car.

To climb Lost Lake Butte for a view of, as the resort's hiking map puts it, "pretty near everything worth seeing," start in the general store's parking area. Walk back up the road and, at the turnoff for the main exit, look for a sign and a trail heading into the woods. You'll come to an unsigned trail intersection; turn right and uphill here. A hundred yards later, you'll cross another road and aim for a sign that says "Lost Lake Butte Trailhead." It can get confusing in here, but when in doubt, keep going uphill. It's a steady climb of 1,300 feet in 2 miles to an old fire lookout. Mount Hood, of course, is the dominant view to the south, but you can also see as far north as Mount Rainier (but not Mount Baker, as the resort map says). Then just come back down the way you went up and get yourself a cool drink in the store as a reward for all your effort. Constant access to refreshments is one of the great things about Lost Lake.

For more information, call the Lost Lake Resort office at (541) 386-6366 or visit **www.lostlakeresort.org**.

33 McNEIL POINT

KEY AT-A-GLANCE INFORMATION

LENGTH: 9.2 miles

CONFIGURATION: Out-and-back

DIFFICULTY: Easy to Bald Mountain viewpoint; strenuous to McNeil Point

SCENERY: Old-growth forest, meadows, rugged mountainside

EXPOSURE: Shady with a few open spots

TRAFFIC: Moderate use on August weekends but light otherwise

TRAIL SURFACE: Packed dirt with roots, a few small stream crossings, some rocks and snow

HIKING TIME: 5.5 hours

DRIVING DISTANCE: 58 miles (1 hour and 30 minutes) from Pioneer Square

SEASON: July–October

ACCESS: Northwest Forest Pass required.

WHEELCHAIR ACCESS: None

MAPS: Mount Hood Wilderness

FACILITIES: None at trailhead; there's water on the trail, but it must be treated.

IN BRIEF

You don't have to do this whole trail to make it worthwhile; it opens with a great view, passes through a cathedral forest to wildflower meadows and alpine ponds, then gets up close and personal with Mount Hood. But if you do go all the way up, you can see the trickle that is the source of the Sandy River and hear glaciers pop and rumble.

DESCRIPTION

This is a honey of a hike! You start out on the Top Spur Trail, which climbs gradually for half a mile to a veritable highway interchange of trails. First you'll reach the Pacific Crest Trail (PCT); turn right on it. In 100 feet you'll get to the Timberline Trail, a trail to Bald Mountain (marked with a sign reading "Viewpoint"), and the PCT leading down 2.2 miles to the Ramona Falls Trail (see page 158).

To simply head for McNeil Point, follow the Timberline Trail (#600) uphill and to the left. But it's well worth it to see the magnificent view from the open side (not actually the top) of Bald Mountain, a mere 0.4 miles past the viewpoint sign, also on the Timberline Trail. Head out there to take in the sweeping view of Mount Hood and the Muddy Fork of the Sandy River. Then keep going, toward Mount Hood, and look for a faint cutoff trail

Directions

From Portland on US 26, drive 36 miles east of I-205 to Zigzag and turn left onto Lolo Pass Road which is 0.6 miles past milepost 41. Go 10.6 miles to Lolo Pass and turn right onto paved FS 1828, which is the first right at the pass. Go 3.1 miles and turn left onto gravel FS 118, following a sign for Top Spur Trail. The trailhead is 1.2 miles ahead on the right.

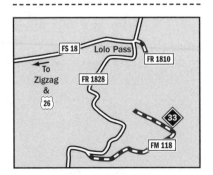

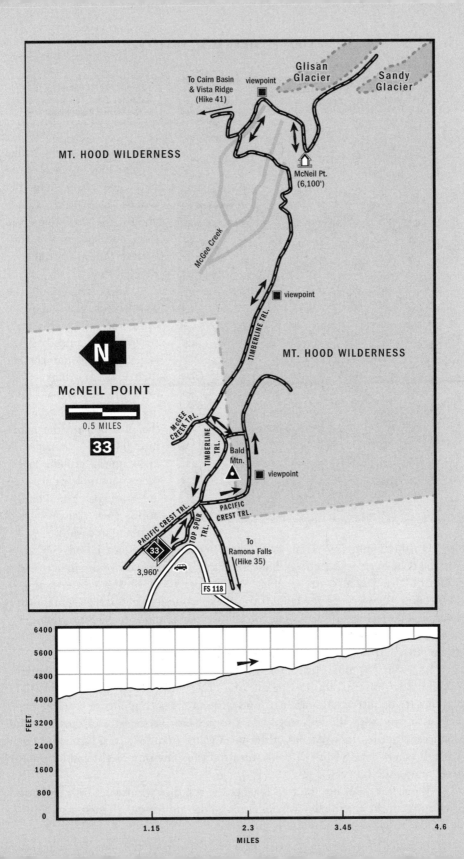

Glisan Glacier

Sandy Glacier

viewpoint

To Cairn Basin
& Vista Ridge
(Hike 41)

MT. HOOD WILDERNESS

McGee Creek

McNeil Pt.
(6,100')

N

McNEIL POINT

0.5 MILES

33

TIMBERLINE TRL.

viewpoint

MT. HOOD WILDERNESS

McGEE CREEK TRL.

TIMBERLINE TRL.

Bald
Mtn.

viewpoint

PACIFIC CREST TRL.

PACIFIC
CREST TRL.

TOP SPUR TRL.

33

3,960'

To
Ramona Falls
(Hike 35)

FS 118

6400
5600
4800
4000
3200
2400
1600
800
0

FEET

1.15   2.3   3.45   4.6

MILES

This view of Mount Hood, from Bald Mountain, can be seen early in the McNeil Point hike.

that goes over the ridge to your left, just before the PCT goes back into the woods. The cutoff extends about 100 yards over the ridge and back to the Timberline Trail; turn right for McNeil Point.

This stretch of the Timberline Trail is in a true cathedral forest—the tall, straight trees, mostly hemlocks, have no branches in their lower portions, creating a forest scene that's both open and lofty. Adding to the pleasure are the many huckleberry bushes that make up the ground cover; their juicy morsels are ripe in late August. You'll hardly notice that you've started climbing in earnest.

On the Timberline Trail, at the first big view of Mount Hood you come to (you'll have gone 2.3 miles), look for the large, unnamed waterfall across the valley on Hood's flank. At 3.5 miles, you'll cross a fork of McGee Creek and, if it's around August, be in the land of wildflowers. Lupines, daisies, pasque flowers, lilies, and butterflies will welcome you to the high country. Just a bit farther are a couple of ponds, which make ideal places to stop for lunch. You can skip and frolic in this area and call it a day, or keep going to the higher country.

At about 3.8 miles, just after the Mazama Trail has come in from the left, you'll reach a tiny stream flowing out of a flower-filled bowl with a snowfield at the top. If you just want more meadows without more climbing, stay on the main trail as it swings to the left, negotiate a somewhat sketchy stream crossing, and connect with the outer reaches of the Vista Ridge hike for Cairn Basin and Eden Park. If you're set on McNeil Point, turn right (up the tiny creek) and follow the trail among the flowers.

About 0.3 miles up, the trail reaches the top of a windswept little ridge and then turns up it, eventually crossing a rockslide and (in most years) a snowfield.

The McNeil Point Trail winds through the flower-filled meadows above the Timberline Trail.

Be careful on both these terrains; they aren't steep, but remember that even big rocks move, and that even packed snow is slippery. The trail keeps going up the ridge face, crossing additional small patches of snow. At a junction near the top, go right for the easiest route or left to stay higher and try your skills at glissading down a small snowfield.

One mile from the turnoff at the creek, you'll reach the 1930s-era stone shelter at McNeil Point. From here the view is stupendous: Mount Hood looming above you, the valley of the Muddy Fork of the Sandy stretching out below you, the other Cascade volcanoes beyond. As you look at Mount Hood, the sprawling glacier on your right is the Sandy Glacier and the trickle coming out the bottom of it is the beginning of the Sandy River, which flows into the Columbia all the way down at Troutdale.

Also, as you look at Mount Hood, you'll notice some more trail going up above you, into the Really High Country. It's not on any maps, but if you follow it you will (A) soon run out of breath as you approach 7,000 feet in elevation with virtually no switchbacks, and (B) find yourself on a narrow, rocky ridge between the Sandy (on your right) and Glisan (on your left) Glaciers.

I sat up there one day listening to the glaciers pop and moan as they slid slowly but relentlessly down the face of the mountain. You might even see massive boulders tumbling down the slope; you can certainly pick out their trails on the snow. At all costs, be careful up there, and most definitely resist the temptation to hop onto the snow.

You may hear or see reports of another, more direct trail between McNeil Point and the Timberline Trail, connecting with the latter at a point west of the

The 1930s-era stone shelter at McNeil Point

ponds. The word from many hikers, including this one, is to avoid that trail. It's steep, rocky, brutal, and unnecessary. The one described here is easier and more scenic.

No matter what the weather is when you start, bring warm clothing if you're going to McNeil Point. It's above the tree line, and weather changes quickly up there. For more information, contact the Mount Hood Visitor Information Center at (503) 622-4822.

NEARBY ACTIVITIES

On the way back on US 26, check out the Oregon Candy Farm. It's not, unfortunately, the mini-world of candy-cane barns and sugar-water streams it sounds like, but it is a store with a heck of a selection of candies and chocolates. Go ahead: you deserve it after going to the high country.

MIRROR LAKE

IN BRIEF

You can go a short way on this hike and join the weekend throngs at a lovely little lake that has a great view of Mount Hood. You can also put in a little more effort and leave the vast majority of the crowds behind to claim an even better view at the top of, believe it or not, Tom, Dick, and Harry Mountain.

DESCRIPTION

When you come around the corner on US 26 and see 75 cars parked on the side of the road, it's not a fair or something: It's the Mirror Lake trailhead. Think about starting early or going on a weekday so you'll have a decent chance for some quiet time. You'll see that the interest in this trail is well justified.

The lower portions of the trail to Mirror Lake have some rhododendrons that will bloom pink in late June, and the upper portions are cool and shady, keeping you from warming up too much as you head up the hill. But it isn't even much of a hill, gaining less than 700 feet in 1.4 well-graded miles. Just below the lake, you'll come to the outlet creek and a trail junction. You can go either way to loop 0.4 miles around the lake, but if you're headed up the ridge, go right. The lake itself is a beauty. The beaches are on the right side, the campsites are on the left, and the view of Mount Hood you're looking for is at the far end, on the boardwalk in a marshy area.

KEY AT-A-GLANCE INFORMATION

LENGTH: 2.8 miles to the lake; 6.4 miles to the top of the ridge

CONFIGURATION: Out-and-back

DIFFICULTY: Easy to the lake, moderate to the ridge

SCENERY: Rhododendrons, deep forest, a small, placid lake, a big view

EXPOSURE: Shady on the way up, open at the lake, wide open atop the ridge

TRAFFIC: Heavy use on summer weekends, moderate otherwise.

TRAIL SURFACE: Packed dirt, rocks

HIKING TIME: 2 hours to the lake; 3.5 hours to the ridgetop

DRIVING DISTANCE: 52 miles (1 hour and 15 minutes) from Pioneer Square

SEASON: Late June–October

ACCESS: Northwest Forest Pass required

WHEELCHAIR ACCESS: None

MAPS: Mount Hood Wilderness; Green Trails #461 (Government Camp); USGS Government Camp

FACILITIES: Sometimes a portable outhouse at the trailhead

SPECIAL COMMENTS: This also makes a great snowshoe trip.

Directions ————————————————→

From Portland on US 26, drive 45 miles east of I-205 and park at the trailhead on the right. It's half a mile past the historic marker for the Laurel Hill Chute on the right.

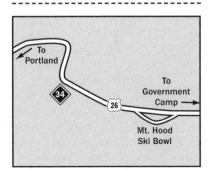

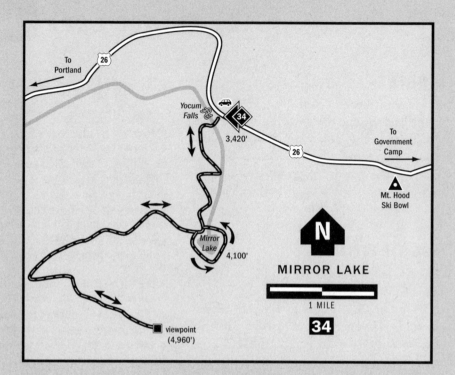

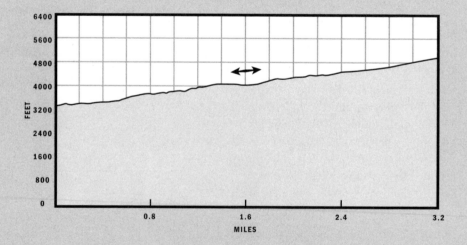

To get to the top of Tom, Dick, and Harry Mountain, walk to the far right side of the lake (as you face it when you arrive), and follow a trail that goes right and slowly climbs the face of the ridge. The place you're headed for is actually right above you, but you have to walk almost 2 miles to get there. As for the name, it indicates the three peaks on the ridge—not, as some would suggest, because every Tom, Dick, and Harry hikes this trail.

The trail is really just two long switchbacks, each one almost a mile long. It's time to turn left when you get to some very odd large piles of rocks, which no one has ever been able to explain. The forest opens up a little more here and, as you approach the summit, it gets a smidge steeper. When you get to a rocky area (neither steep nor dangerous) you're almost there.

The view from on top of this ridge is really something, considering how close you still are to the car. For starters, look how pitifully small Mirror Lake is—and how far down there. It never ceases to amaze me how quickly one gains elevation hiking. Right in front of you, looming across the highway, is Mount Hood in all its glory. Mount Adams is actually blocked by it. To the left is Mount St. Helens. What looks like a shoulder on St. Helens is in fact Mount Rainier, some 100 miles to the north.

In case you're still feeling energetic, resist the temptation to explore the other two peaks on this ridge—Tom and Dick, as it were. They're off-limits because they are home to protected peregrine falcons.

Although this trail is open as early as the first of June, it will often have patches of snow on it until the end of that month, because it is shady and faces north. For more information, call the Mount Hood Visitor Information Center at (503) 622-4822.

NEARBY ACTIVITIES

The easternmost peak of Tom, Dick, and Harry Mountain is the summit of Mount Hood Ski Bowl, which in the summer is like a constant carnival. You can bungee jump, ride the Alpine Slide, play mini-golf, drive go-carts, take a trip in a helicopter, or ride the chairlift to the top of the hill and hike or mountain bike down. The entrance is 1 mile east on US 26.

35 RAMONA FALLS

KEY AT-A-GLANCE INFORMATION

LENGTH: 7.1 miles
CONFIGURATION: Balloon
DIFFICULTY: Easy
SCENERY: A pleasant stream, a historic cabin, and a one-of-a-kind waterfall
EXPOSURE: In the woods all the way, with occasional open spots
TRAFFIC: Heavy use, especially on summer weekends
TRAIL SURFACE: Packed dirt
HIKING TIME: 3.5 hours
DRIVING DISTANCE: 53 miles (1 hour and 10 minutes) from Pioneer Square
SEASON: May–October
ACCESS: Northwest Forest Pass needed
WHEELCHAIR ACCESS: None
MAPS: Mount Hood Wilderness; Green Trails #461 (Government Camp); USGS Bull Run Lake
FACILITIES: None at the trailhead, but a campground with water and toilets is less than a mile away.
SPECIAL COMMENTS: The hike's bridge over the Sandy is only in place from mid-May to mid-October. Also, this area was subject to massive flooding in November 2006, including the destruction of the access road to the trailhead. For up-to-date information, contact the Mount Hood Visitor Information Center at (503) 622-4822.

IN BRIEF

This trail is immensely popular, and it's no wonder. It's a fairly easy hike to a uniquely beautiful falls, with plenty of room for a picnic when you get there. There's even a side trip available that affords a sweeping view of Mount Hood.

DESCRIPTION

This hike starts on a trail that looks like a highway; that's because it's basically flat and thousands of people make the trek to Ramona Falls every year. In 0.2 miles, cross the Sandy River Trail, a connector from the Riley Horse Camp. Keep going on Trail #797 toward Ramona Falls and admire a very large, cracked boulder near the junction. A short walk later you'll see a nice view of Mount Hood up the main stem of the Sandy River.

At 1.2 miles, reach the crossing of the Sandy River. The bridge here will be in place from mid-May to mid-October; call ahead for details, but there are generally signs at the trailhead alerting you to its status. In the fall, the river can often be crossed without the bridge—if there hasn't been much rain lately.

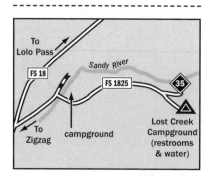

Directions

From Portland on US 26, drive 36 miles east of I-205 to Zigzag. Turn left (north) onto Lolo Pass Road, which is 0.6 miles past milepost 41. Go 4.2 miles and turn right onto FS 1825, which is 0.1 mile past a Mount Hood National Forest sign and marked "campgrounds and trailheads." Stay right at 0.7 miles, cross a bridge, and continue another 1.7 miles to turn left onto Spur Road 100, which leads 0.5 miles to the trailhead. Going right at the last fork would take you 0.3 miles to Lost Creek Campground, where water and toilets are available.

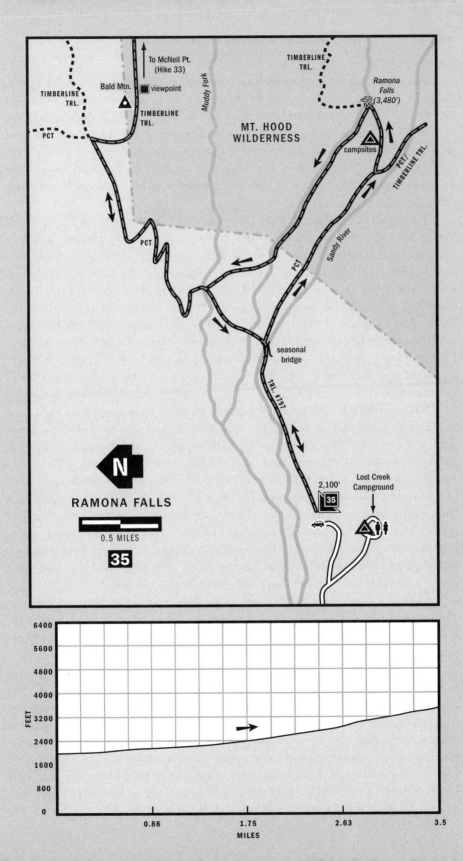

To McNeil Pt. (Hike 33)

TIMBERLINE TRL.

Bald Mtn. ■ viewpoint

TIMBERLINE TRL.

TIMBERLINE TRL.

PCT

Muddy Fork

MT. HOOD WILDERNESS

Ramona Falls (3,480')

campsites

Sandy River

PCT/TIMBERLINE TRL.

PCT

PCT

seasonal bridge

TRL. #197

N

RAMONA FALLS

0.5 MILES

35

2,100'
35

Lost Creek Campground

FEET

6400
5600
4800
4000
3200
2400
1600
800
0

0.88   1.75   2.63   3.5

MILES

After crossing the river, walk a quarter mile to the junction with the Pacific Crest Trail, which here is making its way north around the west side of Mount Hood. This is also where your loop starts, so for now, turn right (south) onto the PCT and continue a gradual climb, over moss-covered ground and under some very large rhododendrons. A mile past the junction, reach the top of a bluff from which the Sandy, below you to the right, is more audible. Also keep an eye out for eroded cliffs across the way, offering a cross-section of Mount Hood's volcanic deposits.

When you're 1.5 miles past the junction, the PCT takes a dip to the right and toward the river; follow this for a little scenic turnoff. At the bottom of a brief descent, reach a campsite near the shore of the Sandy; the crossing here is known among PCT hikers for being treacherous, especially for the early-season crowd. But we don't have to deal with that. At the far end of the campsite, look for log steps leading up the hill to a 1935 Ranger Station, built to keep hikers on the Timberline Trail out of the protected Bull Run watershed. There are no longer rangers stationed here, but hikers can spend the night—though it looks like a haven for mice, and there's no guarantee the roof will keep the rain out. There are some tent sites nearby, though, as well as a nice view of the Sandy River Canyon about 100 yards uphill.

Follow the PCT back up the hill to the Ramona Falls Loop, turn right, and in 0.2 miles come to a horse gate protecting the entrance to the falls area. From here, you can drop down to the left to find campsites; no camping is allowed at the falls. Pass through the gate and enter the falls area in a moment.

Ramona Falls is a perfect example of how a tiny stream can make a heck of a waterfall. The best comparison for these falls is to one of those pyramids of Champagne glasses; as the water cascades over broken columns of basalt, it spreads out into a 120-foot extravaganza of water that emits a cool, misty spray into the open area in front of it. No wonder so many people come here with kids and dogs and picnic supplies! Just beware of the gray jays that haunt the area; they'll take food right out of your hands if you're not careful.

There's a nice story, by the way, behind the naming of Ramona Falls. In 1933 a Forest Service employee came across the falls while scouting the area for a trail; at the time, he was courting his future wife and named the falls after a popular romantic song of the time called "Ramona."

Continue over the bridge, and at the far end reach a junction. To head back to the car, stay straight. Or, if you're looking for an adventure, turn right onto the Timberline Trail, which goes around Mount Hood for 42 miles. Going this way, you'll climb for just under a mile, then begin a looping, 5-mile traverse around the headwaters of the Sandy River's Muddy Fork. There will be some off-route, rocky scrambling and some watery crossings at the head of a very scenic canyon, and eventually you'll wind up on the flanks of Bald Mountain (also part of the McNeil Point hike). From there, you're looking at a 3-mile, 1,600-foot descent back to the Ramona Falls Loop Trail. It's a fine, scenic, occasionally sketchy, and highly recommended trip, and if you do it, your day will be almost 14 miles.

To complete the much simpler loop back to the parking lot from Ramona Falls, follow the trail straight ahead and down lovely Ramona Creek, perhaps singing a romantic tune as you go. It's a gently downhill 1.6 miles back to the PCT near the Muddy Fork; from there, turn left for half a mile back to where your loop started, then backtrack across the Sandy to your car, which is 2 miles down from where you hit the PCT.

36 SALMON BUTTE

KEY AT-A-GLANCE INFORMATION

LENGTH: 8.4 miles

CONFIGURATION: Out-and-back

DIFFICULTY: Moderate

SCENERY: Pleasant forest on the way up, panoramic view on top

EXPOSURE: Shady with occasional open spots, then wide open on top

TRAFFIC: Moderate on weekends, light otherwise

TRAIL SURFACE: Packed dirt, some rocks at the top

HIKING TIME: 4 hours

DRIVING DISTANCE: 70 miles (1 hour and 20 minutes) from Pioneer Square

SEASON: June–October

ACCESS: Northwest Forest Pass required.

WHEELCHAIR ACCESS: None

MAPS: USFS Salmon-Huckleberry Wilderness

FACILITIES: None at the trailhead

SPECIAL COMMENTS: June is the best time for this hike; that's when the rhododendrons are in bloom. For more information, call the Mount Hood Visitor Information Center at (503) 622-4822.

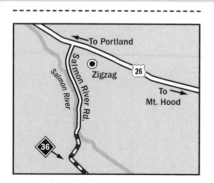

IN BRIEF

This easy-to-get-to trail is a mellow climb through old-growth forest and giant rhododendrons to a viewpoint that takes in Mount Hood, Mount Jefferson, and the heart of the Salmon-Huckleberry Wilderness. And when the rhodies are blooming, it's a treat!

DESCRIPTION

This trail is so well graded, you'll hardly notice you're going uphill, except for occasional views down the valley or up toward the peak. Other trails might climb similar elevation in half the distance, but they'll leave you more tired. So this is a perfect way to get on top of something without spending the whole day or wearing yourself out.

The trail starts out through an area that was clear-cut 30 years ago, so there's not much in the way of old trees, but soon enough you get into the hemlocks and moss-draped Douglas firs, plus some seriously large rhododendrons that will bloom in late June. At 1.3 miles, you'll come to an area at the end of a ridge with a view to the top of the butte and some nice rocks to sit on. Just less than 2 miles up, a trail to the right at a switchback leads to a steep, wildflower-filled meadow with a perfect rock for a photo opportunity. Just past 3 miles up, gain the ridgeline in an open area loaded with rhodies and a view to the left of

Directions

From Portland on US 26, drive 36 miles east of I-205 and turn right onto Salmon River Road, which is 0.1 mile before the Lolo Pass Road on the left. Stay straight on this road for 6.5 miles; you'll come to a small parking area on the left and the trail entering the trees on the right.

SALMON BUTTE

0.5 MILES

36

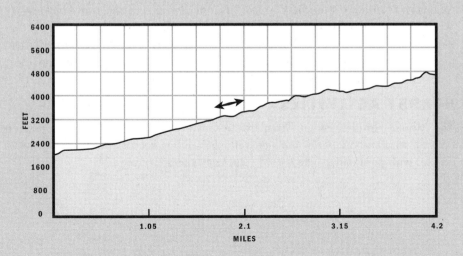

A noble fir stands lookout on Salmon Butte.

the sweeping Salmon River Valley. You'll now have climbed 2,100 of the 2,800 feet in your hike.

Near the top, the trail dead-ends into an old road that once served a lookout tower; turn right and follow the road to the summit, which is reached by a rocky scramble of about 100 feet. From here you're looking south and east, with Mount Hood 15 miles to your left, Mount Jefferson 35 miles to your right, and Mounts Adams and Rainier off on the horizon. In front of you is the Salmon-Huckleberry Wilderness; what a difference a lack of clear-cuts makes, eh? While you're on top, look around for old pieces of glass and metal that are part of the burned-down lookout tower. Then cruise back down the same gentle grade you came up.

NEARBY ACTIVITIES

The Mount Hood Brewing Company in Government Camp (10 miles east on US 26) serves good pizza and generally has about six of the brewery's beers on tap, with cool names like Cloud Cap Amber and Ice Axe IPA.

SALMON RIVER–DEVILS PEAK 37

IN BRIEF

The Salmon River, which starts on the slopes of Timberline Ski Area, is the only river in the lower 48 states to be classified as a Wild and Scenic River from its headwaters to its mouth. (To see its headwaters and cross it where you can skip across, do the Barlow Pass hike.) There are three sections of trail along its lower stretches, two of which are described here. They are extremely easy to get to, and in the fall they host spawning salmon. The upper-most section, accessed by a different road near Trillium Lake, is less interesting than these, tougher to find, and not worth the effort. Its only advantage is that nobody hikes it.

DESCRIPTION

Start with the lower, easier section. From the roadside parking area (the first one you came to while driving in), you'll start out downhill through a beautiful forest of Douglas firs and Western red cedars. You'll be close to the river after 0.1 mile and stay there most of the rest of the way. After two little footbridges over side creeks, you'll come to the first of several trails leading down to the river. You will pass two more small bridges, and in 0.4 miles you'll come to a campsite with a log that sticks out over the river. It's perfectly sturdy, but be sure of your balance before you go out on it.

KEY AT-A-GLANCE INFORMATION

LENGTH: The lower section is 5.2 miles round-trip; the upper section is 6.6 miles round-trip.
CONFIGURATION: Out-and-back
DIFFICULTY: Easy all the way to the campsites in the upper section; moderate beyond that
SCENERY: Old-growth forest; spawning salmon in the spring and fall, a canyon view at the top
EXPOSURE: Shady all the way to the top, then some exposed rocks
TRAFFIC: Heavy all summer long
TRAIL SURFACE: Packed dirt with rocks and roots
HIKING TIME: 2 hours for the lower loop; 3.5 hours for the upper
DRIVING DISTANCE: 50 miles (1 hour and 15 minutes) from Pioneer Square
SEASON: Year-round
ACCESS: Northwest Forest Pass needed
WHEELCHAIR ACCESS: None
MAPS: USFS Salmon-Huckleberry Wilderness
FACILITIES: None at trailheads; water and restrooms at Green Canyon campground
SPECIAL COMMENTS: For more information, contact the Mount Hood Visitor Information Center at (503) 622-4822.

Directions ————————————————→

From Portland on US 26, drive 36 miles east of I-205 and turn right onto Salmon River Road, which is 0.1 mile before the Lolo Pass Road on the left. Stay straight on this road for 2.7 miles to the lower trailhead (just beyond the Mount Hood National Forest sign), or for 4.9 miles to the upper trailhead, at a bridge over the river.

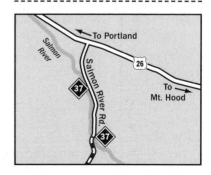

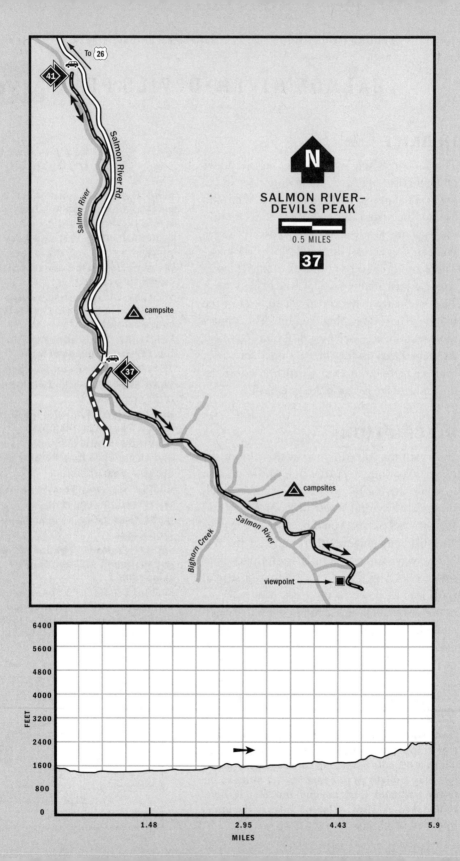

To (26)

41

Salmon River Rd.

Salmon River

N

SALMON RIVER–
DEVILS PEAK

0.5 MILES

37

△ campsite

37

△ campsites

Salmon River

Bighorn Creek

viewpoint ← ■

FEET

6400
5600
4800
4000
3200
2400
1600
800
0

1.48   2.95   4.43   5.9

MILES

There's plenty of old-growth scenery along the Salmon River Trail.

The best thing about this trail, other than its convenience and the river itself, is the nature of the old-growth forest. Look for "nurse" logs, which have fallen and are now the home of new trees. Just past the campsite with the suspended log, you'll go up a set of steps, at the top of which there's an absolutely massive Western red cedar; you can't miss it, as it's right next to the trail and about ten feet thick. At about the 1-mile mark, look for a hollowed-out cedar stump with a new tree growing from it; just past it is the biggest Douglas fir (about eight feet thick) on this stretch of the river.

At about the 1.5-mile mark, you'll come to the first of two sections where the trail joins the road for a brief time. On this first one, you want to take the second trail back into the woods; the first trail is used by anglers and dead-ends at the river. About 50 yards off the road, look for three large trees—two firs and a cedar—almost bonded together. Just past here, where a downed tree lies along the bank, I came across several spawning salmon on a late September hike. They were in the shallows just a few feet from shore. The fish will actually go several miles farther upstream; if you hike the upper section of this trail in the fall, you'll get more chances to see them.

There are two more highlights to this trail. One is a cedar tree so large that a hollowed-out area in its base is big enough to be called a cave. The other is a "nurse" log, cut into three pieces for trail-construction purposes, which is now host to no fewer than eight saplings.

Just past 2 miles out, wind around Green Canyon Campground, with outhouse and water, and after a second section on the roadside, you'll drop back into the woods for another brief spell before emerging at the upper trailhead, where the road crosses the river.

Now, for the upper section. From the trailhead, walk upstream through a forest of Douglas fir. Just less than a half mile up, you'll pass a deep pool where fishermen often gather. A little while past this, when you get another view of the river from about 40 feet above it, look (in September and October) for dark shapes swirling about in the pools. Those are salmon; the black-gray ones are chinook, and the less-often-seen gold ones are cohos. Consider that they have spent their lives in the ocean and have swum all the way up the Columbia River some 75 miles, about 41 miles up the Sandy, then about 20 miles up the Salmon.

At the 2-mile mark, a series of campsites on the right offers yet more chances to get close to the river and look for fish. Just after a trail leads right to a nice little falls and deep pool—both formed by a huge log that fell across the river—you'll embark on just about your only climb of the day, picking up about 600 feet in 1.3 miles to an overlook of the Salmon River Canyon. After you pop out into the open, make sure you go as far as the rock outcrop for the best view. Just be very careful around here, and don't try any of the trails going down toward the river. You might go down farther and faster than you ever intended.

That scenic view is your recommended turnaround, as you're now 3.3 miles from the upper trailhead, but the trail actually goes another 10.8 miles upstream to the road near Trillium Lake. If you're feeling truly industrious, or perhaps you camped back along the river and have more time, consider putting in the big climb to the lookout tower at Devils Peak. Just keep going up the Salmon River Trail for 2.3 miles, turn left (and way up) on the Kinzel Lake Trail (#665), follow that 2.3 miles (and 1,600 feet) up to the Hunchback Trail (#793), which leads 2 miles (and another 700 feet) up to the 5,045-foot lookout. So, if you started at the bridge, you're looking at 14.9 miles round-trip and a climb of 3,400 feet. Good luck with that.

NEARBY ACTIVITIES

Start your day with breakfast at the Zigzag Inn, 0.1 mile east of Salmon River Road on US 26. They do good things with French toast there.

TAMANAWAS FALLS

IN BRIEF

This is a classic falls in a dramatic setting at the end of an easy, beautiful hike. *Tamanawas* (pronounced "ta-MAH-na-was") is a Chinook word for a friendly, guardian spirit, and it's an appropriate name for this nonthreatening, pleasant hike.

DESCRIPTION

So many people like this trail that even a flood in 2000, which wiped out two trail bridges, didn't stop folks from going up there. Officially, the trail was closed that entire summer, but Oregonians displayed their typical respect for the government by hiking the "closed" trail in such numbers that the Forest Service acquiesced and made the new, hiker-created trail the official one.

The funny thing about that flood is that the creek that did the damage, Cold Spring Creek, is primarily spring-fed. I spoke with a ranger who said nobody could figure out how a creek that isn't fed by glaciers could suddenly whip up a flood that actually took out three bridges—two on our trail and one above the falls on the Bluegrass Ridge Trail. She called it a "weird event." Whatever the cause, the Forest Service probably won't rebuild the bridges, so the trail you hike today is what the locals came up with in 2000.

The lower part of the trail was untouched in 2000. From the trailhead, walk to your

KEY AT-A-GLANCE INFORMATION

LENGTH: 3.4 miles

CONFIGURATION: Out-and-back

DIFFICULTY: Easy

SCENERY: A mountain stream, plunging waterfall

EXPOSURE: Shady all the way, then open toward the end

TRAFFIC: Heavy use on summer weekends, moderate otherwise

TRAIL SURFACE: Packed dirt and rocks

HIKING TIME: 2.5 hours

DRIVING DISTANCE: 75 miles (1 hour and 40 minutes) from Pioneer Square

SEASON: April–November

ACCESS: Northwest Forest Pass required.

WHEELCHAIR ACCESS: None

MAPS: Mount Hood Wilderness; Green Trails #462 (Mount Hood); USGS Dog River

FACILITIES: None at the trailhead; water and restrooms are available half a mile south on OR 35 at Sherwood Campground.

SPECIAL COMMENTS: Massive flooding in November 2006 tore up many bridges in this area, so call the Hood River Ranger District, (541) 352-6002, before you go, to make sure the trail is open.

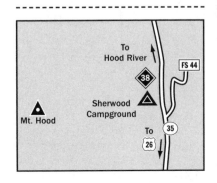

Directions

From Portland on US 26, drive 51 miles east of I-205 and turn north on OR 35, following signs for Hood River. After 15 miles on OR 35, and 0.2 miles past the Sherwood Campground, park at the trailhead on the left.

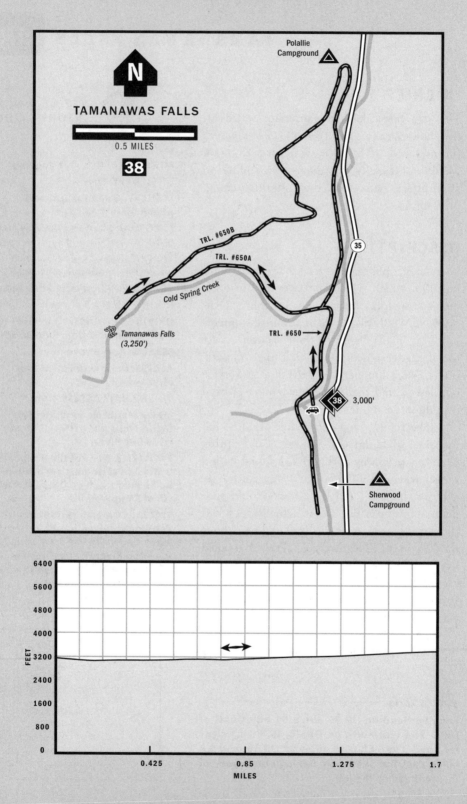

right and cross the East Fork of the Hood River on a one-log bridge with handrails. Note the milky color of this river; that's glacial silt. At the far end of the bridge, join the East Fork Trail (#650) and follow it downstream, contouring to the right and paralleling the road for half a mile.

At 0.7 miles, leave the East Fork Trail and cross Cold Spring Creek on #650A, the Tamanawas Falls Trail. Now enjoy a lovely stretch right along the creek, passing numerous cascades, creekside picnic areas and forest features, and in 0.7 miles come to a rockslide area where #650B (also known as the Tie Trail) splits off to the right. The original Tamanawas Falls Trail went left here and crossed the creek on a bridge, but that bridge was wiped out in 2000. To follow the new route, take #650B for about a minute, until it switches back to the right in the face of a larger, older rockslide. It was here that locals made their new way in 2000.

This larger rockslide has been here for a long time; it is, in fact, the reason the trail used to cross the creek in the first place. The upper bridge that was wiped out crossed back to your current side of the creek, right at the base of the slide. The trail winds through this rockslide, and when you get across it, check out the ruins of the upper bridge lying along the creek. After that, it's about 0.2 miles to the falls.

What makes this falls so special is that even in late summer there's plenty of water coming over it, and also that it's rimmed by basalt walls, much of which are pink because pieces have so recently fallen into the chasm. For this reason, take care if you want to go nearer (or even behind) the falls, as you'll be walking on wet rocks with no official trail and cliffs above you—cliffs that have left ample evidence all around you that pieces of them could come crashing down at any time. These are just little reminders from Mother Nature that we are, after all, visiting her world.

NEARBY ACTIVITIES

Travel north on OR 35 and in 7.5 miles turn left and visit the Hutson Museum in Parkdale. It features local history, Indian artifacts, and memorabilia of the early settlers.

39   TIMBERLINE LODGE

KEY AT-A-GLANCE INFORMATION

LENGTH: 13 miles to Paradise Park; 4.8 miles to Zigzag Canyon overlook; 2.2 miles to Silcox Hut; 1 mile to White River Canyon

CONFIGURATION: Paradise Park, balloon; Zig Zag and White River Canyon, out-and-backs; Silcox Hut, loop

DIFFICULTY: Easy–strenuous

SCENERY: Meadows filled with flowers, deep canyons, glaciers overhead

EXPOSURE: Alternates between shady and open

TRAFFIC: Heavy all summer long

TRAIL SURFACE: Dirt, rock, pavement

HIKING TIME: 0.5–5 hours

DRIVING DISTANCE: 64 miles (1 hour and 30 minutes) from Pioneer Square

SEASON: July–October

ACCESS: No fees or permits needed

WHEELCHAIR ACCESS: A few patches of road around the lodge

MAPS: Mount Hood Wilderness; Green Trails #462 (Mount Hood)

FACILITIES: The lodge is a full-service hotel.

SPECIAL COMMENTS: No matter what the weather looks like, bring warm clothing for this hike. For more information, call the Mount Hood Visitor Information Center at (503) 622-4822.

IN BRIEF

If you spend just one day in Oregon, you should spend it at Timberline Lodge. If you only go on one hike, you should go to Paradise Park in August or early September. But if you aren't up to a 12-mile loop, options abound at this spectacular mountain palace.

DESCRIPTION

Timberline Lodge is the greatest man-made thing in Oregon. It was built in 1937 by the Works Progress Administration and dedicated by President Franklin D. Roosevelt the same day that he dedicated Bonneville Dam. But as astounding as the interior is, it's the setting of the place that requires time to be spent there. Only a few peaks in Oregon are above it, and with few trees around, the views are amazing—especially to the summit of Mount Hood, 3 miles away and the highest point in the state, and to Mount Jefferson, 45 miles to the south. In August, wildflowers bloom all over the place.

Let's start with the shortest hike, to the White River Canyon overlook. Follow a sign to the right of the lodge, pointing you to the Pacific Crest Trail (PCT). You'll walk uphill a couple hundred yards, perhaps wondering why you're suddenly breathing heavily: There's not as much oxygen up here. At the PCT, turn right (that would be toward Mexico) and walk a half mile to the overlook; note

Directions

From Portland on US 26, drive 48 miles east of I-205 and then turn left onto well-marked Timberline Road, 2 miles past Government Camp. Follow Timberline Road 6 winding miles to the parking lot.

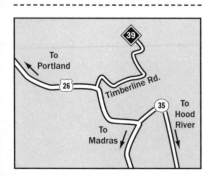

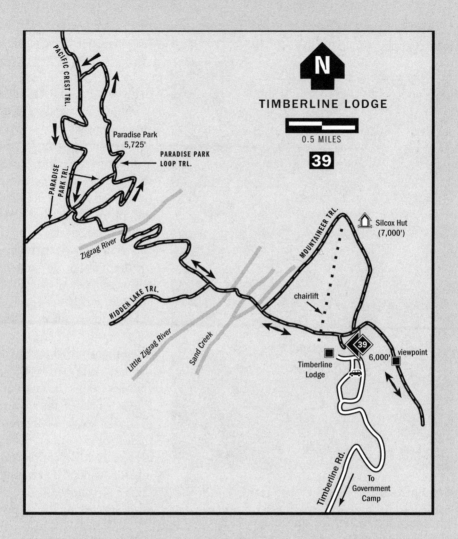

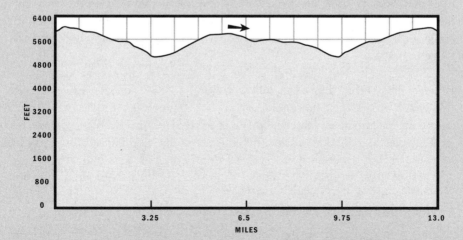

Spectacular Zigzag Canyon is a daunting part of the hike from Timberline Lodge to Paradise Park.

that you'll have to skip over a couple of small creeks along the way.

If you'd like to do a one-way hike with a car shuttle, this trail connects (in another half a mile) with the top of the Barlow Pass hike (see page 130).

For our next toughest destination, go straight when you get to the PCT and follow the road uphill 1.1 miles to Silcox Hut. There seems to be a lot of small trails, but you can see the hut at the top of the chairlift, so just head for it. The last part of the hike is on a dirt road. Timberline Lodge rents this hut out to groups of 12 or more during the winter. For about $100 per person, they take you to the hut by Snow Cat, cook your dinner, then come back in the morning to cook your breakfast. And in the summer, you can ride the Magic Mile chairlift up here, then walk down.

To loop back to the lodge, go back the way you came or take the service road under the chairlift. Or, for a slightly longer loop, take a trail that goes right (as you look down) from the top of the lift. It drops 1 mile to the PCT west of the lodge, in forest broken up by flowered meadows. Turn left and you'll be at the lodge in 0.8 miles.

But enough with the preliminaries: Let's head for Zigzag Canyon and Paradise Park. From the lodge, follow the PCT to your left; it will cross under two chairlifts and start descending slowly as it enters the woods. In 0.8 miles, ignore the Mountaineer Trail leading up to Silcox Hut. In 1.4 miles, ignore a trail to the left leading to Hidden Lake (it's a nice lake, but it's 3 miles below you). Just keep on truckin' through meadows and forests, past flowers and little springs. The best of these are around 2 miles out: great vertical bands of grass and color, the farthest one with a cool view of Ski Bowl and Tom, Dick, and Harry Mountain (described elsewhere in this book as part of the Mirror Lake hike).

At 2.4 miles, you'll find yourself standing agog at the edge of a massive canyon, with Mount Hood looming to your right. This is Zigzag Canyon. If you've had enough at this point, head back, and you'll have done a 4.8-mile out-and-back trip. But for the real prize of this part of the mountain, keep going.

Now, you may have noticed that Paradise Park is actually below Timberline Lodge, making it sound pretty easy. What you need to know, however, is that in the next 3 miles, while crossing Zigzag Canyon and climbing up to Paradise Park, you will go down 600 feet and then up 900. Just believe that it's worth it, and press on. You'll have to hop across the Zigzag River (look for the waterfall just upstream) and, 0.7 miles up the other side, take the first right (the Paradise Park Loop Trail, #757), then, yes, keep climbing toward Paradise Park; that's if you want to climb up to the best attractions. You can also stay on the PCT/Timberline Trail for 2.1 miles to the lower end of our Paradise Park loop, and you'll save yourself several hundred feet of climbing but still see some great waterfalls.

Heading up the Paradise Park Loop (#757), things start to get really spectacular. The number and variety of flowers in this area—lupine, daisies, lilies, and those bushy-looking pasque flowers—as well as the plump sweetness of huckleberries in late summer make it a prime destination. After 1 mile, the Paradise Park Trail comes in from the left; you can take it 0.6 miles down to the PCT and shorten your walk by 3.8 miles. But those 3.8 miles are flat and filled with beauty, so keep going.

Staying on the #757 trail, in a quarter mile you'll cross Lost Creek, spy an amazing campsite on a ledge above it, and 100 yards later come to the site of the old Paradise Park Shelter, one of several built back in the 1930s for people hiking the Timberline Trail.

The trail makes a right turn just before the shelter foundation and starts a long, wonderful, flat traverse through Paradise Park: heather, flowers, creeks, Mount Rainier, Mount St. Helens, a big cliff above you called Mississippi Head, the Zigzag Glacier above that . . . not bad at all for a flat walk. After 1.2 miles of this, you'll drop down into the forest again and intersect the PCT and Timberline Trail; this area has great views down the Sandy River Canyon and across it to Slide Mountain, a literal cross-section of Mount Hood.

Turn left here, and start back toward the lodge. After an easy half a mile, you'll come to Rushing Water Creek and its wonderful canyon, where you pass just under its waterfall; below you is an amazing slot canyon and a view down into the Sandy River Canyon. Another half mile, starting slightly downhill now, brings you back to Lost Creek. Look for a trail that leads uphill just after the crossing; it leads first to a little double waterfall, then to a magical, hidden cove with yet another waterfall. They're everywhere! It's not hard to find campsites in this area, either.

Another 0.7 miles brings you to the lower end of the Paradise Park Trail, where a horse corral will encourage you to keep moving. You'll really start downhill now, and in 0.4 miles come back to the junction where your loop started, the Paradise Park Loop Trail, #757. Follow the PCT back down into the canyon, and, well, hate to tell you, but from here—with 9.5 miles under your belt— you've 3.5 miles to go, gaining 1,200 feet, and you've seen it all before.

But hey, it was worth it, right? Besides, you've got Timberline Lodge to enjoy now. The hot chocolate and coffee drinks are sublime, the food's not bad (or cheap), there's an interesting film about its construction, and its main lobby is about as nice a place to recover from a hike as you could ask for. And you deserve it.

NEARBY ACTIVITIES

Though it's crowded, spend some time exploring Timberline Lodge. Watch the film *The Builders of Timberline* to hear the story of how artists and artisans came together during the Depression to create this masterwork. Then get to know the details of their accomplishment, especially the Head House with its massive central stone tower.

TRILLIUM LAKE 40

IN BRIEF

A prime place to take the kids or just to stretch your legs after driving up from Portland, Trillium Lake is a tiny, friendly lake with a big-time view of Mount Hood. In addition to some short, easy hikes, you can fish, boat, picnic, or just lie around, catch some rays, and feed the ducks.

DESCRIPTION

Most outdoorsy Portlanders know Trillium Lake as a cross-country ski area, famed for the terror felt by many beginners on the long hill you drive down from US 26. But in the summer the lake is a beautiful, peaceful place to get a little taste of what the Mount Hood area has to offer. And if you've got kids along, they can swim, fish, and paddle in the lake all day long.

To hike around it, start at the day-use area located just before the road crosses the dam at the lake's southern end. Stop here and take the picture of Mount Hood that so many other people have taken. In case you're wondering, that square area of snow high up on the mountain is the Palmer Glacier, scene of summer-long skiing and snowboarding at Timberline Ski Area. Walk along the road across the dam, perhaps throwing some crumbs to the ducks, and ask the fishermen how they're doing. At the far end of the dam, follow the trail to the right into the woods.

Directions ————————————————→

From Portland on US 26, drive 49 miles east of I-205 and turn right at a sign for Trillium Lake. At the bottom of the hill, stay straight ahead for the day-use areas. The hiking trail, as described here, starts in the second day-use area you come to on the road.

KEY AT-A-GLANCE INFORMATION

LENGTH: 2 miles

CONFIGURATION: Loop

DIFFICULTY: Easy

SCENERY: Marshes, lake, birds, forest

EXPOSURE: Shady except when crossing the dam

TRAFFIC: Heavy use all summer long, moderate when school is in session

TRAIL SURFACE: Packed dirt, boardwalk, pavement

HIKING TIME: 1 hour

DRIVING DISTANCE: 61 miles (1 hour and 20 minutes) from Pioneer Square

SEASON: May–November

ACCESS: $4 day-use fee per vehicle

WHEELCHAIR ACCESS: The area around the campground has several barrier-free trails.

MAPS: Mount Hood Wilderness; Green Trails #462 (Mount Hood)

FACILITIES: Toilets in the day-use area near the dam; water available in the campground

SPECIAL COMMENTS: For more information, contact the Mount Hood Visitor Information Center at (503) 622-4822.

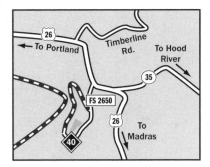

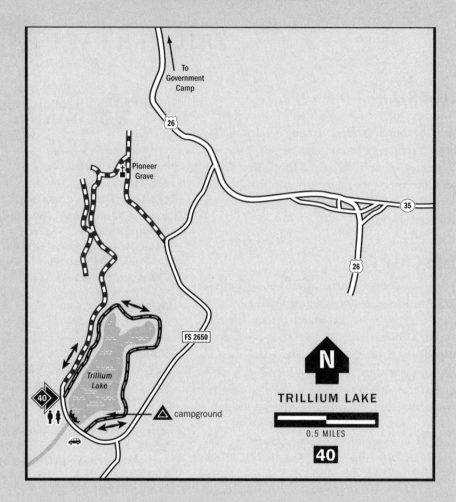

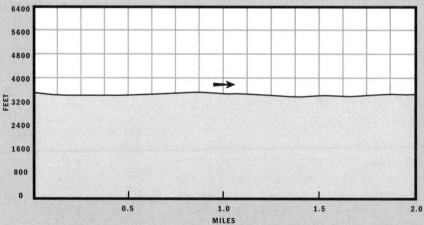

In the first part of the trail, you won't be right by the lake because the shore on that side is marshy and filled with tall grass. So you'll have to enjoy the forest. At 0.6 miles, a short boardwalk goes out to the right, providing a glimpse of the shoreline. At 0.8 miles, there's a campsite on the right with access to a relatively private spot on the lakeshore. Beyond this point, the trail becomes a boardwalk that traverses a marshy area thick with vegetation. It will seem like you're swimming through the wildflowers late in the summer.

As you round the northern end of the lake, you'll pass from marsh to meadow, with a view of a corner of the lake that's covered with lily pads. Then, coming back to the more crowded eastern shore, there are numerous beaches for the kids to romp on or the parents to sun themselves on. At 1.8 miles (which is also just 0.2 miles from where you started, going the other way) there's a boat ramp and another parking lot. Just beyond that is a dock you can walk out onto (it has rails, so you don't have to worry about the kids). I was out there late one summer day with the sun setting and a few pink-hued clouds hanging around Mount Hood across the way, and some grown-ups on the dock were talking about the stock market and housing prices. Some people just don't get it.

When you drive out, go around the lake for a piece of Oregon history. Drive across the dam and go 1 mile on the unpaved road, turn right for half a mile, and then go right again and park immediately on the right near a white picket fence. That's a pioneer-era graveyard. Across the road is Summit Prairie, where Barlow Road travelers rested the day before tackling the infamous Laurel Hill.

Looking for Trillium Lake trout in the shadow of Mount Hood

NEARBY ACTIVITIES

You have to stop at some point at the Huckleberry Inn in Government Camp. They've got huckleberry pies, pancakes, and milk shakes, and they serve pretty serious cheeseburgers, too. I love that place.

VISTA RIDGE 41

IN BRIEF

A short, easy trail to several flower-filled bowls at the tree line on Mount Hood, this hike is surprisingly seldom used. That might be because it's a bit of a drive to the trailhead, but rest assured that it's worth it. You can bring the kids for a short picnic outing or stretch out your legs on an all-day affair.

DESCRIPTION

Exactly why this hike isn't packed all the time has always been a mystery. All you have to do is climb slightly for a couple of miles through quiet woods and you're in wildflower heaven. The bad news is that the beginning and end of this hike can be tedious; the good news is that when you've gone less than 3 miles, you're basically done climbing for the day and can choose among four spectacular areas of flowers, meadows, creeks, and mountain views.

From the trailhead, go 0.2 miles to a sign and turn right onto the Vista Ridge Trail (#626). It's not too exciting in here, and it can get buggy, but when you see Mount Adams through the trees to the left, and the trail gets just a bit steeper, you're almost there. At 2.7 miles from the trailhead, you'll arrive at the Timberline Trail (#600), in an open area with

KEY AT-A-GLANCE INFORMATION

LENGTH: 6 miles to Wy'east Basin; 11 miles to see it all

CONFIGURATION: Balloon

DIFFICULTY: Moderate, but there's one tricky river crossing.

SCENERY: Mountain streams, rocks, glaciers, flowers everywhere

EXPOSURE: Shady for a couple of miles, then in and out of meadows

TRAFFIC: Moderate use on August weekends, light otherwise

TRAIL SURFACE: Packed dirt, roots, rocks

HIKING TIME: 3–6 hours

DRIVING DISTANCE: 77 miles (2 hours and 10 minutes) from Pioneer Square

SEASON: July–October

WHEELCHAIR ACCESS: None

MAPS: Mount Hood Wilderness; Green Trails #462 (Mount Hood)

FACILITIES: None at trailhead; the closest are at the Zigzag Store.

SPECIAL COMMENTS: For more information, contact the Mount Hood Visitor Information Center at (503) 622-4822.

Directions ⟶

From Portland on US 26, drive 36 miles east of I-205 to Zigzag and turn left onto Lolo Pass Road at the Zigzag Store. Continue 10.6 miles to Lolo Pass and turn right onto unpaved FS 1810, which is the second right at the pass. After 5.5 miles, you'll be back on pavement. In 1.8 more miles, you'll enter FS 18. Go 3.3 miles and make a hairpin right onto FS 16. Go 5.4 miles and turn right onto unpaved but signed FS 1650. Stay left at 2.8 miles; the trailhead is 0.8 miles ahead, at the end of the road.

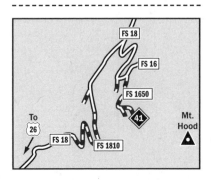

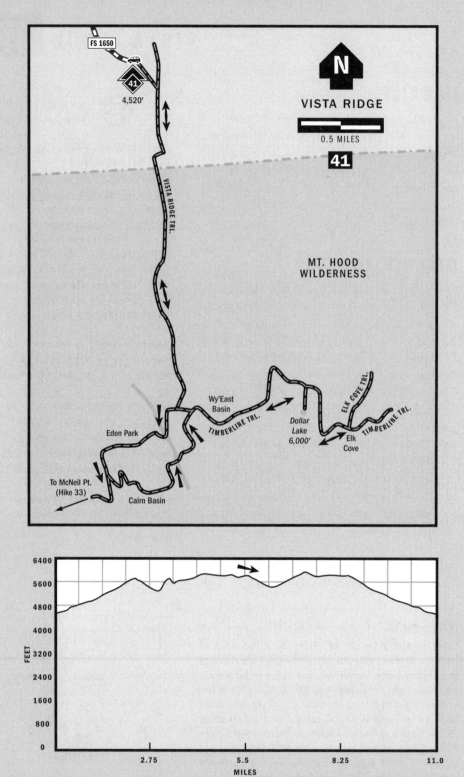

The Timberline Trail drops into Elk Cove on the Vista Ridge hike.

Mount Hood looming right in front of you. Congratulations: You've now climbed the biggest hill of your day—wasn't much, was it? You can go straight ahead for Wy'east Basin and Elk Cove, turn right for Eden Park and Cairn Basin, or go either way and see them all in a big loop.

But let's turn right on the Timberline Trail. You will briefly plunge downhill and then start contouring around to the left, crossing babbling brooks and admiring flowers. After 1 mile of this, you'll cross a larger stream, where logs have usually been placed to make a bridge. A quarter of a mile later, you'll be in Eden Park, which just might be the mountain meadow of your dreams. To preserve the fragile landscape, stay on the trails.

To keep going to Cairn Basin, cross Eden Park and find the trail in the trees as it turns toward Hood. It will climb a small hill, with a view back down to Eden Park, and then pass through a notch and arrive 0.2 miles later in a campsite at Cairn Basin. Here, you can turn right on the Timberline Trail to connect with the McNeil Point hike, which is just 0.3 miles and a tricky river crossing away. Or you can go straight ahead, following a sign for Elk Cove, to complete this loop hike. At the far end of the campsite you'll cross a creek that might be a bit much for the little ones; after that, it's basically a flat mile to Wy'east Basin.

Once there, your car is to your left (go 0.3 miles to the Vista Ridge Trail and turn right) and Elk Cove is to your right. In just a couple minutes on the way to Elk Cove, you'll come to a lovely meadow with a creek and views of Mounts St. Helens, Rainier, and Adams. Just 1.2 flat miles away, Elk Cove might be the most spectacular of these destinations; it's certainly the largest, and Mount Hood seems to rise out of its far side all at once. Here, you'll find wildflowers throughout

August, huckleberries late in the month, and reddish-orange mountain ash in September. I once spoke to a ranger who had seen elk and black bears in Elk Cove. Give either of them their space, and they won't bother you.

As you head back on the Timberline Trail, before you get back to Wy'east Basin, keep an eye out for a side trail leading to Dollar Lake. There's no sign, but it follows a draw uphill in an area of short trees and a tiny stream that's more of a wet spot in the trail. Look for a rocky area uphill of the trail. If you get back as far as the Pinnacle Ridge Trail (#630), you've missed it by about five minutes. Dollar Lake (so named because it's almost perfectly round, like a silver dollar) probably should be called Half-Dollar Lake; you could wade across it in a minute. But it's a quiet, lovely spot to contemplate all the beauty you've seen and say good-bye for now to Mount Hood before heading back to your car.

WILDWOOD RECREATION AREA

IN BRIEF

As much an educational experience as a hiking one, this is a glimpse into the natural world of birds, fish, plants, and water that is, in fact, all around the Pacific Northwest. The crown jewel of Wildwood is the underwater-viewing structure, especially when various species of salmon and trout are returning to the area to spawn.

DESCRIPTION

The 33-mile-long Salmon River is the only river in the lower 48 states that is designated as a National Wild and Scenic River from its headwaters to its mouth, in this case, from Mount Hood to the Sandy River, 3 miles below Wildwood. As far from the sea as it is, it gets several runs each year of anadromous fish—fish that are born in fresh water, go to the ocean, and return to the fresh water of their birth to spawn and die. Although salmon are the most famous of these—and this bend of the Salmon River does get runs of salmon—steelhead do the same thing and beyond even that, there are native trout in this stretch of the river.

To get a sample of this natural wonderland, hike two different loop trails, the 1-mile Wildwood Wetland Trail and the 0.75-mile Cascade Streamwatch Trail. To start the Wetland Trail, start to the left of the parking-lot kiosk, where there are restrooms and free maps

ⓘ KEY AT-A-GLANCE INFORMATION

LENGTH: Two loop trails total 1.75 miles; it's 10.6 miles to Huckleberry Mountain.
CONFIGURATION: Loop, out-and-back
DIFFICULTY: Easy or strenuous
SCENERY: Wetlands, meadows, streams, a big-time summit viewpoint
EXPOSURE: Alternately shady and open on loops; sunny on mountain hike
TRAFFIC: Moderate to heavy use on summer weekends, light otherwise
TRAIL SURFACE: Gravel, pavement, boardwalk (loops); packed dirt (hike to mountain)
HIKING TIME: 2 hours to do both loops; 5 hours for Huckleberry Mountain
DRIVING DISTANCE: 43 miles (1 hour) from Pioneer Square
SEASON: Year-round, but road is gated weekend after Thanksgiving–third Monday in March. During that time, you'll have to park at the gate (free) and walk in; restrooms in the park are left open. The trail up the mountain is generally snow-free May–October.
ACCESS: $5 parking fee per vehicle
WHEELCHAIR ACCESS: Both lower loops
MAPS: Free hiking maps are available in a kiosk at the parking area.
FACILITIES: Water and restrooms at the parking area

Directions ⟶

From Portland on US 26, drive 33 miles east of I-205 and turn right at a large sign: "Cascade Streamwatch." It's half a mile past the Mount Hood RV Park. Following the trailhead sign, drive a mile ahead to the parking area for both trails.

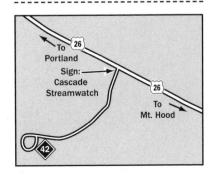

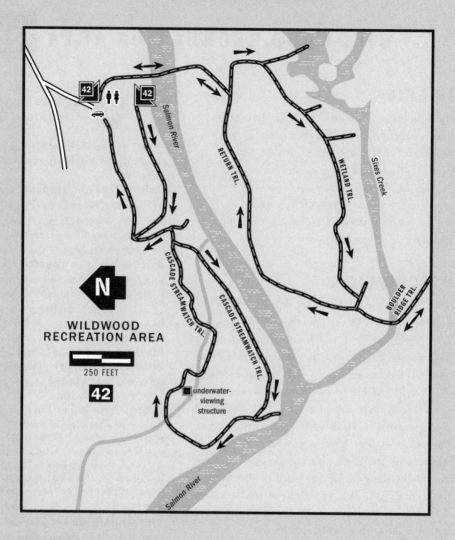

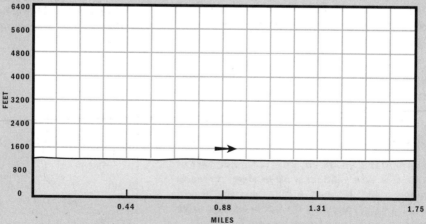

available. You'll cross a 190-foot-long wooden bridge over the lovely Salmon River, where in fall and winter you just might see chinook salmon and steelhead spawning below. Once over the bridge, follow the signs onto the boardwalk. You'll visit several lookouts onto various parts of the wetland: a cattail marsh, an overgrown beaver dam, an area filled with skunk cabbage, and a wetland stream. At each one there's a notebook-style informative display describing the area's wildlife. Also, if you're quiet and go in the morning, there's a good chance you'll see some wildlife. Be sure to take the gravel Return Trail back to the parking lot, if only to admire the size of some 80-year-old stumps.

The Cascade Streamwatch Trail starts at the same kiosk and takes you on a tour of the world of an anadromous fish. In fact, to navigate the trail you just follow the metal fish in the pavement. Along this trail, you'll visit an overlook of the river, a three-dimensional model of the Mount Hood area, several great picnic areas with grills, and then the fantastic underwater-viewing structure. Here, you can see tiny fish most times of the year and try to identify them using the chart on the wall. From late October to mid-December you might even catch a glimpse of an adult coho salmon. You have a better chance of seeing bigger spawning fish a little later on the trail, when it drops down to the riverside. Look for winter steelhead in January; spring chinook salmon in March and April; summer steelhead in May; and coho and fall chinook from late September to mid-November. In case you're wondering, the Salmon River is closed to salmon fishing; you can fish for native trout at limited times, but it's all catch-and-release with artificial lures only.

Now, if it's exercise and a view you're after, take the Boulder Ridge Trail up to Huckleberry Mountain—and I do mean up. It climbs 4,100 feet in 5.3 miles to a tremendous viewpoint. It starts at the far end of the Wetland Trail and climbs a series of switchbacks for just under 2 miles, then offers a nice view of Mount Hood and a slightly less severe grade. Another half mile of climbing puts you at another view in a saddle, and from there you put in another 2 miles to another saddle, then turn right onto the Plaza Trail for a mile to the summit.

For more information, call the Salem District of the Bureau of Land Management at (503) 622-3696.

NEARBY ACTIVITIES

Wildwood is actually a full-service 600-acre recreation area, with picnic areas available for rental, ballfields, and a play area. For rental information, call the National Reservation System at (877) 444-6777.

43 BURNT LAKE-ZIGZAG MOUNTAIN

KEY AT-A-GLANCE INFORMATION

LENGTH: 6.8 miles to the lake, 9.4 miles to the hilltop

CONFIGURATION: Out-and-back

DIFFICULTY: Easy along the creek, moderate to the lake, strenuous to the mountain

SCENERY: Shady creekside forest, a lovely mountain lake, and a spectacular summit view

EXPOSURE: Some ridgetop walking near the top

TRAFFIC: Heavy on summer weekends, moderate otherwise

TRAIL SURFACE: Packed dirt, some rocks

HIKING TIME: 5.5 hours to do it all

DRIVING DISTANCE: 54 miles (1 hour and 20 minutes) from Pioneer Square

SEASON: June–October, though there will be some snow higher up in early summer

ACCESS: Northwest Forest Pass required.

WHEELCHAIR ACCESS: None

MAPS: Green Trails #461 (Government Camp)

FACILITIES: None at the trailhead; stop in Zigzag on the way

SPECIAL COMMENTS: For more information, call the Zigzag Ranger District at (503) 622-3191.

IN BRIEF

This is really three hikes in one: a cool, shady amble along a creek, a steady climb to a beautiful lake with a view of Mount Hood, and a strenuous climb to an old lookout site with a *serious* view of Mount Hood.

DESCRIPTION

Burnt Lake Trail (#772) starts off in an area where there's no lake and it would appear nothing has ever burned. It's all cool, moist, and shady as you wind up through a young forest with a branch of Lost Creek off to your right. If that name sounds familiar, it's because there are enough things called "Lost" in Oregon (as well as Salmon, Elk, and Huckleberry) to fill a whole hiking book.

After a quarter mile, just past a big cedar on the right, the forest gets a little more interesting, and at just under half a mile there's an unmarked trail left leading to a clifftop view toward the main stem of Lost Creek. On the main trail, get your first glimpse of actual water around a mile out, and at just under 2 miles you hop across a tiny creek. Continue climbing ever so gently for half a mile, past some old burned-out snags, and look for a trail dipping left to a picnic site down by a

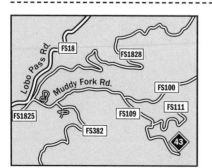

Directions ⟶

From Portland on US 26, drive 36 miles east of I-205 to Zigzag. Turn left (north) onto Lolo Pass Road, which is 0.6 miles past milepost 41. Go 4.2 miles and turn right onto FS 1825, which is 0.1 mile past a Mount Hood National Forest sign and marked "campgrounds and trailheads." Stay right at 0.7 miles, cross a bridge, and 2 miles later, just past the Lost Creek Campground, turn left onto a gravel road for 1.3 miles to trailhead.

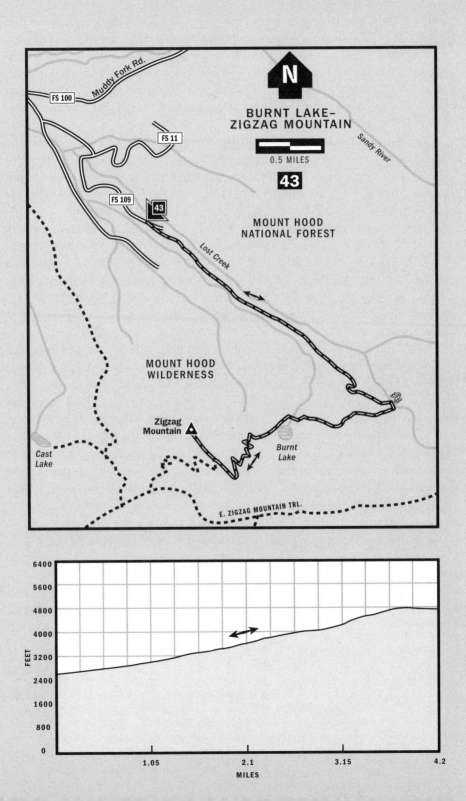

small waterfall. You have now found the main branch of Lost Creek, as well as a good place (2.3 miles out) to turn around if you're tired or you have little kids.

Soon you'll make a switchback to the right and climb for a mile, past several small creeks, some of them in open areas that offer views back along the valley you've been coming up—and Mount Hood over your right shoulder. But the real views start just after you cross Burnt Lake's outlet creek and arrive at the shores of this local wonder.

You'll immediately see that lots of folks come up here; if it's not actually crowded when you arrive, you'll see trails leading all over the place. If you're camping, you must stick to designated spots and not have wood fires. If you're just up for the day, linger a bit, explore the trail around the lake, and soak in the rays and the views of Hood. Turn back here, and you have a 6.8-mile day.

To head up to the lookout, which is another 1.3 miles and 800 feet up, stay right on the trail as it leads away from the lake, following a pointer toward Zigzag Mountain Trail (#775). Cross a marshy area, then switchback up and out of the lake basin, intersecting the #775 trail after 0.8 miles. Turn right here, and things get quite steep for a quarter mile until you reach a viewpoint of Hood with rhododendrons all around you. After the trail goes flat for a few minutes, stay straight at another junction and push up the final 0.3 steep miles to the rocky summit.

From the top, your view runs from two-humped Rainier in the north to Mount Jefferson in the south, with Olallie Butte just to the left of it. To the left of Mount Hood, between it and Mount Adams, look for an open stretch along the side of a ridge, with a piece of trail going through it; that's Bald Mountain and a section of the Timberline Trail you can visit on either the McNeil Point hike or the Ramona Falls hike. The valley below that is the Muddy Fork of the Sandy River, which starts at the Sandy Glacier, clearly visible from here, left of the summit. To the right, beyond the Zigzag Glacier, you can see dramatic Zigzag Canyon, which is visited on the Timberline Lodge hike, and beyond that are two buildings that are part of Timberline Lodge, along the sides of Palmer Glacier.

So it's a two-creek, one-lake, four-volcano, three-glacier day, and yet there are more trails up here to explore. The trail you took to the summit, the Zigzag Mountain Trail, continues west over the summit toward Cast Lake and a veritable noodle bowl of trails, including the continuation of the Burnt Lake Trail (#772), which you left behind at the junction just below this summit. So you could make a loop out of all that, or even head for the lookout atop the west end of Zigzag Mountain—that is, if for some reason what you've already done isn't enough.

THE COAST AND COAST RANGE

44   CAPE FALCON

KEY AT-A-GLANCE INFORMATION

LENGTH: 5 miles

CONFIGURATION: Out-and-back

DIFFICULTY: Easy

SCENERY: Old-growth forest, waterfalls, and several cliff-top vistas of the sea

EXPOSURE: Shady until the last 200 yards

TRAFFIC: Use is heavy all summer, especially weekends; it's moderate otherwise.

TRAIL SURFACE: Packed dirt with some gravel; mud

HIKING TIME: 2.5 hours

DRIVING DISTANCE: 89 miles (1 hour and 40 minutes) from Pioneer Square

SEASON: Year-round

ACCESS: No fees or permits needed.

WHEELCHAIR ACCESS: None

MAPS: USGS Arch Cape

FACILITIES: There are toilets 0.1 mile down the road from the trailhead, but no water. The water on the trail must be treated.

IN BRIEF

This is one of the best hikes on the Oregon coast. It's easy to get to, it's basically flat, and it offers great views and soothing forest. No wonder it's so popular!

DESCRIPTION

Getting out of your car and onto the Cape Falcon Trail is what hiking on the Oregon coast is all about. You're barely an hour from the Portland metro area, and then after about five steps you're in a rare, coastal, old-growth forest, walking a wide, mostly flat path to a wonderful destination. You'll cruise along for 0.4 miles to a junction. Short Sand Beach with restrooms in the campground will be to your left and down the hill about 0.3 miles; Cape Falcon will be to the right. Straight ahead will be a nice view of Smugglers Cove.

After turning right, you'll cross a small creek and start winding in and out with the contours of the land. One highlight along the way is a spectacular pair of downed trees sharing their root structures. The trail splits here for a few feet. The right fork is often muddy. The left fork is cooler: It includes climbing onto one of the downed trees and walking along its trunk for a while.

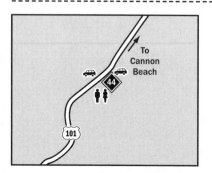

Directions

From Portland on US 26, travel 74 miles west of Interstate 405; turn south on US 101. Trailhead is 14 miles ahead on the right. There are actually three parking areas in succession here. The first (unmarked) one on the right is for Cape Falcon, distinguished by a small median strip along the highway. The second one, 0.1 mile farther on the left, is where the restroom is located. The third is one of the trailheads for Neahkahnie Mountain.

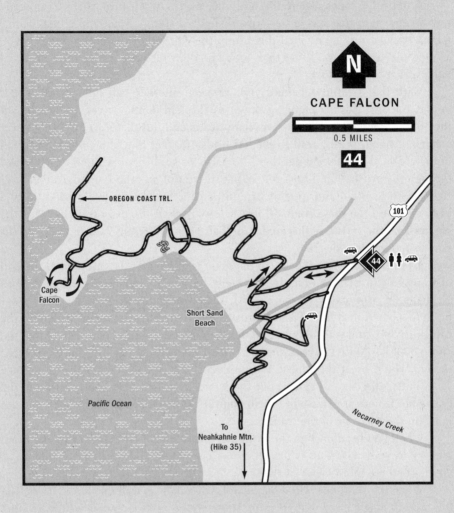

Cape Falcon

N

CAPE FALCON

0.5 MILES

44

OREGON COAST TRL.

101

Cape
Falcon

Short Sand
Beach

Pacific Ocean

Necarney Creek

To
Neahkahnie Mtn.
(Hike 35)

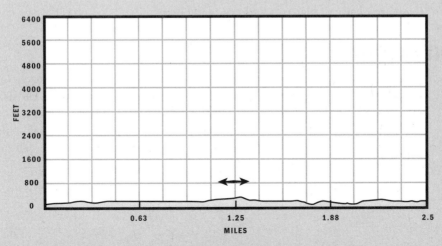

Around 1.3 miles, where the trail makes a sharp left turn, there's a downed tree on the right that has left a large, disfigured stump. Some more imaginative hiking friends of mine dubbed this stump the Throne of the Forest King. If you assume the throne, you'll see that your kingdom includes a nice little grove of Sitka spruce and hemlock.

With that goofiness behind you, proceed another half mile or so. You'll notice a series of trails plunging down to the left. These access the beach, but they're too steep to fool with—especially at the end. Just before a footbridge over a creek, a small, brushy trail to the left leads 100 feet to a hidden little waterfall in the creek. If you take it another 100 yards or so, often having to nearly crawl through the brush, you'll find yourself at the top of an even larger falls that goes right down to the ocean. Just be careful of your footing, or you'll wind up in a heap down on the rocks some 50 feet below. Back at the main trail, look for the big burls on the spruce in this area. You'll also get a different view of the first falls you visited on the side trail.

A few moments later, back on the main trail, you'll start out toward the end of Cape Falcon itself. You'll get nice views back into Smugglers Cove and up to Neahkahnie Mountain (see page 214), then you'll dip through the trees once more to a junction at the edge of a brushy, largely treeless area. For the end of the cape, turn left, and walk about 0.2 miles through the gauntlet of brush. Out at the end, you'll be 200 feet above the sea, with Falcon Rock out in front of you. (At the end you'll be at the top of an unrailed 200-foot cliff.) There are some nice spots under the trees to spread out for a picnic. In late May and early June, the grassy bluffs here are awash in Indian paintbrush and irises. Look for seals and sea lions on the rocks or in the water.

When you head back to the main trail, turn left for a bit and add some more scenery to your day. This is the Oregon Coast Trail, and in the next mile or so you'll get three more views of the sea.

When the trail starts climbing inland, you might as well turn back, unless the old-growth magic has you in its grip. There are no more ocean views for a while, but there are plenty of big trees and not many people.

NEARBY ACTIVITIES

I feel quite strongly that the best clam chowder around is served at the Ecola Seafood Market in Cannon Beach, about 11 miles north of the trailhead on US 101. It's at the corner of Second and Spruce, right across from the visitor center.

Also, this hike is right next to the Neahkahnie Mountain Trail, so you could do both in the same day if you're feeling energetic. For more information, call the Oregon State Parks at (800) 551-6949.

CAPE LOOKOUT STATE PARK 45

IN BRIEF

This park offers everything you'd want from the Oregon coast: old-growth forest, secluded beaches, cliff-top views, and wildlife on land, wing, and water. You've got three options from the trailhead, and with a little energy you could do all three.

DESCRIPTION

When you park at this trailhead, you will need to choose one of multiple options, and it's all downhill from here. Of course, you'll have to come back uphill to get to the car, but even the 800-foot climb from the beach is so well graded you'll hardly be winded when it's done. On our elevation profile for this hike, I've included both the beach route and the cape route.

Start with the best of the trails, the one out the cape (to follow this on the profile, just skip the part between the two "Junction" marks). Take the trail behind the sign at the far end of the lot, and when you get to a junction in 100 yards or so, stay straight. You'll be hiking through that rarest of treats: a coastal old-growth forest. There are some nice Sitka

KEY AT-A-GLANCE INFORMATION

LENGTH: 4.8 miles round-trip to end of cape; 3 miles round-trip to South Beach; 4.6 miles round-trip to picnic area

CONFIGURATION: All 3 hikes are out-and-backs.

DIFFICULTY: All 3 are moderate.

SCENERY: Old-growth forest, cliffs high above the sea, whales in winter and spring

EXPOSURE: Shady, open at end, cliffs

TRAFFIC: Heavy on summer weekends

TRAIL SURFACE: Gravel, dirt, mud

HIKING TIME: 2 hours to the end of the cape; 2 hours to South Beach; 2 hours to the picnic area

DRIVING DISTANCE: 85 miles (1 hour and 40 minutes) from Pioneer Square

SEASON: Year-round, with mud and possibly storms in winter and spring

ACCESS: No fees or permits needed, unless you park in the day-use area near the campground, in which case it's $3 for the day.

WHEELCHAIR ACCESS: None of the hiking trails, but a couple of the campground's yurts and all of its restrooms

MAPS: USGS Sand Lake

FACILITIES: None at trailhead; restrooms and water at campground

Directions

From Portland on US 26, drive 20 miles west of I-405, then bear west on OR 6, following a sign for Tillamook. Drive 51 miles to Tillamook, and at the intersection with US 101 stay straight. At that intersection and from then on, you will be following signs for Cape Lookout State Park and the 3 Capes Scenic Route. After crossing US 101, go two blocks and turn left on Stillwell Street. Go two more blocks and turn right onto 3rd Street. Travel 4.9 miles and turn left. After 5.3 miles you'll pass the state-park campground and day-use area; this is where you can stash a second car to do the shuttle. The free trailhead is 2.7 miles past the campground on the right.

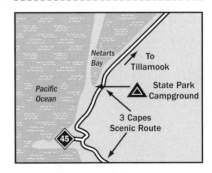

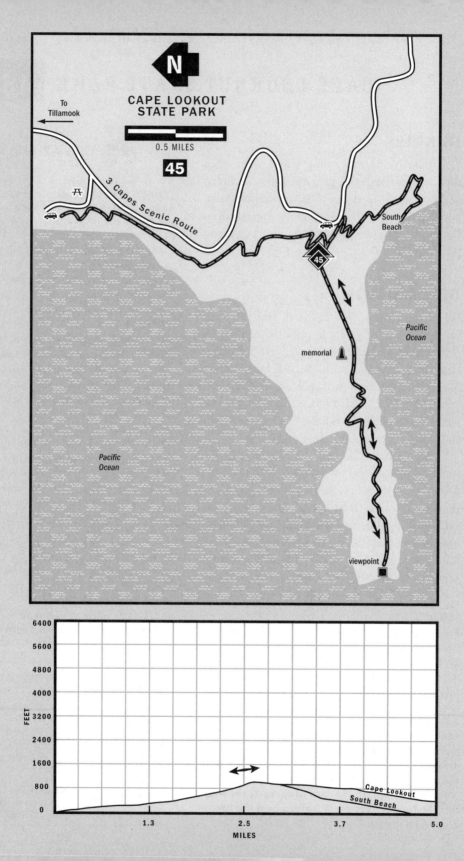

spruces and hemlocks in here, and the whole thing is as peaceful as can be. Just past half a mile out, you'll come to a plaque honoring the flight crew of a B-17 bomber that crashed into the cape just west of there in 1943. After another half a mile you'll get a view north; look for the three rocks just off Cape Meares and the town of Oceanside. You can make out an arch in the middle rock; in fact, all three have such arches, and they're called Three Arch Rocks. When you get to some moderately nerve-racking drop-offs on the left, along with inspiring views south, you're almost done.

At the tip of the cape, you're looking 270 degrees around and 400 feet straight down at the crashing sea. There is a protective cable at the end of the cape, but in other places you'll be right at the top of a cliff. On a calm day— which is rare in a place that gets 100 inches of rain per year—it's not uncommon to see seals or sea lions down there. But the main attraction is the gray whales. Thousands of them make the trip each year from the Bering Sea in Alaska to Baja California, a swim of some 6,000 miles. In late December and early January, when they go south, they tend to be farther out. But in March and April, they're on their way back north with newborn calves, so they go slower and stay closer to shore. At these times of year, bring binoculars (and a raincoat), and you might see dozens of whales in a day. For best viewing, go early in the day, when the sun will be behind you as you look out.

On your way back to the trailhead, when you reach the junction, turn right (downhill) and follow this trail down to South Beach. Avoid the temptation to take all the various cutoff trails, as they add to erosion. If the 1.5-mile, 800-foot-drop trail seems a little tedious (like when the beach looks as though it's just right there below you but you're walking more sideways than down), just believe that you'll be thankful for this easier grade on your way back up.

You can also hike down the beach, which extends 4 miles south to Sand Lake, but eventually you'll get into an area where cars are allowed, which sort of takes away from the wilderness feeling.

The last option from the trailhead is located across the lot, going north on the Oregon Coast Trail. It's 2.3 miles, all downhill, to the picnic area and nature trail, down by the campground. (Note that this trail was damaged by a slide in 2004 and as of spring 2006 had not yet reopened.) You'll pass a couple of view-points on the way, including one of Sphinx Island. If you left another car there, your whole day can be a total of 11.3 manageable miles. If you had only one car, you'll have to come back up to the car at the end of the day, stretching things out to almost 13 miles, so it might not be worth it.

If you have two cars, put one down at the campground–picnic area. You'll have to pay a $3 day-use fee there, but at the end of the day you can walk down-hill just 2.3 miles from the trailhead back to your second car. There's also a short nature trail there. For more information, call Cape Lookout State Park at (503) 842-3182.

South Beach at Cape Lookout State Park

NEARBY ACTIVITIES

As long as you're in Tillamook, take advantage of its tourist stops, most notably the collection of World War II airplanes at the Air Museum south of town and the two cheese factories to the north. The Tillamook Cheese Factory is the best known, but there are slightly more exotic choices at the Blue Heron Cheese Factory.

CASCADE HEAD

IN BRIEF

Imagine standing high atop a windswept, flower-covered prairie, with the sea and the coast spread out below you and not a tree to block the view. Or imagine peeking into a hidden cove where sea lions bark, a waterfall plunges, and waves crash. Well, you don't have to imagine either scene: you can go to Cascade Head and make it happen.

DESCRIPTION

First, the Harts Cove Trail. When it starts out, you might think you've got it made, because it's all downhill and steep—it loses about 500 feet in the first half a mile. Too bad you have to walk back up that at the end of the hike. The forest here is a young one of mostly Sitka spruce; notice how only the tops of trees are green? That's because these lower portions don't get any sun, not because they're unhealthy. Notice also the very large stumps

KEY AT-A-GLANCE INFORMATION

LENGTH: 5.4 miles round-trip to Harts Cove; 2.5 to 4.5 miles round-trip to the Nature Preserve

CONFIGURATION: Out-and-back

DIFFICULTY: Moderate, with an easy option

SCENERY: Old-growth forest, waterfalls, sea cliffs, wildflowers, and wildlife

EXPOSURE: Shaded at first, then open

TRAFFIC: Use is heavy on summer weekends but moderate otherwise.

TRAIL SURFACE: Packed dirt with some roots

HIKING TIME: 3 hours to Harts Cove; 1–2.5 hours for the Nature Preserve

DRIVING DISTANCE: 79 miles (1 hour and 45 minutes) from Pioneer Square

SEASON: The road to the upper trailheads is open July 16 through December 31. The lower trailhead is open year-round.

ACCESS: No fees or permits needed.

WHEELCHAIR ACCESS: None

MAPS: USGS Neskowin

FACILITIES: There is an outhouse at Knight Park, but no facilities at the upper trailheads; there's no drinkable water on the trail.

SPECIAL COMMENTS: No dogs allowed on the Nature Preserve

Directions

From Downtown Portland on I-5, drive 6 miles south and take Exit 294/Tigard/Newberg. Bear right onto OR 99 West and follow it 22 miles. Just before the town of McMinnville, turn left onto OR 18 (following signs for the coast) and follow it for 53 miles to its intersection with US 101. Turn right (north) on US 101. For the lower, year-round trailhead to the Nature Preserve, go 1 mile north and turn left onto Three Rocks Road. Follow this for 2 miles, turn left, and park at Knight Park. To reach the trailhead, follow a trail along the road.

For the two upper trailheads, go 3.8 miles north of OR 18 on US 101 and turn left onto unsigned Forest Service Road 1861, just before the top of a hill on US 101. Stay left at 2.4 miles, still on FS 1861. The upper Nature Preserve trailhead is 0.8 miles after this turn, on the left. The Harts Cove trailhead is at the end of the road, 1 mile later.

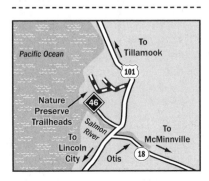

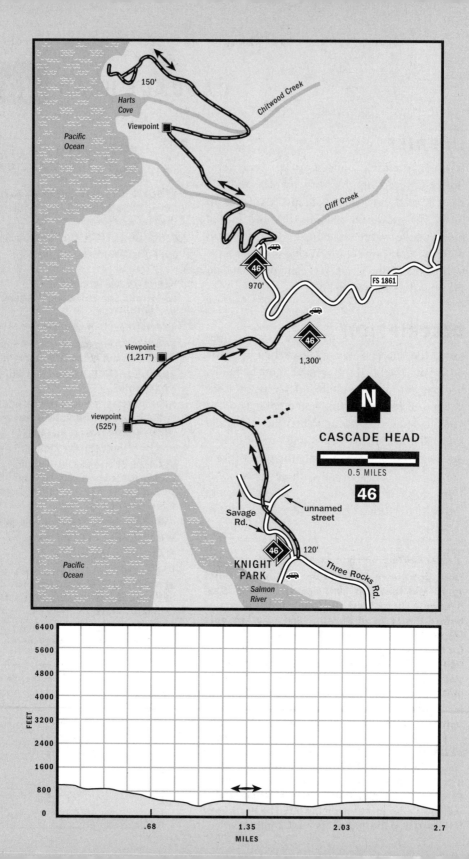

around; there's one right on the side of the trail that you can get on top of and measure for yourself.

After 0.7 miles you'll cross Cliff Creek and walk into a different world. Here you can find out what a Sitka spruce looks like after about 300 years. You'll also get to hear what hundreds of sea lions sound like—they're to the left, and you might get to see some of them later. Now the hiking gets flatter, as you go out to the end of the ridge to a bench with a view of Harts Cove ahead. Then wrap back around to the right, through the drainage of Chitwood Creek. Half a mile after the bench, walk under a massive blown-down spruce and then out into the meadows on top of the bluff—yet another world visited on this hike.

It's important to stay on the trails here; this area is fragile. If you come in August, you'll be wading through a view that looks like it was lifted from the upper reaches of Mount Hood: Look for goldenrod, lupine, Indian paintbrush, and violets. Follow the trail that aims at some trees on the left; there's a wonderful spot to sit down there, and it has a front-row view into Harts Cove. The waterfall you see is that of Chitwood Creek, which you just crossed. As for the sea lions, louder than ever, they are mostly around the point to the south, but if you have binoculars you might be able to see some of them lounging on rocks or the far beach.

There's no real beach access here, but you can get close to the water. From the trees, walk west and stay to the left. There's a steep trail there, almost a slide in spots, that you can take down to the rocky shore. This rock, and all of Cascade Head in fact, is lava that flowed up through the water. If you make your way to the right 100 yards or so on the rock, you'll have a fabulous view of the headland and north to Cape Kiwanda and, farther off, Cape Lookout.

Now, for the Cascade Head Nature Preserve. If the upper road is open and you want an easy, flat, 2.5-mile hike, start up there. The trail, actually an old roadbed, goes through a young and unexciting forest to the main-attraction meadow, arriving at a spot to be described below.

My advice is to start down below; it's a better, more scenic walk, and effort always makes one more appreciative. From the parking lot at Knight Park, start near the interpretive sign and walk up the access road. After 100 yards, cross Three Rocks Road and, following signs, head up Savage Road. At the top of a hill a few minutes later, turn left, then walk across the road and down its far side. Where the road turns left at the bottom of the hill, enter the woods to the right. This is 0.6 miles from Knight Park.

The trail starts out steep, over steps and roots, then mellows after 0.1 mile, where a massive spruce guards the trail. Enjoy typical coastal scenery—spruces and ferns, skunk cabbage and devil's club, a small meadow filled with foxglove—as you cross several small streams on boardwalks and continue climbing, now more moderately. When you reach a trail junction just less than a mile out, stay left, and a few moments later a sign will tell you you're entering National Forest property. At 1.2 miles you'll come to a registration station and donation box.

The mouth of the Salmon River, from the nature preserve at Cascade Head

For a while now, you've probably been hearing the ocean, and at 1.3 miles you'll finally come out of the vegetation tunnel and see the Pacific and the mouth of the Salmon River, some 600 feet below you. The trail is flat and wonderful for a quarter mile—look for elk on the bluffs and bald eagles in the sky—and then, when it makes a switchback to the right, it starts climbing pretty seriously.

In summer, this climb will be through waist-high flowers, with birds chirping, swallows swooping, and butterflies and bumblebees buzzing. From any of the switchbacks, wander out, carefully, toward the cliff edge to take a look to the north, possibly spotting sea lions down below. When you see a sign saying "Danger: Hazardous Cliffs," you've gone 2 miles and gained 1,000 feet. Only a quarter mile and a couple hundred feet to the top! The spot where the upper trail emerges from the woods is 0.3 miles past the summit.

As you take it all in from the top of the hill, consider this: More than 30 years ago, this meadow was slated to become a housing development, but conservation-minded folks banded together, bought it, and donated it to the Nature Conservancy. Now also designated as a United Nations Biosphere Reserve, it's protected as the home of the Oregon silverspot butterfly, whose caterpillar will eat only a rare violet that lives in these meadows. That's why FS 1861 and the upper part of the trail is closed from January 1 through July 15. The silverspots emerge in late August and fly for about a month.

For more information, contact the Nature Conservancy at (503) 230-1221 or the Hebo Ranger District at (503) 392-3161.

Looking north at the ocean from the nature preserve at Cascade Head

NEARBY ACTIVITIES

Back on OR 18, a mile before you came to US 101, you went through the town of Otis. You might not have noticed it (it has only about a dozen buildings), but it's the home of an Oregon coast tradition, the Otis Café. It's got 28 seats, a line outside, and the biggest portions this side of a logging camp. It's famous for sourdough pancakes, German potatoes, and whole-wheat molasses toast. They also make wonderful pies in the back. Plus, if you're interested, the whole town of Otis is for sale—for $3 million.

47 DRIFT CREEK FALLS

KEY AT-A-GLANCE INFORMATION

LENGTH: 3.5 miles

CONFIGURATION: Out-and-back

DIFFICULTY: Easy

SCENERY: Quiet forest, a meandering stream, and one seriously amazing bridge

EXPOSURE: In the woods, then on a narrow, high bridge—which you can get swinging, if you want

TRAFFIC: Moderate on summer weekends, light otherwise

TRAIL SURFACE: Packed dirt, muddy in winter and spring

HIKING TIME: 2 hours

DRIVING DISTANCE: 91 miles (2 hours) from Pioneer Square

SEASON: Year-round, but there could be snow in winter.

ACCESS: Northwest Forest Pass required.

WHEELCHAIR ACCESS: None

MAPS: Siuslaw National Forest; USGS Devils Lake covers the area, but this trail isn't on it.

FACILITIES: Toilets at the trailhead

IN BRIEF

This is a long drive, best done as part of a day at the coast, and there is just about nothing to this hike. If it weren't for the suspension bridge it crosses, nobody would ever hike it. But what a bridge! There are a couple of places to hang out by the stream, and a nice waterfall . . . but what a bridge!

DESCRIPTION

It's a long drive to this trail, so do it on a day when you're headed to the coast anyway—especially in spring or late fall, when there will be plenty of water in the creek. It's all about the bridge.

From the trailhead, you start down (what a novel concept!) and, in a little more than 200 yards come to . . . a trash can! Why it isn't at the trailhead is anyone's guess, but its existence (along with the sign and restroom at the trailhead) probably owes entirely to the fact that you need a pass to park at this trailhead; new regulations require such things where a pass is required.

You'll see a bench at 0.4 miles as you wind down through a young forest that may remind you of Forest Park in Portland. At half a mile, cross a small footbridge that was built

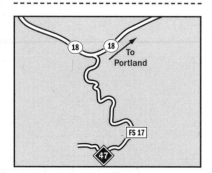

Directions

From downtown Portland on I-5, drive 6 miles south and take Exit 294, Tigard/Newberg. Bear right onto OR 99W; drive 23 miles. Just before McMinnville, turn left onto OR 18 (follow a sign for Oregon Coast). After 49 miles, turn left onto Bear Creek County Road (follow a sign for Drift Creek Falls Trail). In 2 miles you'll leave the pavement. At 3.3 miles, stay straight, again following a sign for the trail; you're now on FS 17. Trailhead is 10 miles ahead on the left.

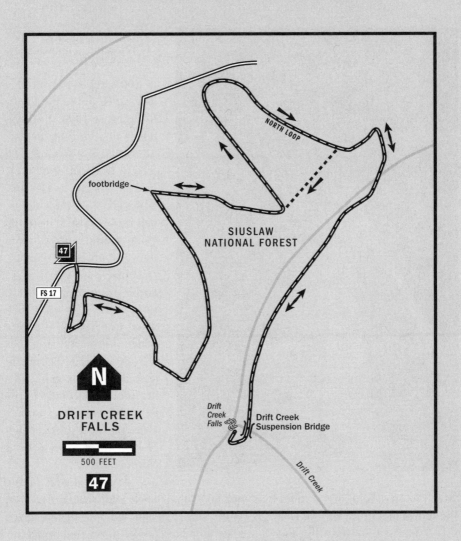

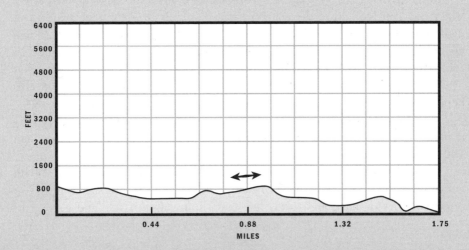

in 2003, replacing one that was wiped out in the floods of February 1996. That was when, in a four-day period, 30 inches of warm rain fell on top of two feet of snow in the coastal mountains, and when it all came down, hell broke loose. Tillamook County alone suffered more than $50 million in damage.

Just past this bridge, come to a new "North Loop," the sign for which does not really indicate where it goes. What it does is loop out to the north, then back to this trail, adding about a half-mile to the trip. But it's easy, and it visits the only (tiny) patch of old forest around, so I recommend it.

At the far end of the North Loop, a total of 1.4 miles into your hike, come back to the original trail on the shores of a north fork of Drift Creek, in a mossy, fern-filled bottomland. Cross this creek 0.1 mile after this, then a quarter-mile later, come to the real bridge.

Built in 1997, the Drift Creek Falls Suspension Bridge is 240 feet long, 3 feet wide, and 100 feet above the canyon floor. The falls to your right are 80 feet high—and you're above them! A few more technical details: the towers are 29 feet tall and made of Douglas fir beams 12 by 18 inches thick. The anchors include 28 cubic yards of concrete and 10-foot rock bolts. The mainlines are 1¼-inch galvanized wire rope. Also of note is that the same company that built this bridge also built the one over Lava Canyon, another hike in this book.

And how do they build such a thing, you might wonder? (I did.) They flew in materials with a helicopter, and built the main span from a "skyline" more than 100 feet off the ground—not a business for anybody afraid of heights.

Enough with the technical talk. It's a wonderful bridge, spanning the canyon and at the same time visiting the tree canopy. And, if you're into such things, you can get it rocking back and forth. Just put a foot on each side and have at it.

I couldn't get it to bounce, though—thanks to the stiffening truss underneath it. The bridge is dedicated to the late Scott Paul, a Forest Service trail builder who was foreman of this job and died in an accident during construction of the bridge.

If you keep going a quarter-mile past the bridge, you can get down to the creek and look up at both the falls and the bridge. There's a nice little pool where I saw some tiny trout kicking around, and a patch of grass across the creek that was pleasant for a picnic. I was there in October, though—probably the lowest water time of year. In the spring it would be a bit more of an adventure to cross.

NEARBY ACTIVITIES

Perhaps you noticed another bridge on the way down Bear Creek Road. The Drift Creek Covered Bridge is one of only four in Lincoln County, and it has an interesting history; for starters, it was built in 2001, and it's not over Drift Creek. There was a Drift Creek Covered Bridge (over Drift Creek) built in 1914 (hence the date on the sign), but it turns out the one still in existence in 1997 was built in 1933, after the original two got washed out. The county voted to tear it down, because it was beyond repair, but a couple named the Sweitzes offered to haul away the pieces and rebuild it here, over Bear Creek. The rest is a truly amazing story, related in a flyer on the bridge, complete with miracles and a near-divorce and tears and more miracles. Seriously; you should read it. The bridge reopened July 14, 2001, and is open to the public, though not cars. The place across the way is the Sweitz home.

48   KINGS MOUNTAIN-ELK MOUNTAIN

KEY AT-A-GLANCE INFORMATION

LENGTH: 5.4 miles to Kings Mountain, or 13 miles to include Elk Mountain

CONFIGURATION: Out-and-back, loop

DIFFICULTY: Difficult

SCENERY: Second-growth forest, regrowth after fires, wildflower meadows, a couple of panoramas on top

EXPOSURE: Shady on the way up, open on top. No dangerous sections, unless you go to Elk Mountain, in which case you'll traverse a thin ridgetop on the way there, then face a steep, rocky slope down the other side.

TRAFFIC: Use is moderate on summer weekends, light otherwise

TRAIL SURFACE: Packed dirt with some rock; if you continue to Elk Mountain, you'll face sheer rock and steep scrambles too.

HIKING TIME: 3.5 hours to Kings Mountain, 8 hours for longer loop

DRIVING DISTANCE: 47 miles (55 minutes) from Pioneer Square

SEASON: Year-round, but there may be snow on top in winter. Recent rains make some slopes slippery.

ACCESS: No fees or permits

WHEELCHAIR ACCESS: None

MAPS: USGS Jordan Creek

FACILITIES: None at the trailhead, and no water on the trail

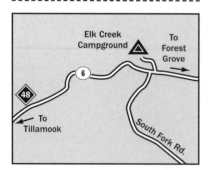

IN BRIEF

There are two options here: the trip up Kings Mountain is simple but steep, but the loop that includes Elk Mountain borders on an adventure, with exposed scrambles and insanely steep hiking over a 13-mile good time. If you're doing it all, consider going the other way, opposite this description, so you'll go up the steep Elk Mountain Trail, rather than down it.

DESCRIPTION

This entire hike is in the Tillamook State Forest, which might not sound that impressive compared with a national park or wilderness area, but there is a fascinating story behind this forest.

On a hot August day in 1933, a fire started at a logging operation in Gales Creek Canyon. The temperatures had been in the 90s for weeks, and humidity was at an all-time low. The forest, therefore, was a bomb waiting to go off. The Gales Creek fire started as a fairly standard fire, but then a hot, dry wind came from the east, and the 40,000-acre fire turned, in less than 24 hours, into a 240,000-acre fire. This "explosion" threw up a mushroom cloud 40 miles wide that rained debris two feet thick on a 30-mile stretch of the Oregon coast. Three more major fires would strike every six years until 1951, by which time 355,000 acres and 13 billion board feet

Directions ————————————→

From Portland on US 26, drive 20 miles west of I-405, then bear west on OR 6, following a sign for Tillamook. Continue 26 more miles and, just before milepost 25, park at the trailhead on the right.

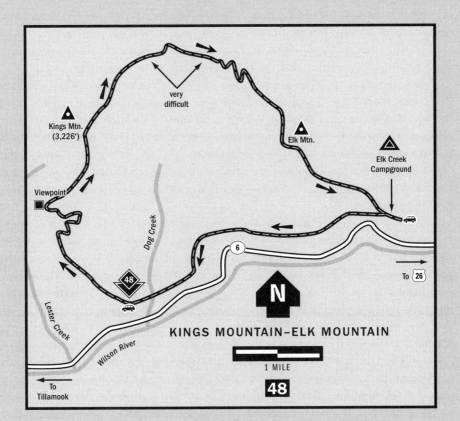

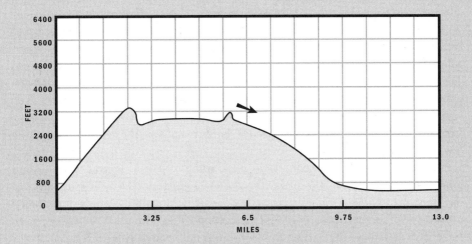

of timber (enough for more than one million five-room homes) had been completely destroyed. Logging came to a halt, wildlife was decimated, rivers were choked with sediment and debris, and most importantly for the forest, seedcones were annihilated, meaning that the forest wouldn't grow back on its own.

But starting with a bond measure in 1949, a recovery effort was launched. Eventually, more than 72 million seedlings were planted by hand, and in 1973 what had been known as the Tillamook Burn was renamed Tillamook State Forest. Now the question facing the state is whether or not to start logging it again. You won't have to worry about that; your job is to explore one of the highest points in the forest and have a look at how the place has recovered. Keep an eye out for charred logs, for example, and remember that 50 years ago most of this area was bare of vegetation.

With an elevation of 670 feet at the trailhead and a climb to 3,226 feet at the top of Kings Mountain, get ready for a workout. This trail starts steep and gets steeper. But first you have to admire the signs at the trailhead. What do you suppose are the odds that it's exactly 2.46 miles to the summit of Kings Mountain? And I don't know who considers this a "one-quart trip," but I'd start out with more than that, especially if you're also going to Elk Mountain.

You begin in a forest of alder and fern with Dog Creek off to your right. At 0.1 mile, you'll see (but not take) the Wilson River Trail on your right; if you're going to Elk Mountain, you'll be coming back this way. Around 1 mile, things get nasty steep; the next mile gains about 1,300 feet, as opposed to the 800 feet you've gained in the first mile. When the trail makes a sharp turn to the right and a small trail goes left, go out there for your first real view to the north. Lester Creek, below you, flows into the Wilson River to your left; Kings Mountain is directly behind you, higher than the rocky peak you can see from here. There are also some large, charred stumps on this ridge. The live trees were all planted after the big fires.

The last 0.6 miles of this hike gain about 900 feet, so just take your time and believe it's worth the effort. If you're here in May or June, you'll have no doubt about that when you walk past a picnic table (many thanks to Troop 299 from Tigard!) and out into the meadows, which in early summer are filled with beargrass, lupine, Indian paintbrush, and seemingly a billion other tiny flowers. The summit is now just 0.3 miles straight ahead, marked by a wonderful sign. The view stretches from the ocean to the Cascades; be sure and sign the register, one of the few in Oregon.

Now, if you've had enough, go back while you can. If you want to add 9 miles and tons of fun to your day, head on to Elk Mountain by continuing over the summit of Kings Mountain, traveling east. The downhill slope will get steep quickly, which might make you miss the trip up Kings Mountain. There are even some rock scrambles and ledges to keep things interesting. After 0.8 miles of this loveliness, you'll cross the ridge through a rock slot and join an old roadbed that traverses the ridge for 0.5 miles to a junction. Stay right for the last 2 miles to Elk Mountain, a tiny summit with a big view.

From here, you might wish you had a parachute. The Elk Mountain Trail is the steepest thing in this book. At times, you'll have to practically slide down rocky slopes, and in some places it will look like you're about to hike off the end of the world. Just take it easy, and you'll get down in one piece. When you reach the Wilson River Trail, turn right onto it, and you're 3.7 miles from the trailhead. There's a nice meadow on the way (this trail has it all!), and the only direction you need is that just after you cross a bridge, you'll encounter a road that you ignore; stay on the trail until you hit the Kings Mountain Trail, then turn left for 0.1 mile to the car. *Whew.*

For more information call Tillamook State Forest, (503) 357-2191.

49 NEAHKAHNIE MOUNTAIN

KEY AT-A-GLANCE INFORMATION

LENGTH: Several options from 2.5 to 9 miles

CONFIGURATION: Out-and-back or one-way

DIFFICULTY: Moderate–strenuous

SCENERY: A lovely beach, lookouts over the sea, old-growth forest

EXPOSURE: Shady all the way up

TRAFFIC: Use is heavy all summer, especially on weekends, but moderate otherwise.

TRAIL SURFACE: Gravel, packed dirt with some roots, muddy in sections, rocks on top

HIKING TIME: 2 hours for short options; 4 hours if you start at beach

DRIVING DISTANCE: 89 miles (1 hour and 40 minutes) from Pioneer Square

SEASON: Year-round, but beware of nasty weather and muddy trails in winter and spring.

ACCESS: No fees or permits needed.

WHEELCHAIR ACCESS: No paved trails, but beach might be reachable.

MAPS: USGS Arch Cape and Nehalem

FACILITIES: Restroom at northern trailhead

SPECIAL COMMENTS: For more information, call the Oregon State Parks office at (800) 551-6949.

IN BRIEF

One of the classic views on the Oregon coast is from the top of this 1,600-foot peak, which juts straight above the sea. And here you have three options for reaching it, plus a one-way alternative that covers the whole thing.

DESCRIPTION

Perhaps all these trailheads have you confused. Well, don't be. It's really very simple. Neahkahnie Mountain has a killer view, from 1,600 feet above the ocean, and you have three options for how to get there: The simplest is a 2.5-mile round-trip from the southernmost trailhead, gaining 850 feet; the middle option is the steepest section at 1,200 feet over 1.5 miles; and the longest option starts at the beach and offers more to see on the way up. It gains 1,600 feet in 3.3 miles. With two cars, you could do all three and put in only 4.5 miles; this would mean hiking our entire elevation profile.

First, the shortest option, starting at the southernmost trailhead. Start by switchbacking up through open areas filled with tasty red thimbleberries in late summer, and, after 0.7 miles, reach a junction with a road that leads left to some radio towers. Cross the road and follow

Directions ————————————➤

From Portland on US 26, travel 74 miles west of I-405 and turn south on US 101. The campground trailhead (where you'd park to go to the beach) is 14 miles ahead on the right. The middle trailhead for Neahkahnie Mountain is 0.9 miles farther up US 101 on the right before the viewpoint. For the southernmost trailhead, drive 1 mile past the middle trailhead and turn left onto a gravel road by a brown hiker sign. The trailhead is 0.4 miles up on the left.

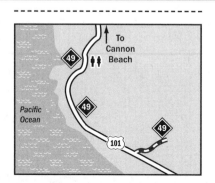

To Cannon Beach

Pacific Ocean

101

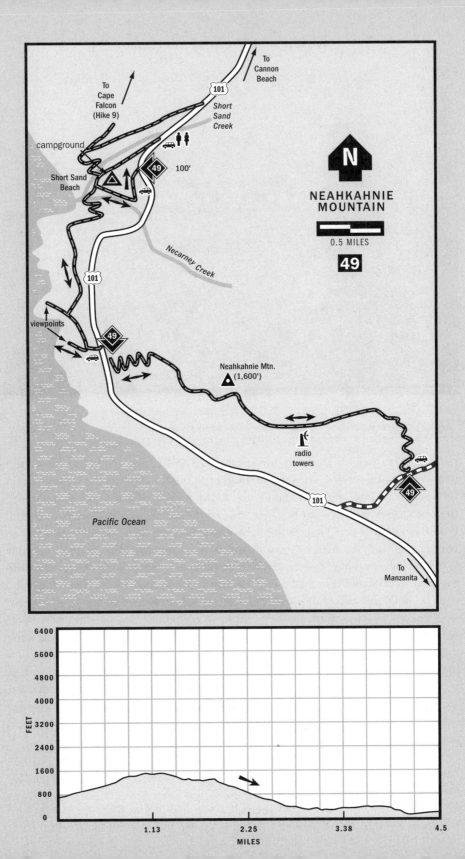

Looking down at the town of Manzanita from Neahkhanie Mountain

the trail. You'll climb gradually for another 0.3 miles, pass to the north of (and below) the radio towers, and then in another 0.2 miles come to the summit. It's a little rocky scramble, but nothing intense. Right in the spot where you pop out into the open, after you cross to the west side of the ridgeline, you'll see a little trail heading up and to your right. You might also notice that the same trail continues to your left, skirting the ridge to the south. You can follow this little scramble on your way back, if you'd like; just be aware that there are thorns at the start, one little exposed section, and then half a mile of easy going to the towers. Walk down the road 0.1 mile past them, and you'll see the trail where you came up.

For the beach option, the best and most scenic one, start at the parking lot for the Oswald West State Park campground. Walk down the trail, among some awesome Sitka spruces, toward Short Sand Beach. In 0.1 mile you'll come to a junction offering a choice between beach and campground; choose beach, unless you'd like to use the restroom in the campground. In another 0.1 mile, turn left at another junction, this time crossing a wonderfully bouncy suspension bridge over Necarney Creek. Take a few minutes to explore the lovely beach, which has some pretty decent tidepools around to the left.

Now, back on the trail to Neahkahnie Mountain, you'll climb up a ridge covered with massive Sitka spruces. About 0.2 miles up the trail you'll actually go through one of them.

When you get to the top of the ridge, you may notice there are some more hemlocks around. These trees and Douglas firs are the only ones you'll find from sea level to higher elevations in the Cascades. When the walk-through tree is 0.3 miles behind you, look for a large western red cedar just by the trail on the left, and just beyond that two ridiculously large Sitka spruces, with foot-thick branches that have turned upward and become trees in their own right. If you think they can't get any bigger, the largest spruce of the hike, with several trunks, is 0.2 miles farther along.

When you pop out into the open, in a meadow more than 200 feet above the sea, you'll have come 1.3 miles since leaving your car. Just ahead you'll see a trail splitting off to the right; it leads to a cliff-top viewpoint among the trees, looking down at Devils Cauldron. You'll actually see two of these trails to the right; the second one is the one to take. And don't wander around in these meadows. I know a guy who fell into a 15-foot hole here and had to be pulled out with a rope.

When you reach US 101, cross it carefully, and start into the woods at a trail sign that reads "Neahkahnie Mountain: 1.5 miles." Note that you could park here; this is the "middle" option.

Climb in the open for 0.6 miles before going back into the trees. At this point, you're at about 1,000 feet above sea level. You'll keep climbing gradually after this, and then if the trail seems to be dipping downward, don't worry. You're just traversing around to the far side of the mountain, where the view is. When you come to a junction where two large trees fell, stay to the right. Eventually you'll be back into the open and see a small trail heading up to the left; that's the summit.

From the top of Neahkahnie, you can see all the way south to Cape Meares; look for Three Arch Rocks offshore there. If it's a really clear day, you might make out Cape Lookout south of Cape Meares. The beach town seemingly at your feet is Manzanita, and the body of water beyond it is Nehalem Bay. During the invasion-scare days of World War II, the Coast Guard had a lookout up here, while soldiers patrolled the beaches on horseback and blimps from Tillamook cruised offshore.

If you have a car at the southern trailhead, time your arrival on the summit for just before sundown. It's quite a show from up there, and even at dusk it's no problem getting to your car.

If you want to do an even longer one-way shuttle, combine this with our Cape Falcon Hike (see page 194), or really go nuts and start up in the town of Arch Cape. The Oregon Coast Trail comes all the way down from there; it's 7 miles from the town to Short Sand Beach.

50 SALMONBERRY RIVER

KEY AT-A-GLANCE INFORMATION

LENGTH: Up to 16 miles with a shuttle

CONFIGURATION: One-way or out-and-back

DIFFICULTY: Easy aside from distance

SCENERY: Remote forested canyon, mountain stream, high bridges, tunnels, railroad tracks, occasional train

EXPOSURE: One high trestle, several tunnels, possibly a train or two

TRAFFIC: Light

TRAIL SURFACE: Railroad tracks, gravel

HIKING TIME: 7 hours to do it all

DRIVING DISTANCE: From Pioneer Square, Cochran is 48 miles (1 hour, 5 minutes), and Salmonberry is 77 miles (1 hour, 35 minutes).

SEASON: Access is typically closed from early July to mid-October for fire season; call the railroad for details. Possible snow in winter.

ACCESS: No passes required.

WHEELCHAIR ACCESS: None

MAPS: USGS Rogers Peak, Cook Creek

FACILITIES: None at either trailhead; there's water on the trail, but it would have to be treated.

SPECIAL COMMENTS: Bring a flashlight, since you'll be going through some tunnels.

After this edition was printed, massive storms destroyed sections of this railroad. Trains no longer operate here, and hikers must exercise extreme caution. The lower end of the hike appeared to be more accessible than the upper, but hikers should know that entire sections of the railroad were wiped out and safety may be an issue. The rest of this chapter remains as it was written before the storms.

IN BRIEF

Have you ever wanted to wander off down the railroad tracks? This is your chance. The Port of Tillamook Bay allows hiking access on this (still-active) 16-mile section through a roadless canyon in the Coast Range. You'll see old equipment, a seriously remote settlement, and lots of river loveliness.

DESCRIPTION

First things first: yes, there are still trains going through here, roughly one per day. But official railroad policy is that (a) hikers are welcome

Directions

For the upper trailhead at Cochran, from Portland on US 26, drive 37 miles west of I-405 to Timber Junction and turn left onto Timber Road, following a sign for Timber. Go 3 miles to Timber and then turn right onto Cochran Road. The pavement will end in a half mile; stay right at a junction in 3.7 miles, then left at 6.2 miles and left again at 6.3 miles, this time leaving Cochran Road and following a sign for Standard Grade Road. Park 0.1 mile ahead, where the road crosses the tracks.

For the lower trailhead at Salmonberry, stay on US 26 for 17 more miles and turn left onto Lower Nehalem Road, following a sign for Lower Nehalem River. Go a half mile and turn left at a stop sign, then continue 12 miles to where the road crosses the tracks. There's parking on the left.

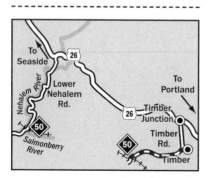

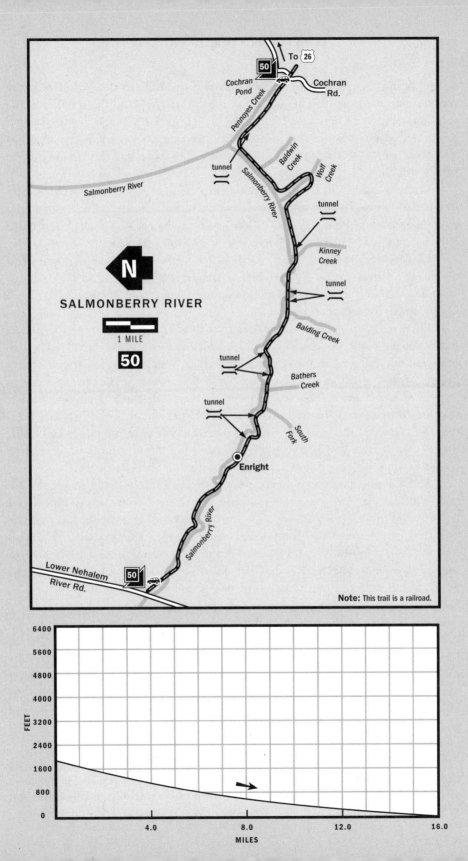

except during fire season, and (b) trains are required to blow their whistles all the way through the canyon. The grade and the curves also keep the trains slow, so you'll have plenty of time to get out of the way. I speak from experience: you *will* hear a train coming! Some of the smaller maintenance vehicles are quieter, but they also stop a whole lot quicker. Just call the railroad to make sure the canyon is open before you go.

Warnings aside, this is a unique hiking experience. Come in the spring or early summer for lush greenery and roaring water, or in October for fall colors and migrating salmon. Either way, you're likely to have the place to yourself, since I've only encountered a handful of people who know about this place.

I'll describe the way I like to do it, which is one-way from Cochran to Salmonberry, with a car or (preferably) a friend waiting at the other end. It's 16 miles, downhill, and such a mellow grade (about 100 feet per mile) you'll hardly notice the elevation change.

From the crossing at Cochran, head off to your right, following the pair of tracks down the hill. In 0.1 mile you'll see Cochran Pond on the right, and by this time you will have figured out something about walking on a railroad: Unless you're 5-feet-1 or 6-feet-9, walking on the ties is awkward. They're too short to step on each one and too far apart to step on every other one. The good news is that for 90 percent of the walk, there's enough dirt and/or gravel between them that the surface is flat. Just be careful that you don't twist anything, and know that in many places you'll have gravel or even a slight trail to walk on beside the tracks. Besides, walking down the tracks is just so . . . Woody Guthrie.

About a mile down, you'll encounter the first of many small tunnels. All but one (which comes later) are short enough that a train won't sneak up on you while you're in there, so just give a listen and then head on through. Just past this one is the first trestle. The second tunnel leads onto the highest trestle of the hike, a good 100 feet above Baldwin Creek. For the next several miles it's just more of the same—tunnels and trestles and ties and trees. Watch for herons along the river and old train equipment along the tracks, and enjoy the solitude.

Around 7 miles out you'll encounter a 1925 steel bridge, and less than a mile later you'll come to the long tunnel that you're not to go through. The reason you're not to go through it is that it's about 500 feet long and has a curve to it, so if a vehicle was coming, you might not know it. On the downhill end of this tunnel, there's a sign showing the way to the trail, but on the uphill end you'll just have to scramble through some brush on the right side, actually following an old railroad track, until the trail becomes a little clearer. Just hug the hillside, and you'll be back on the tracks in a few minutes; you might even enjoy the brief spell of walking on actual ground.

A few miles later you'll come to—surprise!—the "town" of Enright, apparently only two houses. It was actually a train station with a post office in the early 1920s, and it has no road access. There's an old water tower at the downhill end of it. If you're headed downhill, you're about two-thirds of the way done here.

A couple miles beyond Enright, you'll come to another steel bridge, this one over a long, deep pool. Officially, I can't recommend anybody jump off the bridge and into this deep, inviting pool, but the thought did occur to me. The water is quite refreshing. While I was contemplating the leap on an October afternoon, I noticed a large fish swimming around down there. On closer inspection, I found about a half dozen chinook salmon in the pool, mostly on the downstream side of the bridge. I watched for half an hour as they swam in circles, chased each other, and splashed around. One of them must have been 30 inches long.

At this point, you're only about 2 miles from Salmonberry, so you may start to see other people. When I hiked the whole stretch on a Saturday, I encountered only two hunters and two fishermen the whole day. A half mile or so below the salmon pool, look for a cable crossing the river; it leads to a house in the woods. Can you imagine living there?

When you start to see houses—in the comparatively huge "town" of Salmonberry, across the river to your left—you're about a half mile from the road, and walking on something other than railroad tracks will probably feel pretty nice. But if you're looking to relax a little, there's a nice little section of beach on the far side of the Nehalem River. Just keep going on the tracks across the Nehalem, then scramble down to the right and follow a faint trail though a batch of snowberry bushes to a sandy little nap spot. It's probably under water in spring and summer, but I had a pleasant autumn lie-down there after my walk. And here's an interesting thing about the Nehalem River: it actually starts just on the other side of Cochran, flows through Timber, then travels some 100 miles in a great northern loop through four counties to get to this point, which is only 16 miles from where it started. Go figure.

51   SADDLE MOUNTAIN

KEY AT-A-GLANCE INFORMATION

LENGTH: 5.2 miles

CONFIGURATION: Out-and-back

DIFFICULTY: Strenuous

SCENERY: Deep forest, wildflowers, panoramic view

EXPOSURE: In the forest, then out in the open on top, occasionally steep on some loose rocks

TRAFFIC: Use is very heavy on summer weekends, heavy on other summer days, and moderate otherwise.

TRAIL SURFACE: Packed dirt with rocks, then just rocks

HIKING TIME: 3.5 hours

DRIVING DISTANCE: 74 miles (1 hour and 30 minutes) from Pioneer Square

SEASON: Year-round, but it does get snow in the winter

ACCESS: No fees or permits needed.

WHEELCHAIR ACCESS: None

MAPS: USGS Saddle Mountain

FACILITIES: Toilets at the trailhead but no water there or anywhere on the trail

SPECIAL COMMENTS: For more information, contact the Oregon State Parks office at (800) 551-6949.

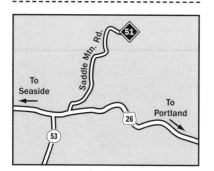

IN BRIEF

The highest point in northwest Oregon, Saddle Mountain is also one of the most popular hiking trails in the state. It goes through flower-filled meadows unparalleled in this part of the state and has a view on top that stretches from the ocean to the mouth of the Columbia River to the Cascades.

DESCRIPTION

Saddle Mountain just doesn't seem to belong in its surroundings. It's the highest point in this part of the state, but the other hills around it aren't even close. It doesn't even look like them, with its two-headed, rocky summit of "pillow lava," which looks like that because it erupted under water, millions of years ago when this area was the sea floor. Then, when you get on top of it, you might think you're on Mount Hood, with the faraway views and the wildflowers all over. Of course, with the crowds on summer weekends, you might think you're in a city park right after 5 p.m. on a weekday. Whatever—it's a great hike, so start early in the morning and get there ahead of everybody else.

When you get out of your car, you might be a little intimidated as you look up at the mountain. You might even see some speck-sized people up there. The good news is, you'll be up there soon enough; the bad news is, that's not the summit.

Directions ———————→

From Portland on US 26, travel 66 miles west of I-405 and turn right at a sign for Saddle Mountain State Park. The trailhead is 7 miles ahead, at the end of the road.

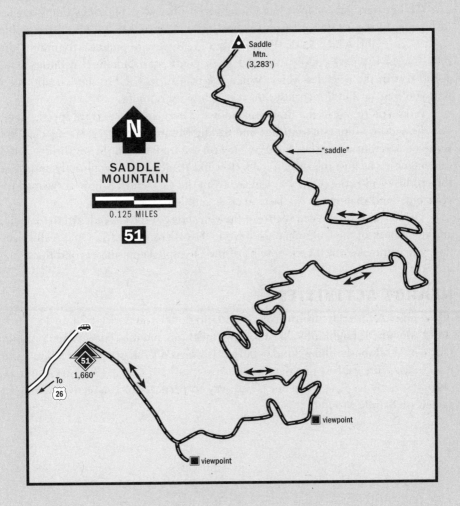

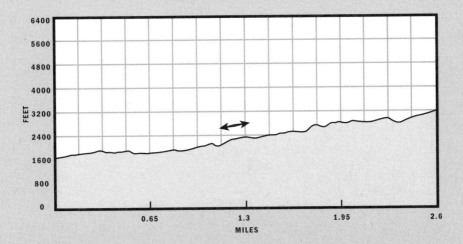

Things start out mellow, in a young forest filled with big, old stumps—relics of logging in the 1920s and fires in the 1930s. After 0.2 miles, you'll see a side trail to the right, which leads 0.1 mile to a great view of Saddle Mountain—the only one in the park, oddly enough. Then you'll start climbing, gaining about 1,100 feet in the next 1.4 miles. When the trail turns back to the left and stays flat, you'll be at 2,900 feet, just 300 feet below the summit.

Now you're out in the flower meadows. There are several rare species here, like the Saddle Mountain saxifrage and Saddle Mountain bittercress—species that survived here during the last Ice Age. Stay on the trail and on the footbridges, and remember it's against the rules to pick flowers. You'll drop down briefly and cross the saddle—this is the point you can see from the car, which is now very small on your left—and then climb the last, steep scramble to the summit.

On a clear day, you can see from the volcanoes of the Cascades to the Pacific, and the mouth of the Columbia just beyond Astoria to the north. On a really clear day, you can make out the mountains of the Olympic Peninsula beyond that.

NEARBY ACTIVITIES

A few miles before the turnoff from US 26, no doubt you noticed Camp 18. How could you not? It might look like a logging museum, and it is, but it's also a restaurant with a famously filling Sunday buffet. It's served from 10 a.m. to 2 p.m., and it includes prime rib! As one newspaper story put it, at Camp 18 "you can throw on one serious feedbag." It's not a bad way to prepare for (or recover from) an assault on Saddle Mountain.

TILLAMOOK HEAD

IN BRIEF

Hiking options abound among the scenic splendor of Tillamook Head and Ecola State Park. You can sample a beach stroll, dramatic viewpoints, and pieces of history on trail segments, and you're guaranteed to come home amazed. If you make the moderate hike up Tillamook Head, you can even follow in the footsteps of the Lewis and Clark expedition.

DESCRIPTION

If you were measuring great views per mile of walking, this would be the most efficient area you could visit. Just walking the easy, 3-mile round-trip from the picnic area to Indian Beach, you'll get several views of the rock-and-sand-and-water magnificence below. Do as much hiking as you feel up to here, and then kick back on a beach somewhere or stroll around Cannon Beach or Seaside.

First, a little history. On January 7, 1806, William Clark was on his way to see a beached whale the natives had told him about. He and 12 others, including Sacajawea, went over Tillamook Head (he humbly named it "Clark's Mountain") on a trail that forms the basis of

KEY AT-A-GLANCE INFORMATION

LENGTH: 3–7.8 miles

CONFIGURATION: Out-and-back or one-way with a car shuttle

DIFFICULTY: Easy–strenuous

SCENERY: Beaches, cliffs above the sea, historic lighthouse

EXPOSURE: Mostly in the shade

TRAFFIC: Use is heavy all summer, more so on weekends; it's moderate otherwise.

TRAIL SURFACE: Packed dirt with roots; year-round mud in some places

HIKING TIME: 1–5 hours

DRIVING DISTANCE: 80 miles (1 hour and 25 minutes) from Pioneer Square

SEASON: Year-round, but muddy in winter

ACCESS: To park at Indian Beach or the Ecola Picnic Area, there's a $3-per-vehicle day-use fee.

WHEELCHAIR ACCESS: Only the short trail from main parking area to the lookout in Ecola State Park.

MAPS: USGS Tillamook Head

FACILITIES: Trailheads at Ecola State Park and Indian Beach have toilets.

SPECIAL COMMENTS: For more information, call the Ecola State Park office at (503) 436-2844.

Directions

From Portland on US 26, travel 74 miles west of I-405 and turn south on US 101. Go 4 miles and take the first Cannon Beach exit. At the bottom of the hill, turn right, following a sign for Ecola State Park. (*Note:* To avoid paying the $3 fee and to add a couple of viewpoints to your day, park at the "park and ride" lot at the bottom of this hill, walk up the state park road 0.9 miles, and take a 1.1-mile trail on the left to the picnic area.) After driving up the road 2 miles, you'll come to the entrance booth. The picnic area is on the left, and Indian Beach is 1.5 miles to the right.

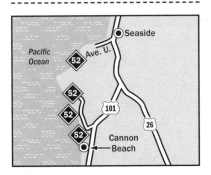

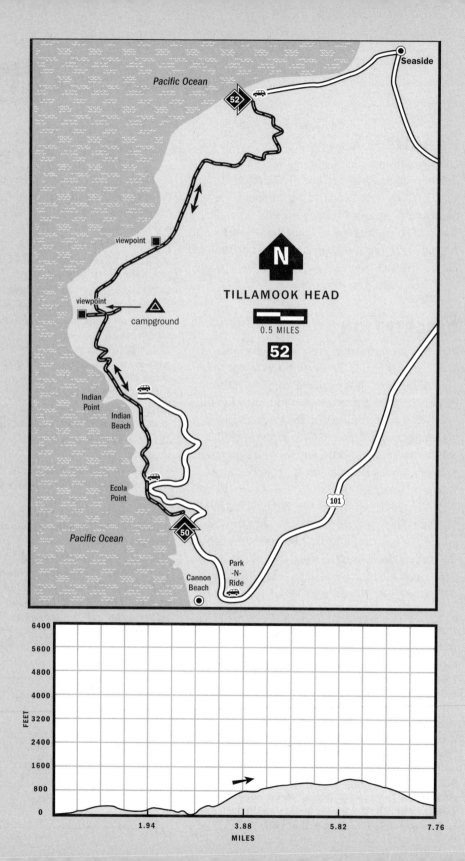

the modern-day path. Clark wrote of the view, "From this point I beheld the grandest and most pleasing prospects which my eyes ever surveyed." He also said the coast had "a most romantic appearance." From his description, it's fairly certain that the exact piece of land he stood on washed into the sea decades ago, but you can still experience pretty much the same view.

If you're wondering about the name Ecola, it comes from the local Indians' word for "whale," not anything to do with the deadly bacteria that sounds similar.

From the Ecola State Park picnic area, take a well-marked trail to the north. In its easy 1.5 miles it never gets far from the view, and at a couple of points it's right at the edge of the cliff—though with fences. When you get to Indian Beach, a favorite among surfers, go left and wander down to the sand for a bit.

The trail north of Indian Beach, tougher than the trail south of it, starts just beyond the restroom. After 100 yards, turn left onto a trail that starts climbing pretty quickly. You'll pass another view or two, but you'll also go through muddy patches. After 1.6 miles you'll come to an old road. Turn left for an ocean view from more than 700 feet up, and also to see a World War II–era bunker that housed radar equipment. The lighthouse—which, no matter what it looks like, is a full mile from the coast—was built in 1881 but decommissioned in 1957. It was called "Terrible Tilly" by the unfortunate souls who used to live out there and maintain the light. Strangely enough, in 1980 it was bought and converted into a repository for the ashes of cremated bodies. The owners make deliveries by helicopter.

Back up the road, turn right to head back to your car, or left for more forest and more views. Half a mile past the road, and after some switchback climbing, you'll come to a series of viewpoints out to the left, one of which is officially known as Clark's Point of View. Trouble is, a sign marking the spot tends to disappear, presumably tossed into the sea by yahoos.

The official summit of Tillamook Head is 1,130 feet above the sea and 1.5 miles north of this point. You'll be traveling through mixed forest with the usual views, but my recommendation is to turn back unless you have a car at the Seaside trailhead. At this point, you are 2.1 miles from Indian Beach, 3.6 miles from the picnic area, and 5.6 miles from Cannon Beach. If you did stash a car at Seaside, you're 2 miles from there. The trail will continue until the viewless summit, then switchback down for 1.7 miles to the trailhead.

NEARBY ACTIVITIES

Seaside is a beachside tourist town. It's worth a stroll, if only to choose from among all the fudge, corn-dog, and elephant-ear outlets on its "Million-Dollar Walk." If you're looking for a little history, there's a model of Lewis and Clark's saltworks (a stove to extract salt from seawater) in Seaside as well.

IN PORTLAND AND
THE WILLAMETTE VALLEY

53 | MACLEAY TRAIL

KEY AT-A-GLANCE INFORMATION

LENGTH: 2.2 miles to Upper Macleay Park; 4.5 miles to Pittock Mansion

CONFIGURATION: Out-and-back

DIFFICULTY: Easy to Upper Macleay Park and the Audubon Society; moderate to Pittock Mansion

SCENERY: Quiet woods, predatory birds (in cages), three must-see trees

EXPOSURE: Shady

TRAFFIC: Light use on the trail but moderate on weekends; heavy at the mansion

TRAIL SURFACE: Packed dirt with some gravel

HIKING TIME: 1 hour to the Audubon Society; 2.5 hours for the whole thing

DRIVING DISTANCE: 3 miles (10 minutes) from Pioneer Square

SEASON: Year-round

ACCESS: No fees or permits needed.

WHEELCHAIR ACCESS: The lower quarter mile is paved.

MAPS: USGS Portland

FACILITIES: Water and toilets at trailhead, Audubon Society and mansion

IN BRIEF

If you just take the easier trip to the Audubon Society, you'll get some quiet time in the woods, including two monumental trees, and close-up views of (caged) wildlife. If you put in a little more effort, you'll get that and some history with a great view—and another monumental tree. And it's all right in the middle of town!

DESCRIPTION

If the headquarters of the Forest Park Ivy Removal Project is open, it's worth a look inside. It has cleared hundreds of acres and saved thousands of trees in Forest Park from invasive English ivy, which creates "ivy deserts" where no native plants can survive. In this building the crews house some of their "trophies," ivy roots bigger than you can imagine such things being. Gawk, get some water, and head up the trail.

What you're walking up here is Balch Creek, named for the man who once owned this land—also the first man in Portland to be tried and hanged for murder. Small as it is, the creek was the original water supply for the city of Portland. As astounding as that may

Directions ⟶

From downtown Portland, drive 1 mile west on Burnside Street and turn right on NW 23rd Avenue. Proceed 0.8 miles and turn left on Thurman Street. Go six blocks to NW 28th Avenue and turn right. Go one block, turn left on NW Upshur, and follow it three blocks to the trailhead at the end of the road. This trailhead can also be reached via Tri-Met. From downtown, take the #15 bus (NW 23rd Avenue), but make sure it's headed for Thurman Street and not Montgomery Park. Get off at Thurman and 28th, walk one more block, and descend a flight of steps at the side of the bridge.

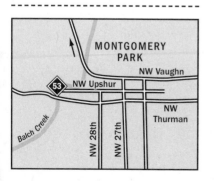

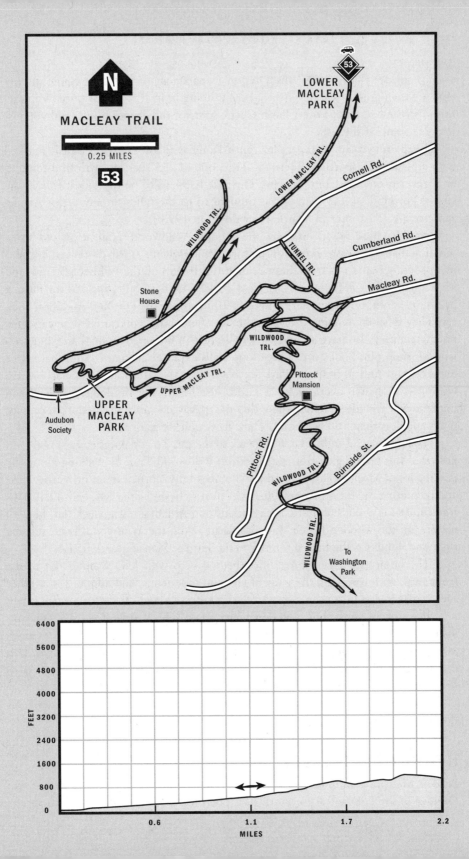

seem, consider that in 1987 the Oregon Department of Fish and Game discovered a native population of cutthroat trout living in it. It is one of only two year-round streams in all of Forest Park. Check some of the deeper pools, and you just may see some of the fish.

Keep an eye out, at 0.4 miles, for a Douglas fir on your left that is marked with a plaque as a Portland Heritage Tree, one of 235 such trees around town to be forever protected from the saw. This one happens to be the tallest tree in the city of Portland, at 241 feet, and is thought to be the tallest in any major American city. (A 255-footer in Seattle blew down in 1993.)

At 0.9 miles, you'll intersect the 30-mile Wildwood Trail at an old stone building that was a restroom until the early 1960s when a storm destroyed its pipes by uprooting numerous trees. Stay straight (upstream) on the Wildwood Trail, and after a half mile you'll come to Macleay Park. Whether you're headed for Pittock Mansion or not, turn right here and walk 100 yards to the Portland Audubon Society. They rehabilitate injured owls and hawks here, birds you can view in cages for no charge; they also have an extensive collection of mounted animals and an excellent gift shop plus bookstore. Three loop trails explore sanctuaries from here; free maps of those and all of Forest Park are available at the gift shop. Particularly worth visiting is a shelter overlooking a pond, just below the headquarters. You can impress your friends by telling them that the massive sequoia beside the parking lot is actually less than 100 years old. They grow quickly at first.

To just do a 2.2-mile hike, head back to the car. To add another 2.7 miles (and just over 400 feet in elevation), stay on the Wildwood Trail by walking along the parking lot of Macleay Park, crossing sometimes-busy Cornell Road on a crosswalk, and reentering the forest. After 100 yards, turn right on Upper Macleay Trail. This trail climbs for about 0.2 miles, then flattens out. At half a mile, check out the cool pattern on the wooden bench. Just past that, rejoin the Wildwood Trail, turning right and uphill for the final 0.6 miles to the Pittock Mansion parking lot.

The home (see Nearby Activities, below) is to your left. Wander out to the front yard, with roses and the view of city and mountains, and admire yet another spectacular tree: a European white birch that offers enough shade for a small town.

If you were on the bus, you don't have to walk back down the trail. You can, instead, walk down the road from the mansion to Burnside Street, about 0.3 miles away, cross over it (quickly), and take the #20 (Burnside) bus to downtown. You can also continue on the Wildwood Trail for 1 mile (and down 300 feet) to connect with the Washington Park–Hoyt Arboretum hike (see page 250).

For more information, contact the Portland Parks and Recreation office at (503) 823-7529.

NEARBY ACTIVITIES

Pittock Mansion, built in 1914 by the owner-publisher of the *Oregonian* and founder of the Portland Rose Festival, is open for tours daily.

MARQUAM TRAIL TO COUNCIL CREST · 54

IN BRIEF

This pleasant trail through a wooded canyon just minutes from downtown leads to the highest point in town, where you can take in a view of four volcanoes.

DESCRIPTION

Council Crest got its name in 1898 when a group of visiting ministers met there after a two-hour wagon drive. They assumed the locals must have held many a council there. In the early and mid-20th century you could ride a trolley to the top and visit an amusement park. Today you can get there by car or bus, but the best way is to walk up the Marquam Trail through a wooded canyon.

At the trailhead shelter, two signs lead you to the Marquam Trail. If you got a brochure and feel like adding the Nature Trail, take the path on the left that says 0.7 miles, instead of the one on the right that says 0.4 miles. This leads you 0.3 miles up the creek to a junction; here, turn right and enter the Nature Trail. Numbered signs along the way point out various local flora and fauna as you traverse back to the right on a flat 0.4-mile cutoff to the Marquam Trail, which leads to Council Crest.

KEY AT-A-GLANCE INFORMATION

LENGTH: 3.7 miles
CONFIGURATION: Out-and-back with a side loop
DIFFICULTY: Easy on the Nature Trail; moderate to Council Crest
SCENERY: Through the woods, past some impressive homes, and then a sweeping vista on top
EXPOSURE: Shady all the way up, open on top
TRAFFIC: Heavy on weekends and workday evenings but light otherwise
TRAIL SURFACE: Packed dirt and gravel
HIKING TIME: 2 hours
DRIVING DISTANCE: 1 mile (5 minutes) from Pioneer Square
SEASON: Year-round
ACCESS: No fees or permits needed.
WHEELCHAIR ACCESS: None
MAPS: USGS Portland; guides to the Nature Trail are available at the trailhead.
FACILITIES: Water at the trailhead and at Council Crest

Directions

From downtown Portland, drive south on Broadway Avenue. After it crosses Interstate 405, take the second right onto SW 6th Avenue, following the blue H signs leading to the hospital. (Don't take the right with the sign saying "Council Crest.") Stay straight through three lights in the next half mile, passing two large concrete water towers on your right. When the road cuts back to the left, turn right into a parking lot. You can also take Tri-Met bus #8 to the third light, Sam Jackson and Terwilliger, and walk 200 yards to the trailhead.

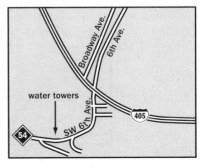

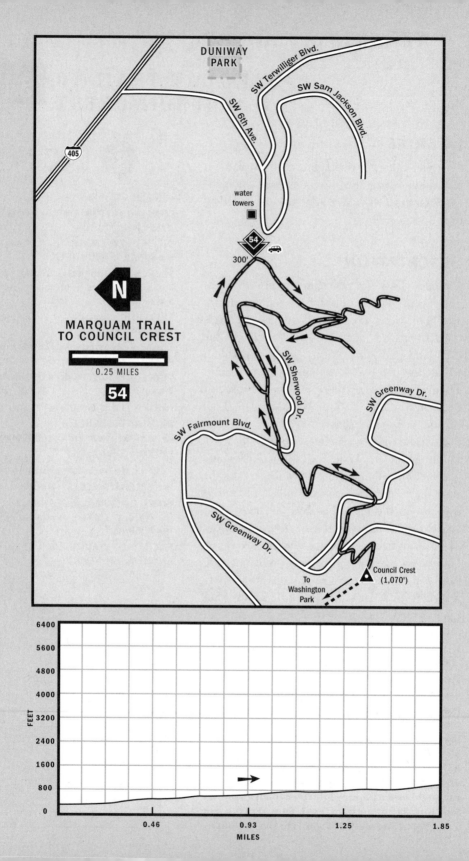

DUNIWAY PARK

SW Terwilliger Blvd.

SW Sam Jackson Blvd.

SW 6th Ave.

405

water towers

54

300'

N

MARQUAM TRAIL
TO COUNCIL CREST

0.25 MILES

54

SW Sherwood Dr.

SW Greenway Dr.

SW Fairmount Blvd.

SW Greenway Dr.

To Washington Park

Council Crest (1,070')

6400
5600
4800
4000
3200
2400
1600
800
0

FEET

0.46   0.93   1.25   1.85

MILES

At this junction, if you don't feel like going up the hill, stay right and you'll be back at the car in 0.4 miles (this is the right-hand trail you skipped at the trailhead). But for the best view in town, turn left and follow the trail up Marquam Gulch. You don't really need a map for this one, because you'll be following Council Crest signs at several junctions. The first is a right turn after 0.2 miles; the second is a left turn 0.6 miles later. At this point you'll start going uphill a bit. Just before you cross a road at the 1-mile mark, keep your eyes peeled for an extremely cool tree house on your left. Oh, to be a kid in a neighborhood like this!

After crossing yet another road, in an area planted decades ago with May-blooming rhododendrons, you'll come into the wide, open area atop Council Crest, where couples come to snuggle and kids come to throw the Frisbee. Take a moment on the two benches in front of you to admire the view of Mount Hood and the dates of the people the benches were dedicated to: They both made it to age 98 and died within a year of each other.

Now, go up to the stone circle at the top of the park. Plaques there point out the four volcanoes and give a native name for each. Also to the east you can see into the Columbia River Gorge. The view to the west goes out to Beaverton and, on a clear day, the Coast Range. For an odd, secret treat, find the small metal disc in the middle of this stone enclosure, stand on it and say, "Portland rocks."

You can connect this trail to the Washington Park hike, if you're up for something a little longer. As you start back down the trail, take a left just after you enter the trees, turning to the northwest. This trail will traverse the hill for a few minutes, then turn downhill and to the left, eventually reaching the intersection of Southwest Talbot and Southwest Fairmount. Walk down Talbot about 0.3 miles to the intersection with Southwest Patton. Cross Patton, then turn right onto it, and in 200 feet you'll see a trail heading down the hill to the left. Follow it 1 mile down through the forest until you reach an access road along US 26. Walk left 50 yards, cross the bridge over the expressway, then look on the left for a trail going up the hill, into the trees again. This will lead you through a meadow, behind the World Forestry Center, and eventually (in 0.2 miles or so) to an intersection with the Wildwood Trail. (This is also the end of the Marquam Trail.) Turn right on the Wildwood Trail, and in 0.1 mile you'll be at the parking lot; across that is the MAX station, where you can catch a train back to town.

To just go back from Council Crest, head back down the trail, following signs for Marquam Shelter, and after 1.3 miles, when you get to a junction pointing left 0.4 miles to Marquam Park, take it. That's the shorter route back to the car that you skipped earlier in favor of the Nature Trail.

For more information, contact the Portland Parks and Recreation office at (503) 823-7529.

NEARBY ACTIVITIES

If it's a Saturday between May and October, don't miss the Portland Farmer's Market at Portland State, just a few blocks north.

55 OAKS BOTTOM

KEY AT-A-GLANCE INFORMATION

LENGTH: 3 miles

CONFIGURATION: Loop

DIFFICULTY: Easy

SCENERY: Wildlife, woods, water, and even an amusement park

EXPOSURE: Shady for the most part, but occasionally in the open

TRAFFIC: Heavy use on weekends, moderate otherwise

TRAIL SURFACE: Packed dirt and gravel

HIKING TIME: 2 hours, but only because you'll want to bird-watch

DRIVING DISTANCE: 4 miles (10 minutes) from Pioneer Square

SEASON: Year-round, but it will get muddy in winter and spring.

ACCESS: No fees or permits needed.

WHEELCHAIR ACCESS: A paved loop is possible.

MAPS: USGS Lake Oswego; there's also a map on a sign at the trailhead.

FACILITIES: Water at the trailhead; restrooms and water along the way

SPECIAL COMMENTS: For more information, call the Portland Parks and Recreation office at (503) 823-7529.

IN BRIEF

The heart of this trail is essentially a viewing platform around the edge of a watery wildlife preserve. It's home to dozens of bird species, especially in spring and fall, and it couldn't be more conveniently located.

DESCRIPTION

It is so easy, when living in a city, to think that we are "here" and nature is out "there" somewhere, in the hills or on the coast. Occasionally you'll be walking down the street and see some Canada geese fly overhead, and you'll remember that nature is actually all around us. Whenever you need a reminder, just go down to Oaks Bottom.

Oaks Bottom is 160 acres of wildlife habitat just a few miles from downtown. It supports some 140 species of birds at various times of the year, especially in the spring and fall migration seasons. At any time of year you can expect to see herons and ducks, and if you're lucky, you might catch a glimpse of beavers, deer, cormorants, woodpeckers, ospreys, kingfishers, or bald eagles.

From the trailhead, walk downhill on a moderate grade. At 0.1 mile, you'll see a wide trail going into an open area to the right. This is a series of meadows between the main trail and the railroad tracks—actually landfill from

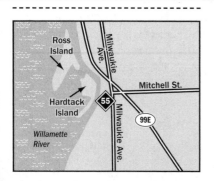

Directions ⟶

From downtown Portland, go south on Broadway Avenue and follow the signs for the Ross Island Bridge (US 26 East). After crossing the bridge, turn right at the first light (Milwaukie Avenue). Go south 1.1 mile on Milwaukie and park in the signed trailhead on the right, just past Mitchell Street. You can also take Tri-Met's #19 Woodstock bus from downtown to the trailhead.

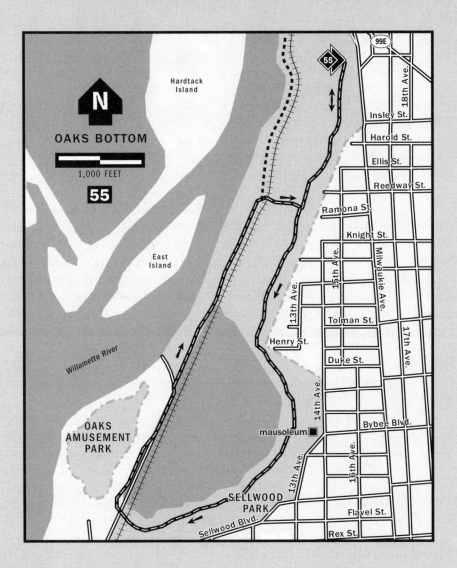

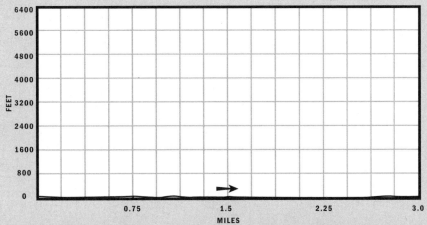

before this was a city park. Explore them in search of birds, or spread out a blanket for a picnic.

Back on the main trail, you'll reach a fork at 0.3 miles. The trail to the right leads under the railroad tracks and to a paved section of the Willamette River Trail (see page 253). Staying left at the fork, you'll pass through an area that was the subject of an ivy-removal project in 2000. English ivy, not native to the Pacific Northwest, has taken over many of Portland's parks, creating "ivy deserts" where no native plants can grow. So the city went in, removed ivy from this section, and planted native conifers, especially western red cedar, in an attempt to re-establish the native plants. You can judge for yourself how it worked.

The trail crosses a bridge and begins to skirt a marsh–meadow area (depending on the time of year) of alder, blackberry, dogwoods, and reed grass—and oaks, of course. After a few minutes you'll come to Oaks Bottom proper, a large pond that was part of the Willamette River before the construction of the railroad cut it off from the main river in the late 19th century. What is now the park was used as a dumping ground for asphalt and other construction materials. But the area was purchased by the city in 1969 and turned into a wildlife-reclamation area. The pond is best viewed in spring and late fall, when the maximum amount of water is present—both in the pond and on the trail, by the way. Wear sturdy boots and bring binoculars. At all times of the year, look for great blue herons standing still in the water, awaiting a meal, and in the summer, Canada geese swooping in for a landing on their way north or south.

When the trail reaches the end of the lake, one branch cuts off to the right and heads for Oaks Amusement Park (see Nearby Activities, below). Another continues straight ahead to a trailhead at the southern end of the park. A third, the smallest one, climbs a small hill to the left to Sellwood Park, where there are water fountains and restrooms. Turn right here and head toward the amusement park, then consider making a loop out of it by turning right on the paved trail along the railroad tracks. In just less than a mile, you'll see the underpass leading to the right and back toward your trailhead. There's also, on your left, an interesting area of artwork in the woods.

Remember to be thankful for your little reminder that Mother Nature isn't always that far away.

NEARBY ACTIVITIES

If you hear the screams of children coming from across the pond, don't call 911 on your cell phone; it's just Oaks Amusement Park, in continuous operation since 1905. They've got all the midway thrill rides, the Northwest's oldest skating rink, and a kids' area.

SAUVIE ISLAND 56

IN BRIEF

Two casual strolls on the edge of the city offer a glimpse into the local world of wildlife—and back into the past. Both of them are easy to reach and easy to do, and there's plenty of other stuff to do on the island while you're out there.

DESCRIPTION

First, let's go to Oak Island, which is actually a peninsula in a lake on an island in a river.

Some hikes are in the wilderness, some are walks through history, some are educational, some offer a distant view. This one feels like just being out in the country. You'll even skirt a couple of crops! The whole scene might remind you of visiting your grandparents in the country. But even the crops are part of a plan

---

Directions ————————➤

From Portland on US 30, drive 10 miles west of I-405 and turn right to cross the Sauvie Island Bridge. The Sauvie Island Market (where you buy your parking pass) is on your left, 0.1 mile beyond the far end of the bridge. Go 2 more miles and turn right on Reeder Road.

FOR OAK ISLAND: After 1.3 miles on Reeder Road, turn left onto Oak Island Road—but since Reeder goes off to the right here, it's more like keeping straight. After 1.9 miles you'll leave the pavement, and 0.8 miles later you'll cross a dike. At the bottom of the dike, go straight; the trailhead is 0.4 miles ahead at the end of the road.

FOR WARRIOR ROCK: After 10 miles on Reeder Road, you'll leave the pavement and come to a series of parking areas for Welton Beach, just over the dike to your right. Past that is parking for Collins Beach, which happens to be clothing-optional but is blocked from the road by forest. At 2.3 miles after you left the pavement, the road ends at the parking area for Warrior Rock.

KEY AT-A-GLANCE INFORMATION

LENGTH: 3 miles for Oak Island, 7 miles for Warrior Rock

CONFIGURATION: Oak Island is a loop; Warrior Rock is out-and-back.

DIFFICULTY: Easy

SCENERY: Lakeshore, woods, meadows, beaches, and birds

EXPOSURE: Oak Island is mostly open; Warrior Rock is mostly wooded.

TRAFFIC: Use is moderate on summer weekends, light otherwise

TRAIL SURFACE: Packed dirt and grass, some beach

HIKING TIME: 1 hour for Oak Island, 3 hours for Warrior Rock

DRIVING DISTANCE: Oak Island is 19 miles (30 minutes) from Pioneer Square; Warrior Rock is 22 miles (45 minutes).

SEASON: Oak Island is open April 16– September 30; Warrior Rock is open year-round.

ACCESS: A parking pass is required for all of Sauvie Island. Buy a $3 day pass at the Sauvie Island Market.

WHEELCHAIR ACCESS: None

MAPS: USGS St Helens; get a free hiking map at the Sauvie Island Market.

FACILITIES: There's an outhouse at each trailhead; the nearest water is at the Sauvie Island Market

SPECIAL COMMENTS: Sauvie Island Information Center, (503) 621-3488.

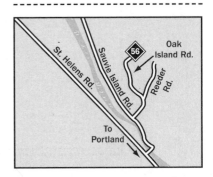

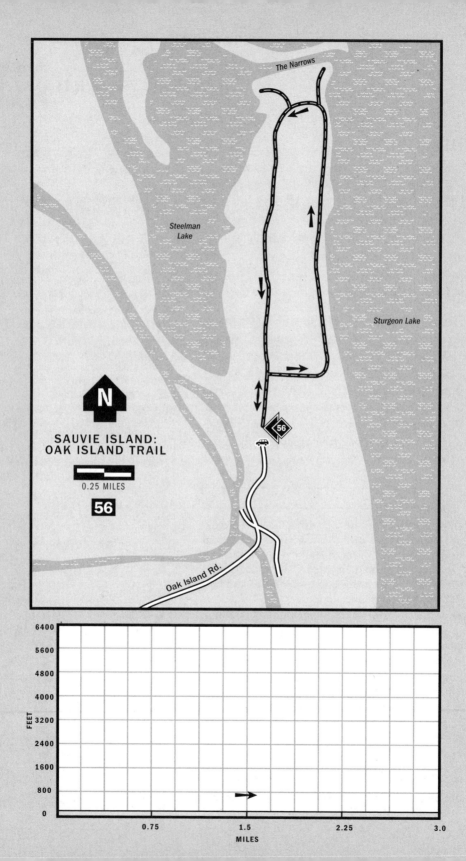

The Narrows

Steelman
Lake

Sturgeon Lake

N

SAUVIE ISLAND:
OAK ISLAND TRAIL

0.25 MILES

56

56

Oak Island Rd.

6400
5600
4800
4000
3200
FEET
2400
1600
800
0

0.75   1.5   2.25   3.0
MILES

by the Oregon Department of Fish and Wildlife to manage waterfowl in this area—and waterfowl are what Oak Island is all about.

Sauvie Island (named for a French-Canadian employee of the Hudson's Bay Company) has, for thousands of years, been a resting place for migratory birds. At the peak of the fall migration, some 150,000 ducks and geese are here. Several thousand sandhill cranes come, as well. In all, some 250 species of birds spend some amount of time on the island each year, including bald eagles by the score in the winter. So if you were to go to Oak Island in the middle of a summer day, you might wonder what the big deal is. But if you come in the spring, or early on a summer day when the animals haven't hidden from the heat yet, you just might see a whole different world. And in fact, even though the bulk of the migratory birds are gone when the trail is open, there are numerous songbirds here, as well as ducks, geese, and even bald eagles who spend the whole summer.

From the trailhead, you walk a few minutes on the mowed roadway-trail to a junction. Be sure to grab a guide from the box; it corresponds to several signs around the trail. Go either way you wish, or strike off into the grassy meadows or woods. If you stay on the trail, going right will take you to a view of Sturgeon Lake, which at some times of the year might be a long way off because it's so shallow. Turn left here and in 0.9 miles, when the signed trail turns left, follow another trail to the right, 200 yards to The Narrows, a—you guessed it—narrow body of water that connects Sturgeon Lake to the east with Steelman Lake to the west.

Continuing on the loop trail, you'll head back to the left and walk along a plowed area; Fish and Wildlife actually farms some 1,000 acres of its land on Sauvie Island as part of a cycle that brings alfalfa, corn, millet, and other foods to migratory birds in the winter and cattle in the summer.

And now for the other stroll—Warrior Rock.

In the fall of 1805 Lewis and Clark's Corps of Discovery floated down the Columbia River and managed to miss the Willamette River entirely. It wasn't that they were fools; it's just that the Willamette's entry was blocked from view by the forested wetland which is now called Sauvie Island. While much of it has long since been diked, and some is now farmed, about half of it is managed by the Oregon Department of Fish and Wildlife.

Lewis and Clark, while exploring the island that was the summer and fall home of the Multnomah Indians, camped on the beach that is just beyond the parking area. If for some reason you would like to skip the beach entirely, walk over a low point in the fence at the southern end of the parking lot, then walk through the pasture, parallel to the river, to the trees. You'll find the road there.

To start on the beach, follow the trail out onto it and stroll along, considering what it must have looked like in 1805, but also how quiet it is today. Look also for animal tracks leading from the woods to the water; raccoons, deer, and fox are all common here. But those critters move around mostly at night, and if the hunters and fishermen aren't out, you may have the place to yourselves.

If it's late summer or early fall when the river is low, you can make it almost the whole 3 miles to the lighthouse on Warrior Rock just staying on the beach. Otherwise, go as far as you want, and then look for a place to head up into the woods. Once up on the bluff, you will encounter a trail that once served as a service road to the lighthouse. Follow it through a world of blackberries, oak, alder, and maple. After about 2.5 miles, at a point where the trail is right at the top of the bluff, look to the right for an old shipwreck on the beach. Just a few minutes later, you'll come to a large meadow; stay right for 0.2 miles to the lighthouse.

Warrior Rock got its name when members of a 1792 English expedition up the Columbia (the party that named the river for their ship and Mount Hood for the head of the English navy) found themselves surrounded on this rock by dozens of native warriors. They made peace and lived to tell the tale. The lighthouse was maintained by the U.S. Coast Guard to warn ships of the rock. And speaking of ships, there's a decent chance you'll see an oceangoing vessel making its way roughly 70 river miles from Portland to the Pacific Ocean at Astoria.

A hundred yards up the sandy beach to the left, somebody cut a perfect little bench into a large piece of driftwood; with any luck, the river will not have reclaimed it before you get there. A few minutes beyond that, at the northwestern tip of Sauvie Island, you'll come to old pilings which no one seems able to explain. Leading theories are it was a fish processing plant, a boat works, or a loading dock for shipping milk from island dairies. Whatever it was, it offers a viewpoint of the town of Saint Helens, Oregon, which was founded in 1845—and in case you're wondering why the town and the nearby mountain are called Saint Helens, well, the same English sailors who named Hood and the Columbia named Mount Saint Helens for the English ambassador to Spain at the time, a certain Baron Saint Helens. His real name was Fitzherbert; thank goodness they chose his official name.

Nothing like some useless trivia to think about while you're walking back to the car. And speaking of which, if you stay on the trail all the way, you'll come to the cow pasture above the beach where you started. Just walk across it—careful where you step—to the fenced parking area and step over the low portion of the fence to your right, next to the hunters' check-in stand.

And, for the record, Lewis and Clark saw the Willamette on the way home, in the spring of 1806. Clark stood on a bluff where the University of Portland is today.

NEARBY ACTIVITIES

Many of the farms on Sauvie Island are "you pick 'em" operations, with treats like berries, flowers, pumpkins, and corn. One of them, on Reeder Road, has a corn maze (or a maize maze). You can't miss it. Stop and get a little something for dinner on your way home, if you don't get lost. Also, the 1856 Bybee-Howell House, the oldest home in Multnomah County, is now a museum including farm implements from the old days. It's open weekends from June 3 through September 3.

SILVER FALLS STATE PARK

IN BRIEF

If it's waterfalls you're after—especially the chance to get behind them—this is the hike of your dreams. It's an easy loop that's known as the Trail of Ten Falls. There are also shorter loops available, all of which take in views of one or more waterfalls.

DESCRIPTION

This is the crown jewel of the Oregon State Parks system; it's also the most visited park in the state. Unless it's a rainy weekday in the winter, you probably won't be close to alone here, but it hardly matters. It's one of the finest walks around, especially if you're into waterfalls. By the way, Silver Creek was named not for its color but for a pioneer who settled here in the 1840s. He was known as "Silver" Smith because it was said he brought a bushel of silver dollars with him from back east.

Be sure to visit the South Falls Lodge, 0.1 mile from the parking lot. It was built of native stone and wood by the Civilian Conservation Corps (CCC) in 1941. You can warm yourself by two massive fireplaces, enjoy photos of the park and some of the tools used by the CCC, and take advantage of that most modern of conveniences: a snack bar with espresso stand.

KEY AT-A-GLANCE INFORMATION

LENGTH: Up to 7 miles

CONFIGURATION: Loop

DIFFICULTY: Easy

SCENERY: Every type of waterfall in a forested canyon

EXPOSURE: Shady all the way

TRAFFIC: Heavy spring and summer, moderate–light otherwise

TRAIL SURFACE: Pavement, gravel, dirt

HIKING TIME: 3 hours to hike it all

DRIVING DISTANCE: 61 miles (1 hour and 30 minutes) from Pioneer Square

SEASON: Year-round, but wet in winter and spring with occasional snow

ACCESS: $3 day-use fee per vehicle

WHEELCHAIR ACCESS: Much of the recommended loop is not accessible, but some falls are, as are many other trails. Call the park for more info.

MAPS: USGS Drake Crossing; free maps are available in the South Falls Lodge at the trailhead.

FACILITIES: Water, restrooms, snack bar, and gift shop at the trailhead

SPECIAL COMMENTS: Dogs, even on a leash, are not allowed on this loop, though they're welcome on other trails in the park. For more information, contact the Silver Falls State Park office at (503) 873-8681.

Directions

From Portland on I-5, drive 17 miles south of I-205 and take Exit 271/Woodburn. Turn left and follow OR 214 for 14 miles to Silverton. Note that you'll be turning right at 2.7 miles, then left at 3.9 miles. Both intersections have signs, but they could still be missed. In Silverton, follow signs for Silver Falls State Park, staying on OR 214 for 15 more miles. After entering the park, continue on OR 214 for 2.3 miles and park on the right at the South Falls parking area.

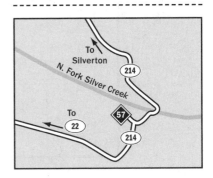

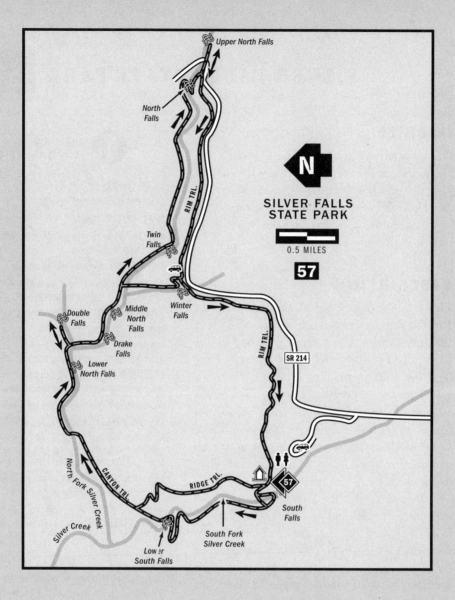

Upper North Falls

North Falls

RIM TRL.

N

SILVER FALLS
STATE PARK

0.5 MILES

57

Twin Falls

Double Falls

Middle North Falls

Winter Falls

Drake Falls

RIM TRL.

SR 214

Lower North Falls

North Fork Silver Creek

CANYON TRL.

RIDGE TRL.

Silver Creek

Lower South Falls

South Fork Silver Creek

57

South Falls

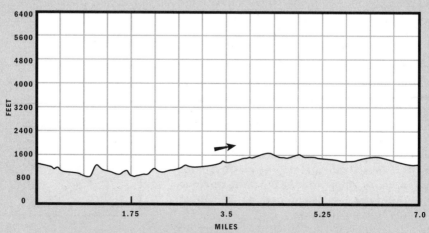

With your hot drink in hand, walk toward 177-foot South Falls, take in the view from the top, and contemplate the fact that in the 1920s a man used to send old automobiles over the falls as a Fourth of July stunt. It's said that fishermen pulled car parts out of the pool for decades. Now, take the trail behind the sign. (Note: This is as far as your dogs can go, even if they're on a leash.) The trail will switchback down for 0.2 miles, then go behind South Falls. The cavelike setting was created over the millennia, when water seeped through the rocks above, froze and expanded, and then cracked away the rocks that now lie at your feet.

When the trail comes to a bridge 100 yards later, you can cross it and make it a day with a 0.6-mile loop. It's the first of several opportunities to cut the loop short. But keep going for 0.7 miles to see 93-foot Lower South Falls. Just before you start down to it on the main trail, you'll see a trail plunging down to the right; that one goes to the top of the falls, but beware that there's no rail to keep you from a fearsome fall. The main trail descends a number of steps, often wet even in summer, and passes behind Lower South Falls, a combination of curtain and cascade falls.

In 0.2 miles you'll come to your second chance to cut the loop short. Turn right, and it's 1 mile along the Ridge Trail back to the lodge; stay straight, and it's 0.7 miles to Lower North Falls, a 30-foot slide. At this point you've left the South Fork of Silver Creek for the North Fork; the two combine downstream of you to form Silver Creek—this is why you're suddenly walking upstream rather than down. (I like to pose this "mystery" to follow hikers, to see who's paying attention.) Keep an eye out for deer and beaver, both of which live in the park. Human tree-cutters left their mark, too; on some of the big cedar stumps you can still make out springboard slots, where loggers stood to cut the trees by hand.

Just past Lower North Falls, make sure to go left for a 0.1-mile side trip to see Double Falls, at 178 feet. Its shallow splash pool, which you can get in if you'd like, almost always hosts a rainbow when the sun is out. Back on the main trail, in the next 0.4 miles, you'll pass 27-foot Drake Falls (named for a photographer whose images were instrumental in the creation of the park), and 103-foot Middle North Falls, which you can almost go behind. When you get to a bridge (the halfway point for the full loop), you can turn right for one last chance to cut the loop short. Take this trail for 0.3 miles to Winter Falls, and then continue past it; turn right onto the Rim Trail for 1.2 miles back to the lodge, and your day is done at 4.2 miles.

If you ignore the bridge and stay straight, in 0.3 miles you'll come to 31-foot Twin Falls, which at low-water times of the year is just one falls, but which does have the hike's best picnic spot, right at the creek's edge. After another 0.9 miles (look for the rocks in the creek with ferns growing on top!), you come to North Falls, which you'll see coming for a while before you get there and which is probably the most spectacular falls in the park. Once again, the trail takes you behind the falls. Back there, look for the columns in the rock overhead, left when lava cooled around trees and then the trees rotted—15 million years ago!

Lower South Falls, behind which the Canyon Trail goes at Silver Falls State Park

After that, climb up some steps, then along a railing with another view back down to North Falls. When you get to the Rim Trail on the right, go ahead and put in the 0.4-mile loop to Upper North Falls, a seldom-visited 65-foot drop in an area with ample opportunity to wander around on the rocks.

On the Rim Trail's 2.3-mile trip back to the lodge, you'll pass by the top of Winter Falls (more of a damp spot in the late summer and fall, but worth dropping down to) and through some pleasant forest where I have encountered deer on three occasions. When you get to the picnic area, stay straight on a nice, new trail, and you'll be back at the lodge in no time. I recommend another coffee drink.

NEARBY ACTIVITIES

Just upstream from the parking area, there's an official swimming area in Silver Creek. The kids will love it, and if it's a hot day, grown-ups could probably use a dip in the creek as well. The park also has cabins you can rent for the night, and horses are available for rent from May to September.

TRYON CREEK STATE PARK 58

IN BRIEF

Tryon Creek—Oregon's only state park in a major city—is the kind of place you want to come to over and over, just to see what's going on. Are the steelhead in? Are the fall colors hitting yet? Are the trilliums blooming? Any beavers around?

DESCRIPTION

An iron company logged this whole area in the 1880s to provide fuel for their smelter, so what you see today is what's known as second-growth forest. But that shouldn't sound like it's a second-class forest; if nothing else, some of those old tree trunks are amazing! Tryon Creek, a 645-acre park in a ravine between Portland and Lake Oswego, hosts 50 species of birds plus deer, beaver, fox, and a winter steelhead trout run. There have even been sightings of coyote, badger, and bobcat.

Numerous hiking options start at the Nature Center, so pick up a free map and make your own way, or call the park for a schedule of ranger-led activities. For our suggested loop, when you come out of the Nature Center, turn left, walk past the Jackson Shelter, and start on the Maple Ridge Trail. As the name implies, this area is home to many vine maples, which put on quite a red and orange show in the fall.

After 0.2 miles, take a right onto the Middle Creek Trail and descend 0.2 miles to

KEY AT-A-GLANCE INFORMATION

LENGTH: The loop described here is 3.25 miles; there are 8 miles of hiking trails in the park.

CONFIGURATION: Loop

DIFFICULTY: Easy

SCENERY: A woodsy ravine with a creek, lots of springtime wildflowers

EXPOSURE: Shady

TRAFFIC: Heavy on weekends, moderate otherwise

TRAIL SURFACE: Packed dirt, gravel

HIKING TIME: 1 hour for this loop

DRIVING DISTANCE: 6 miles (15 minutes) from Pioneer Square

SEASON: Year-round

ACCESS: No fees or permits needed.

WHEELCHAIR ACCESS: The Trillium Trail offers several barrier-free loops and viewpoints of the forest.

MAPS: Free maps are available at the park's Nature Center.

FACILITIES: Water and toilets are available at the Nature Center.

SPECIAL COMMENTS: For more information, call the Tryon Creek State Park office at (503) 636-9886. The nonprofit Friends of Tryon Creek puts on numerous events in the park, from day camps to nighttime hikes to classes and lectures. To find out what's going on, call (503) 636-4398.

Directions

From Portland, drive south on I-5 for 3 miles and take Exit 297/Terwilliger. Turn right at the end of the ramp, then take the first right onto Terwilliger Boulevard. Stay on Terwilliger for 2.5 miles; the main entrance to the park is on the right.

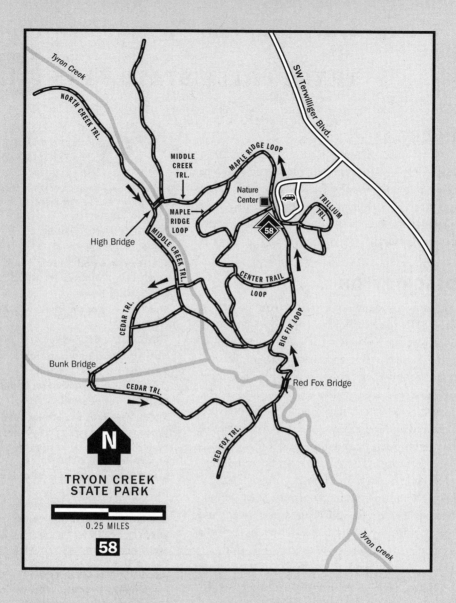

Tyron Creek

NORTH CREEK TRL.

SW Terwilliger Blvd.

MIDDLE
CREEK
TRL.

MAPLE RIDGE LOOP

Nature
Center

TRILLIUM TRL.

MAPLE
RIDGE
LOOP

High Bridge

MIDDLE CREEK TRL.

CENTER TRAIL LOOP

CEDAR TRL.

BIG FIR LOOP

Bunk Bridge

CEDAR TRL.

Red Fox Bridge

RED FOX TRL.

N

**TRYON CREEK
STATE PARK**

0.25 MILES

58

Tyron Creek

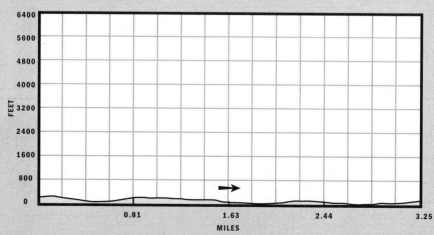

cross Tryon Creek at High Bridge. It's worth it to turn right here and explore up the 0.4-mile North Creek Trail, if only for the astonishing fields of impatiens (also known as jewelweed) and a few places to access the creek, one of them a deep pool at a bend. Return to the Middle Creek Trail and follow it 0.2 miles to an intersection with the Cedar Trail. Follow this trail to the right as it crosses a horse trail (careful where you step!) and then climbs briefly into a more open forest. Keep an eye out for a downed cedar trunk on the right that has obviously been explored by many an adventuresome child.

The Cedar Trail crosses the Bunk Bridge, then continues 0.8 miles to a junction with the Red Fox Trail. Turn left here and cross the Red Fox Bridge; if it's winter, keep an eye out for spawning steelhead. Climb briefly to the Old Main Trail, and then turn right and follow it back to the Nature Center.

NEARBY ACTIVITIES

The Original Pancake House, founded in 1953, is located not far away at 8601 SW 24th Avenue. A third-generation family business that has spawned more than 80 franchises in 22 states, this one won the 1999 James Beard America's Regional Classics Award. Go there, get an apple pancake or a Dutch boy, and know what breakfast can truly be.

59 WASHINGTON PARK– HOYT ARBORETUM

KEY AT-A-GLANCE INFORMATION

LENGTH: 4 miles

CONFIGURATION: Loop

DIFFICULTY: Easy

SCENERY: 950 species and varieties of plants, with labels on more than 5,000 trees and shrubs

EXPOSURE: Shady, with the occasional open spot for city views or contemplation

TRAFFIC: Use is heavy on weekends but moderate during the workday or when the weather is inclement.

TRAIL SURFACE: Pavement, packed dirt, gravel

HIKING TIME: 2 hours for the recommended loop

DRIVING DISTANCE: 2 miles (5 minutes) from Pioneer Square

SEASON: Year-round

ACCESS: No fees or permits needed.

WHEELCHAIR ACCESS: There are several barrier-free trails in the area; ask at the visitor center for details.

MAPS: The Hoyt Arboretum Visitor Center offers a trail guide.

FACILITIES: Water and restrooms are available throughout the park.

SPECIAL COMMENTS: For more information, contact the Portland Parks and Recreation office at (503) 823-7529.

IN BRIEF

A family could spend a weekend in Washington Park and never run out of things to do. The park has a zoo, a children's museum, the World Forestry Center, the Oregon Vietnam Veterans Memorial, a world-class Japanese garden, the Hoyt Arboretum, and miles of hiking trails. TriMet runs a shuttle bus that connects it all. The loop described here is only a suggestion.

DESCRIPTION

This loop hike can be your base for exploring and an introduction to all that Washington Park has to offer. From a hiker's perspective, the heart of the park is Hoyt Arboretum (literally meaning "tree museum"), founded in 1928 on land that was completely clear-cut in the early 20th century. Be sure to stop in the visitor center (which is on this loop) for one of its helpful maps.

Beginning your walk at the Oregon Vietnam Veterans Memorial, follow the trail under and then across the bridge and through a circular series of memorials describing events at home and in Southeast Asia from 1959 to

---

Directions

The best way to get to this trailhead is actually to take the Max Light Rail. It takes you from downtown to the deepest transit station in North America (260 feet—second deepest in the world) with artwork and displays on the geological history of the region. An elevator puts you right next to the World Forestry Center. To drive from downtown Portland, head west on US 26 and take Exit 72/Zoo after 1.3 miles. At the end of the ramp, turn right on SW Canyon Road. Then stay to the left, circling the parking lot, and turn left at the MAX station. The trailhead is at the Vietnam Veterans Memorial on your left 0.1 mile later. Driving time is 5 minutes.

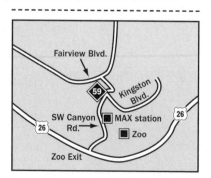

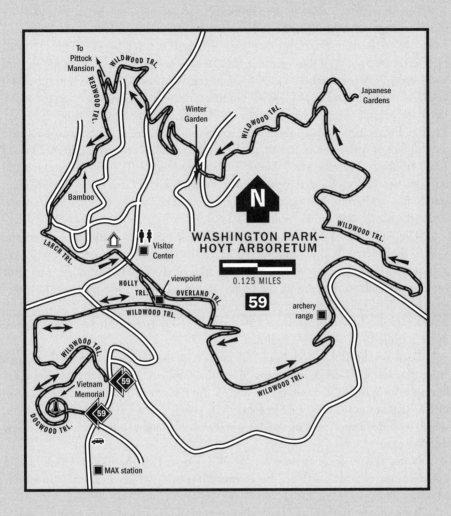

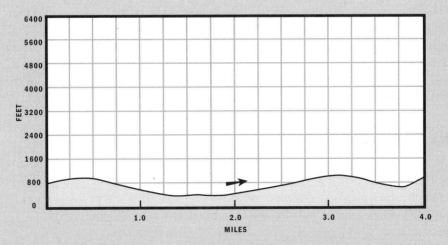

1972. At this point, you're in the arboretum—specifically, on the Dogwood Trail. (Each arboretum trail is named for the trees that dominate it.) Follow the Dogwood Trail out of the memorial, and then turn left onto the Wildwood Trail. (To your right is the beginning of this "wonder trail" that wanders through Washington Park and Forest Park for some 30 miles. Stay on the Wildwood Trail for 0.4 miles as it circles to the right and climbs a small hill to a viewpoint between two water towers. Look for Mount Saint Helens and Mount Rainier, and then turn left on the Holly Trail and walk 100 yards to the visitor center, where there's water, restrooms, and a mountain of information. Return to the viewpoint and turn left on the Wildwood Trail. In about 200 feet you'll come to the Magnolia Trail on the left; take it 0.3 miles to the Winter Garden if you'd like to cut about 1.6 miles off your hike and stay in the arboretum. For a pleasant, woodsy stroll and access to other Washington Park attractions, stay on the Wildwood Trail.

The wide, flat Wildwood Trail loops out for 1.5 miles, with access along the way to the Cherry, Walnut, and Maple Trails. At the 1.2-mile mark, you will have a view down to the right at the waterfall area of the Japanese garden; just after that a trail leads to the garden, the largest in the world outside Japan and a must-see. Just down a hill beyond that is the International Rose Test Garden, with 8,000 rose bushes in more than 550 varieties. Did I mention you could spend quite a while in Washington Park?

Back on the Wildwood Trail, 0.3 miles past the Japanese Garden Trail, you enter the Winter Garden, where the Magnolia Trail cutoff re-enters. Just 0.6 miles later on the Wildwood Trail, take a left on the Redwood Trail for an exploration of the sequoia collection. Just beyond that, you'll enter the redwood collection, which includes a specimen of the dawn redwood, thought to be extinct until a few decades ago.

Note: If you were to stay on the Wildwood Trail here, you would add a 2.4-mile out-and-back trip to the Pittock Mansion, which is at the top of the Macleay Trail (see page 230).

Back on the Redwood Trail, when you come to a trail on the right marked "To Creek Trail," take that, and you'll be in the middle of the bamboo collection. From redwoods to bamboo—culture shock is now a possibility. The Creek Trail dead-ends at a road; pick up the Redwood Trail at the far side, and you'll pass through the larch collection on your way to the picnic shelter. Cross the road, and you're back at the visitor center. Turn right, take the Holly Trail back to the Wildwood Trail, turn right on it, and follow it a half mile back to your car.

NEARBY ACTIVITIES

Of all the attractions in Washington Park, the Children's Museum is the newest and hottest. It opened at this location in 2001 and features hands-on exhibits in a "center for creativity, designed for kids age 6 months through 12 years old." Kids can climb, swim, toss balls, and even produce a movie there.

WILLAMETTE RIVER 60

IN BRIEF

Take a tour of central Portland and the Willamette River on a series of interconnected paved walkways. You can piece this one together on different days, mixing in tourist activities, or do it all in a pleasant day of wandering.

DESCRIPTION

Portland is so cool. Whether it's tearing out a major road and replacing with it a park, or building a floating walkway in the middle of downtown, the city just takes care of its walkers.

Here's a loop through downtown and the area to the south that takes in river views, hustle and bustle, entertainment, education, and even some solitude. There are numerous places to start, but I've decided to start at the west end (downtown side) of the Hawthorne Bridge—for the simple reasons that it's my favorite bridge in town and the park just to the south of it is a great place to be. How many downtowns have Canada geese hanging out in them?

The big platform on the south side of the bridge has a great view of the boats at RiverPlace, as well as a sign talking about Tom McCall Waterfront Park, which stretches from here north to the Steel Bridge. In the early 20th century, a plan was proposed to make this

Directions ⟶

There are numerous ways to access this hike. A parking lot between SE Madison and Salmon streets, with entrances at Main and Salmon, requires payment for parking. The easiest way to access it is via public transit. From downtown Portland, take bus #4, #10, or #14 on SW Fifth Avenue and get off at SW Madison and First Avenue, then walk one block toward the river.

ⓘ KEY AT-A-GLANCE INFORMATION

LENGTH: Anything up to 11 miles

CONFIGURATION: Loop

DIFFICULTY: Easy

SCENERY: Condos and cormorants, high-rises and herons, bridges and beavers, boats and butterflies . . .

EXPOSURE: Open most of the way, occasionally in the shade, with one mildly nerve-racking bridge crossing

TRAFFIC: Use is heavy on summer weekends and after work on a nice day, moderate otherwise.

TRAIL SURFACE: Paved

HIKING TIME: 5 hours

DRIVING DISTANCE: 7 blocks (a 5-minute walk) from Pioneer Square

SEASON: Year-round

ACCESS: No fees or passes required, but you'll probably pay to park.

WHEELCHAIR ACCESS: All of it

FACILITIES: Water and toilets at numerous locations

MAPS: There's no good map of the whole thing (other than in this book). Find a map of Waterfront Park and the Eastbank Esplanade at www .parks.ci.portland.oregon.us.

SPECIAL COMMENTS: Portland Parks and Recreation, (503) 823-7529

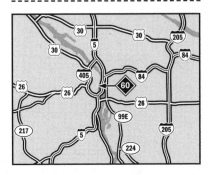

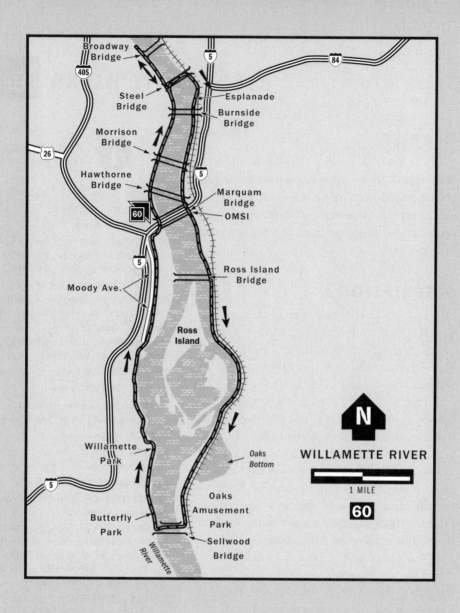

Broadway
Bridge

405

Steel
Bridge

Morrison
Bridge

26

Hawthorne
Bridge

5

60

5

Moody Ave.

Esplanade

Burnside
Bridge

5

Marquam
Bridge

OMSI

Ross Island
Bridge

Ross
Island

Willamette
Park

Butterfly
Park

Oaks
Bottom

Oaks
Amusement
Park

Sellwood
Bridge

Willamette
River

5

84

N

WILLAMETTE RIVER

1 MILE

60

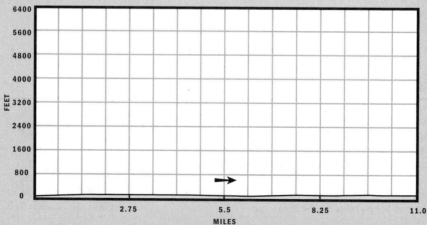

FEET

6400
5600
4800
4000
3200
2400
1600
800
0

2.75   5.5   8.25   11.0

MILES

a waterfront park, but in the 1920s a seawall was built to control floods, and then Harbor Drive was built in the 1940s. But when the Marquam (I-5) Bridge opened in 1966, Harbor Drive was made obsolete. So Governor Tom McCall proposed a public open space to go there, and that park opened in 1978. The city named it for McCall in 1984.

There are restrooms under the Hawthorne Bridge, if you need them; otherwise, walk north, dodging joggers and bikers and enjoying the summertime festivals, if one is going on. You'll also pass by Salmon Street Springs, which usually has kids romping in it.

Look, on the left, for the battleship *Oregon* Memorial, built in 1956 to honor an 1893 ship nicknamed "the Bulldog of the United States Navy." On July 4, 1976, a time capsule was sealed in the base of the memorial; it's set to be opened July 5, 2076. Look also for The Founders' Stone, which honors Portland's founders (William Pettygrove and Asa Lovejoy), who tossed a coin to decide whether the new town would be named New Boston or Portland (for the city in Maine). You'll also see the Oregon Maritime Center and Museum, housed in the sternwheeler *Portland.*

Under the Burnside Bridge and one block to the left, you can hit Saturday Market, open weekends from March through Christmas, for food and handmade crafts. You can also cross the river by taking a flight of steps located in the market onto the bridge. Just before the Steel Bridge, you'll come to the Japanese American Historical Plaza and its wonderful cherry trees. Come here in March and be amazed by the pink blossoms.

The walkway crosses the Steel Bridge, but it's worth it to take a little detour to the north. Just follow the walkway as it goes under the bridge near the steps, then cross the railroad tracks and continue in front of the condominiums along the river. There's a little beach here, and rocks and pilings which often host herons, geese, and ducks. I've even seen salmon jump in this stretch of river. The path passes in front of the condos (does it make you feel like a voyeur?), visits a lookout platform, goes under the Broadway Bridge, and eventually reaches a big deck with a nice view north toward the Fremont Bridge.

Now go back to the Steel Bridge (built in 1912) and cross over it, either down on the lower level or up on top. You might choose based on the view, or because the lower section is raised to let a boat through. The Steel Bridge is one of the few in the world (and the only one in the United States) with two lift spans; the lower part lifts into the upper part. The total weight lifted between the two spans is nine million pounds.

At the east end of the 890-foot walkway, turn right, and you'll be on the 1.5-mile-long Eastbank Esplanade. Enjoy some of the 280 trees and 43,695 shrubs (most native) planted along the trail; local beavers sure did when they first went in, so now many of them are covered by fence—the plants, not the beavers. Also, enjoy the 13 "urban markers" along the way; they mark where streets are, and each one has a unique light fixture on it, as well.

In just a few minutes you'll come to the fanciest feature of the Esplanade, the floating walkway. At 1,200 feet, it's the longest in the world. It's held in place by 65 pylons, each one sunk 30 feet into the bottom of the river. Each section of the walkway weighs 800,000 pounds, and you can still feel it bobbing up and down when the wind is tossing up the river.

If you want to head back to the west side, you can do so on the Burnside Bridge via a staircase on the south side.

Just north of the Morrison Bridge, you'll see what looks like a strange rock formation; in fact, this is leftover concrete, dumped when the Morrison Bridge was being built. What kind of fines do you think that would generate these days?

If you're wondering about some other oddities—the little bumps on the seats of benches—those are to keep skateboarders from practicing tricks on them.

Just past the Hawthorne Bridge, which has a nice lookout point on the north side and access to cross back over the river, you'll come to the Oregon Museum of Science and Industry (OMSI). The path goes right across the front of OMSI (past the submarine), and if you like, you can step inside for a snack, a drink, or some education. (The Omnimax Theater is especially recommended.)

You've now officially left the Esplanade, but don't worry. Just follow the path as it loops around to the left and turns into Southeast Carruthers Street. Take a right on Southeast Fourth Avenue, and in two blocks you'll be on the Springwater Corridor Trail. This trail will eventually be improved all the way to the town of Boring, and possibly even be extended to Estacada, and maybe even into the National Forest along the Clackamas River, and maybe even to the Pacific Crest Trail—all depending on which enthusiastic civic leader you ask.

Just past a lovely concrete plant on the right, you'll come to an area that was replanted with native shrubs and flowers from the fall of 2003 to the spring of 2004, so you can see how it worked out—and enjoy the first real taste of quiet on the trip. For most of the next 3 miles, you will feel free of the city.

Just less than 2 miles along, you'll come to a trail that goes under the railroad tracks to the left; this is a connector to the Oaks Bottom Trail (see page 236). Soon thereafter, you'll come to Oaks Bottom on the left; I've seen as many as two dozen herons in there at once. On the right, you'll pass Oaks Amusement Park, then just before the Sellwood Bridge, turn left onto Spokane. Look for a cute little church in the trees on the left; that's Oaks Pioneer Museum, which was originally the 1851 St. John's Episcopal Church and was moved to this location in 1961.

Go two blocks and turn right on Southeast Sixth, then you'll arrive at Southeast Tacoma. If you need a break, there's a coffee shop four blocks to your left; otherwise, turn right and head over the 1925 Sellwood Bridge. Look for a statue of an owl on a roof to your right, and then look out for traffic. This is a pretty dicey bridge crossing, especially when a big truck goes by and the whole bridge bounces.

At the west end of the bridge, take some steps down to the right, cross under the road, then follow signs for the Willamette Greenway Trail. You'll walk along the side of Macadam Avenue, then turn right at a sign for the Macadam Bay Club. Just before the gate for this club, turn left to get back onto the trail.

In less than half a mile, you'll come to Butterfly Park, which is really just an undeveloped piece of riverside filled with cottonwood trees, where a lot of butterflies live. Volunteers maintain it to keep it attractive to the winged critters. An interpretive sign explores more, but it's nice to know you live in a city that has a Butterfly Park.

About a quarter mile north, you'll come into 30-acre Willamette Park, where the trail hugs the riverside next to fields full of dogs, discs, and barbecuers. At the north end of that park, you'll come into an area of condos and office buildings— and enough "Stay on the Trails" signs to make you crazy. Pay attention to the trail, because at times you have to hug buildings and duck through parking lots, but it's all well-marked with the Willamette Greenway Trail signs.

Eventually, you pop out onto Southwest Moody Avenue in an industrial area that was the scene of massive construction as this book went to press. It wasn't entirely clear where the trail would go or how it would be marked, but last we saw, it followed Moody under I-405, then turned right onto Southwest Sheridan. However you get there, before you know it, you'll be walking through the shops and marinas of RiverPlace, and just north of that is where all this adventure started, the Hawthorne Bridge.

APPENDIXES
AND INDEX

APPENDIX A:
HIKING STORES

Columbia Sportswear
911 SW Broadway
(503) 226-6800

G.I. Joe's
3900 SE 82nd Avenue
(503) 777-4526

Next Adventure
(*includes used items*)
426 SE Grand Avenue
(503) 233-0706

Oregon Mountain Community
2975 NE Sandy Boulevard
(503) 227-1038

Patagonia
907 NW Irving Street
(503) 525-2552

REI–Portland
1405 NW Johnson Street
(503) 221-1938

The Mountain Shop
628 NE Broadway
(503) 288-6768

US Outdoor Store
219 SW Broadway
(503) 223-5937

APPENDIX B:
PLACES TO BUY MAPS

Nature of the Northwest
800 NE Oregon Street
Suite 177
(503) 731-4444

Oregon Mountain Community
2975 NE Sandy Boulevard
(503) 227-1038

REI–Tigard
7410 SW Bridgeport Road
(503) 624-8600

APPENDIX C:
HIKING CLUBS

Bergfreunde Ski Club
(503) 245-8543
www.bergfreunde.org

Columbia River Volkssport Club
www.ava.org/clubs/crvc

Friends of Forest Park
(503) 223-5449
www.friendsofforestpark.org

Mazamas
527 SE 43rd Avenue
(503) 227-2345
www.mazamas.org

Trails Club of Oregon
(503) 233-2740
www.trailsclub.org

Oregon Chapter Sierra Club
2950 SE Stark Street, Suite 110
(503) 238-0442
oregon.sierraclub.org

Portland Parks and Recreation
(503) 823-7529
www.portlandonline.com/parks

Ptarmigans
1220 NE 68th Street
Vancouver, Washington
Meet at 7 p.m. on the second Tuesday of each month at the First Congregational Church in Vancouver.
www.ptarmigans.org

INDEX

DAY AND OVERNIGHT HIKES ON THE PACIFIC CREST TRAIL

by Paul Gerald
ISBN-10: 0-89732-973-2
ISBN-13: 978-0-89732-973-6
$13.95
192 pages

This new guide is complete with GPS-based trail maps and elevation profiles, directions to the trailhead, and trail descriptions guide hikers of all attitudes and abilities on the PCT through Oregon.

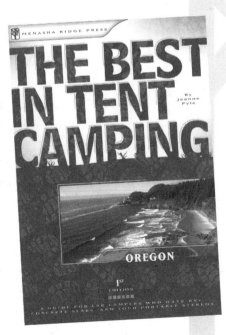

BEST IN TENT CAMPING: OREGON

by Jeanne Pyle
ISBN 10: 0-89732-570-2
ISBN 13: 978-0-89732-570-7
$14.95
192 pages

From the rocky coastlines in the western part of the state to the sagebrush deserts of the east, Oregon has hundreds of campgrounds, but only the quietest, most beautiful and secure sites were selected for this guide.

DEAR CUSTOMERS AND FRIENDS,

SUPPORTING YOUR INTEREST IN OUTDOOR ADVENTURE, travel, and an active lifestyle is central to our operations, from the authors we choose to the locations we detail to the way we design our books. Menasha Ridge Press was incorporated in 1982 by a group of veteran outdoorsmen and professional outfitters. For 25 years now, we've specialized in creating books that benefit the outdoors enthusiast.

Almost immediately, Menasha Ridge Press earned a reputation for revolutionizing outdoors- and travel-guidebook publishing. For such activities as canoeing, kayaking, hiking, backpacking, and mountain biking, we established new standards of quality that transformed the whole genre, resulting in outdoor-recreation guides of great sophistication and solid content. Menasha Ridge continues to be outdoor publishing's greatest innovator.

The folks at Menasha Ridge Press are as at home on a white-water river or mountain trail as they are editing a manuscript. The books we build for you are the best they can be, because we're responding to your needs. Plus, we use and depend on them ourselves.

We look forward to seeing you on the river or the trail. If you'd like to contact us directly, join in at www.trekalong.com or visit us at www.menasharidge.com. We thank you for your interest in our books and the natural world around us all.

SAFE TRAVELS,

BOB SEHLINGER
PUBLISHER